Hong Kong as an International Financial Centre

Hong Kong has been one of the most exciting and dynamic economies in the last half century. The rags-to-riches story of Hong Kong's manufacturing has inspired historians, economists and business people. Now, however, Hong Kong is better known as a premier international financial centre. This book uncovers previously inaccessible data on the origins of Hong Kong's post-war rise to global prominence in the international financial system by exploring the expansion of the gold market, stock market, banking system, foreign exchange market and insurance in the years 1945–65.

This book addresses key questions such as how did the close relationship with China develop after the war? What have been the benefits and costs of the laissez-faire policy for the Hong Kong financial system? And to what extent was the local industry disadvantaged by the international outlook of the financial sector?

Catherine R. Schenk exposes deep conflicts between the British government and the Hong Kong government, and also between local financial institutions and the Hong Kong government. The resolution of these conflicts had a profound impact on the development of the financial system in Hong Kong; moreover, the book argues that Hong Kong's unique position in the 1950s and 1960s in the international monetary system gave it advantages that promoted it to a global importance it would not recapture until the 1980s.

Based on previously unpublished archival records, this book makes a significant contribution to our understanding of the development of Hong Kong, the impact of financial regulation, and more broadly the role of financial centres in the international economy in the post-war period. It will be important new material for students of international finance, historians, specialists in Asian studies and the development of the Pacific Rim.

Catherine R. Schenk is Senior Lecturer in Economic History at the University of Glasgow. She has published widely on Hong Kong's financial history, as well as on British and European international monetary relations. She is the author of *Britain and the Sterling Area: From Devaluation to Convertibility in the 1950s.*

Routledge studies in the growth economies of Asia

Hong Kong as an International Financial Centre

Emergence and development 1945–65

Catherine R. Schenk

London and New York

Repl

First published 2001 by Routledge
11 New Fetter Lane, London EC4P 4EE

Simultaneously published in the USA and Canada
by Routledge
29 West 35th Street, New York, NY 10001

Transferred to Digital Printing 2002

Routledge is an imprint of the Taylor & Francis Group

© 2001 Catherine R. Schenk

Typeset in 10/12 pt AGaramond by Newgen Imaging Systems (P) Ltd.,
Chennai, India

Printed and bound in Great Britain by TJI Digital, Padstow, Cornwall

British Library Cataloguing in Publication Data
A catalogue record for this book is available from the British Library

Library of Congress Cataloguing in Publication Data
Schenk, Catherine R. (Catherine Ruth), 1964–
    Hong Kong as an international financial centre: emergence and development
    1945–1965/Catherine R. Schenk.
    p. cm. – (Routledge studies in the growth economies of Asia; 31)
    Includes bibliographical references and index.
    1. Finance – China – Hong Kong. 2. International finance – China –
    Hong Kong. 3. Hong Kong – Economic conditions. I. Title. II. Series.

    HG187.C62 H667 2001
    332′.095125 – dc21

                                                            00-062799

ISBN 0-415-20583-2

This book is dedicated to the memory of my father, a model of fine scholarship, who died as this manuscript was completed.

Contents

Figures

Tables

Acknowledgements

The research for this book has received generous support from the Department of Economic and Social History, University of Glasgow, the British Academy, the British Council, the Carnegie Trust for the Universities of Scotland, and the Centre for Business History in Scotland. I would like to thank Tony Stockwell, Andrea McElderry, Kathleen Burk and Tom Tomlinson for their support of my applications to these institutions. I would also like to thank the Centre for Asian Studies, University of Hong Kong for their hospitality, and especially Elizabeth Sinn for her advice. The Standard Chartered Bank, and the Hongkong and Shanghai Bank generously allowed me access to their records. Various archives and archivists have contributed to the work in this book, including Henry Gillett at the Bank of England, Edwin Green and Sara Kinsey at the Hongkong and Shanghai Bank Group, Victor Mok of the Stock Market History Project, University of Hong Kong, and the Keeper of Manuscripts at the Guildhall Library, holders of the records of the Chartered Bank. I am also grateful to the Public Records Office, London, for access to their records. Finally, I would like to thank my colleagues for their encouragement and for unselfishly giving up their time to help me: Gregg Huff and Duncan Ross at the University of Glasgow, Chris Munn and Lee Pui-tak in Hong Kong. None of these individuals, of course, bear any responsibility for the errors and poor grammar that remain.

1   Hong Kong in the international economy

Hong Kong has occupied a unique position in the international economy since its initial occupation by British traders in 1842. As a haven for Western traders engaged in commerce with China, the colony of Hong Kong developed into the most important entrepot in East Asia. By the end of the nineteenth century, the island's reputation as an outpost of colonial influence and free market opportunities attracted thousands of European and Chinese merchants to the colony.[1] In the first half of the twentieth century, however, these merchants began to feel the impact that international politics would have on the colony over the next century. The Sino-Japanese War, the Japanese occupation of China and then of Hong Kong from 1941 halted the colony's development for close to a decade. After the surrender of the Japanese in August 1945, Hong Kong was poised to resume its traditional role as the hub of the Asian economy. However, the economic environment into which Asia emerged in 1945 was changed irrevocably, and the subsequent shifts in the global economy propelled Hong Kong towards a new role in East Asia.

The importance of Hong Kong as an international trade entrepot in the nineteenth century is widely researched but (with some exceptions) the history of Hong Kong in the international economy then skips from the early twentieth century to the 1970s.[2] The financial history of the 1950s and 1960s is usually neglected in favour of the more dynamic and easily documented period from the 1970s. Jao's classic *Banking and Currency in Hong Kong* remains the authoritative text, although it deals mainly with the 1960s and 1970s and is now more than 25 years old. Another important contribution is King's *The Hongkong Bank in the Period of Development and Nationalism, 1941–1984*. The bulk of this volume deals with the period up to 1962 but it is clearly a history of the bank and not of Hong Kong.[3] There are also several early economic histories of Hong Kong which cover the 1950s and 1960s from a contemporary viewpoint, but they lack the access to new data and archival resources.[4] Another group of histories discuss Hong Kong as a by-product of studies on China.[5]

The neglect of financial history contrasts sharply with the increasing interest in Hong Kong as a manufacturing centre. This was fuelled by the frenzy that surrounded the analysis of Hong Kong, Singapore, South Korea and Taiwan when these 'Four Little Dragons' seemed to offer the world a model for modern development (until the financial crisis of 1997).[6] The return of Hong Kong to Chinese control in 1997 also sparked a rush of political histories, partly to feed public curiosity about the historical importance of this moment in British imperial history.[7]

The historical development of financial centres generally has been relatively underresearched, although the development of international financial centres (IFCs) began to attract academic attention in the 1970s with the publication of Kindleberger's seminal study.[8] New interest no doubt stemmed from the dramatic increase in international financial activity brought on by deregulation and the rise of the Euromarkets in this decade. Since then, there has been considerable interest in the defining characteristics of IFCs as well as their development and rank of importance.[9] The defining characteristics include whether the banking business is actually performed in the territory, or if it is merely a tax haven, 'brass plate', or 'paper' centre. Other important features are whether the centre is a capital importer or a capital exporter, and whether there is a regulatory barrier between domestic and international financial activities. Another set of criteria revolve around the geographical range of activity as well as the range of services offered.

A quick glance at Hong Kong's international financial services in the period 1945–65 confirms three key characteristics: that the colony was not a 'brass plate' centre, that it was a net capital importer, and that there was no regulatory barrier between domestic and international transactions. Hong Kong's financial institutions served the local region as well as customers in the USA and Europe, and the services offered were mainly banking, foreign exchange and insurance. It is the purpose of this book to focus on the role of Hong Kong in the international monetary and financial system in the first two decades after the war, and in the process to expose a new side of Hong Kong's post-war economic development.

The rise of Hong Kong as an international financial centre is usually measured from its position in the 1970s. This decade saw an influx of foreign banking interests and the mushrooming of non-banking financial institutions that sought to share in the 'miracle' economic growth of the colony. In 1979, China emerged from three decades of relative isolation and attracted the attention of international investors the world over. As a wave of optimism swept through capital markets in anticipation of huge profits that the Chinese market seemed to offer, Hong Kong was ideally prepared to become the primary route for Western capital to enter China. Through the 1980s the investments met with mixed fortunes, but Hong Kong firms themselves became substantial investors as they sought to take advantage of cheaper labour costs across the border. As a consequence, the economic integration of Hong Kong with southeast China intensified and presaged political integration. By 1997, when the political handover was completed, 60 per cent of the total overseas capital raised by China came through Hong Kong.[10]

The role of Hong Kong as a financial centre since the 1970s has been most vigorously researched by Jao.[11] He has convincingly argued that Hong Kong became an *important regional* financial centre in this decade, and that its presence increased even more in the 1980s. This reflected the open-door policy of China from 1979 as well as the general boom in international financial activity due to globalisation. Between 1980 and 1990, Hong Kong banks' assets increased from US$38 billion to

US$464 billion (from 2 per cent to almost 7 per cent of the world total) by which time Hong Kong ranked fourth in the world, trailing only the UK, USA and Japan. By 1990 Hong Kong was host to 138 licensed foreign banks, compared with 30 in 1965. In terms of the number of foreign banking offices, Hong Kong ranked second only to London with a total of 357 in 1995.[12]

The boom in financial activities in Hong Kong from the 1980s is impressive indeed but the international financial services of Hong Kong have a much longer history, which has not been adequately explored. It is Jao's contention that 'Hong Kong's rise as a regional financial centre began circa 1969/70 and not earlier' and he attributes the start of Hong Kong's establishment to the political rapprochement between the USA and China in 1971.[13] In contrast, the present study will argue that in the first two decades after 1945, Hong Kong's financial sector increased in importance largely because of the colony's unique position in the Bretton Woods system. The banking crisis of 1965 and the political riots of 1966/7 combined to undermine international confidence, and Hong Kong's relative position declined. In the 1970s, Singapore significantly increased its presence as an international financial centre through government incentives which included encouraging the Asia dollar market. Nevertheless, the financial expertise that developed in the 1950s and 1960s in Hong Kong formed the basis for the subsequent boom in the 1980s. Banking continued to be the foundation of Hong Kong's international financial activities through the 1990s.[14]

Evolution of Hong Kong's economy 1945–65

Hong Kong has gone through various manifestations in the post-war period. In the 1940s it was a bastion of the empire, and a political as well as economic link to China in revolution. This latter aspect was felt most keenly in the influx of immigrants from China between 1946 and 1950. The increased population put extreme pressure on the resources of the colony, but at the same time created the basis for successful industrialisation.[15] Throughout the 1950s, the energies of its new population transformed the economy by creating a substantial labour-intensive manufacturing base alongside the traditional financial and commercial services sector. During the 1960s, the global importance of Hong Kong became more widely recognised as these exports made inroads into the mature markets of Europe and the USA. This generated considerable trade friction between Hong Kong and some of its traditional Western trading partners, but industrialists in Hong Kong showed their famous flexibility and continued to flourish. Hong Kong's famously changing skyline, which became the potent symbol of prosperity achieved with few natural resources, began to take shape in this period. In the 1970s, the industrial restructuring of Hong Kong included the promotion of financial services, and this sector was given added impetus after the opening of the Chinese economy to the West from 1979.

While this rags-to-riches story of Hong Kong's development is now familiar, tracing the detailed development of the economy is a rather more speculative business than is the case for most other countries. The reluctance of the government to intervene in the economy extended to an unwillingness to collect statistics unless strictly necessary for business or welfare purposes. For this reason, for example, no official balance of payments or national income accounts are available before 1961. Gross Domestic Product (GDP) began to be calculated only from the early 1970s. The government's interest in the external orientation of the colony is shown in the very detailed statistics of international trade, which were collected to give business intelligence on potential markets. In the absence of official records, historians and economists have generated a variety of estimates. From these diverse sources, a fairly consistent picture of the post-war development of Hong Kong can be established.

Figure 1.1 shows estimates of real and nominal GDP per capita (p.c.) from 1948 to 1967 based on Table A in the Appendix. After the initial boom associated with recovery and the Korean War, an influx of refugees combined with a trade slump in 1952–4 caused the only fall in per capita GDP in this entire period. The economy recovered gradually through the middle of the decade as industry adjusted to the new international environment. A second influx of refugees surged into Hong Kong in 1958 as a result of the Great Leap Forward and famine in China. This pushed nominal per capita growth rates down below 1 per cent.[16] After 1959, however, growth accelerated and nominal GDP p.c. grew at an average rate of 10 per cent per annum (p.a.) from 1959 to 1965. Much of this growth appears to have been achieved through high rates of Gross Domestic Capital Formation, which averaged 12 per cent of GDP in 1948–58 and 20 per cent of GDP in 1959–65. The economy suffered a series of setbacks due to the banking crisis in 1965, the collapse of a building boom, the imposition of an import surcharge on Hong Kong goods by Britain, and the political disturbances of 1966/7. These events reduced the rate of growth considerably, but by 1969 the annual growth rate had returned to 16 per cent p.a.

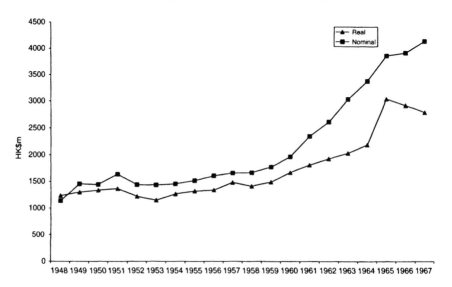

Figure 1.1 Real and nominal GDP p.c. 1948–67.

A variety of estimates of the sector breakdown of GDP are shown in Table 1.1.[17] These estimates suggest that the financial sector directly contributed about 10 per cent of GDP at this time. Chang reckoned that about half of the financial sector's output was from banking, 10 per cent from insurance, and the rest from real estate and business rental.[18] In comparison, the share of financial services in GDP in the 1970s fluctuated between 15 per cent and 22 per cent according to official estimates, rising to 26 per cent by 1995.[19] Employment in the financial sector is relatively small since it is not a labour-intensive activity (note the large proportion of the workforce engaged in manufacturing). By 1975 only 2.2 per cent of the workforce was employed in the banking, finance and insurance sector, although this increased to 5 per cent by 1995.[20]

Chau calculated the growth of the various sectors of the economy based largely on Chang's estimates.[21] Income from banking was assumed to grow at the same rate as revenue-producing assets invested locally. Income from property was calculated from the growth of revenue from rates. Insurance income was assumed to grow at the same rate as international trade. These estimates (albeit sketchy) suggest that the rate of growth of the financial sector was slowing down through the 1960s, but was still persistently higher than the growth rate of manufacturing output. On average through the 1960s, Chau calculated that manufacturing contributed to 34.5 per cent of GDP growth and the financial sector contributed 13 per cent.

McCarthy and Johnson suggest a variety of ways in which an IFC may affect the domestic economy of the host, by contributing indirectly to GDP.[22] The potential benefits relevant to Hong Kong include local expenditure on wages and incomes, a

Table 1.1 Output and employment by economic activity (%)

Sector	GNP 1954/5	GDP 1960/1	GDP 1961/2	Employment 1961
Agriculture, forestry, fishing	3.0	3.3	3.4	7.3
Mining and quarrying	0.3	0.3	0.3	0.7
Manufacturing	33.0	24.7	23.6	43.0
Utilities		2.4	2.4	1.1
Construction	3.3	5.3	6.1	4.9
Transport, storage and communication	7.5	9.4	9.6	7.3
Wholesale and retail trade	17.7[a]	20.4	19.5	14.4
Banking, insurance and real estate		9.7	10.8	1.6
Other services	20[b]	11.4	11.5	18.3
Public administration/defence	8.5	6.6	6.2	
Ownership of dwellings	6.5	6.5	6.6	

Notes
a Includes utilities.
b Includes banking, insurance and real estate.
Sources: GDP by economic activity, 1954–5, E. Szczepanik, *The Economic Growth of Hong Kong*, Oxford, Oxford University Press, 1958, p. 178. 1960/1 and 1961/2, E. R. Chang, *Report on the National Income Survey of Hong Kong*, HK Government Printer, 1969. Employment figures from L. C. Chau, *Hong Kong: A Unique Case of Development*, Washington, World Bank, 1993, p. 5.

more skilled labour force, tax revenue, capital gains for local property-owners, more efficient local banking, and the development of 'business tourism'. The costs include the rise of rental and property prices, and the 'squeezing out' of local financial institutions. The direct gains through wages are limited because the financial sector is not labour-intensive, and many of the highest paid employees are expatriates, rather than from the local population. In 1961 there were 164,303 workers in the categories of Managerial, Professional, Office and Clerical in Hong Kong. The large number of Chinese-controlled banks engaged in international financial activity suggests that the gains to the local population might be more significant than was the case in other centres such as Panama. Johnson also suggests that the construction industry benefits from the IFC, although in Hong Kong's case construction booms arose from the expansion of domestic manufacturing as well as the financial sector. Certainly property and real estate markets soared in the 1960s, due partly to speculative capital attracted to the IFC, but this could be destabilising for the economy as a whole because of periodic slumps in the market. Tax revenue related to the IFC is difficult to specify. Interest tax totalled HK$96 million between 1950 and 1965, but was only 5 per cent of tax revenue in 1965, and 1 per cent total government revenue. Since one half of total bank deposits were probably from overseas, about HK$48 million was generated for the government. It is not possible to isolate the profits and property tax related to international financial activity. The IFC probably did contribute to the development of Hong Kong's services as a business tourism centre, but again it is difficult to isolate this from the role of the manufactured export sector, which also attracted tourists through regular trade fairs. The impact of the development of the IFC on domestic financial institutions, and its effects on the provision of capital for industry will be discussed in Chapter 6.

The 1950s and 1960s are best known as the era in which Hong Kong abandoned its entrepot role and became a manufacturer. By 1960, 85 per cent of Hong Kong's domestic exports were manufactured goods, which amounted to over HK$2.4 billion. Table 1.2 gives some indication of the growth of manufacturing, particularly in textiles.

The protection from Chinese competition afforded by political events, combined with support from the Hong Kong government, might be interpreted as the

Table 1.2 Some indicators of the growth of Hong Kong manufacturing

	1955	1965
Number of manufacturing establishments	2,437	8,137
Number employed in registered factories	110,574	329,214
Number of spinning factories	21	40
Number of weaving factories	116	202
Production of cotton yarn (1,000 lb)	82,450	288,893
Production of cotton piece goods (1,000 sq. yd)	139,355	723,586
Value of manufactured exports	HK$1.6b	HK$4.3b

Sources: General manufacturing sector from S.-h. Ng and V. Sit, *Labour Relations and Labour Conditions in Hong Kong*, London, Macmillan, 1989, p. 6. Textile sector from *Hong Kong Statistics 1947–67*, Hong Kong, Census and Statistics Department, 1969.

'import-substitution' phase of Hong Kong's industrialisation. Until 1949, the government imported and rationed scarce cotton yarn to keep its price down in order to protect the textile industry. Prices subsequently dropped due to dumping of Chinese and Indian stocks, but began to rise again during the Korean War boom in the second half of 1950. The government then imposed a ban on re-exports of yarn from Hong Kong until 1953 to protect supplies to local factories. The government also imposed a ban on Japanese cotton imports to protect domestic producers. The early support offered by the government through these policies is generally ignored by those critical of the state's neglect of industry.[23]

Textile weaving dates back to 1922, when the first factory was opened in Hong Kong by the East Asia Clothing Factory of Macao.[24] Power looms were first introduced in 1928. Entrepreneurs from Fujian and Guangdong were active investors in this sector during the Sino-Japanese War. A wave of consolidation after 1945 saw the disappearance of many of the smaller factories as the average size rose. By 1953 it was estimated that HK$70–80 million had been invested in this sector.[25] Almost all of Hong Kong's production was exported, mainly to markets in Southeast Asia, but also to Africa, the Middle East and the UK. The famous efforts of Shanghai immigrants created the cotton spinning industry after the war.[26] In 1947 there were no spinning mills in Hong Kong but by 1953 there were 13, and an estimated HK$300 million had been invested in this industry.[27]

Hong Kong is traditionally viewed as an example of export-led growth[28] and Figure 1.2 shows the value of the colony's trade from 1947 to 1965 (based on Table B in the Appendix). Re-exports were only separated from the total from 1959. This shows the quick recovery of Hong Kong's exports after the war until embargoes by

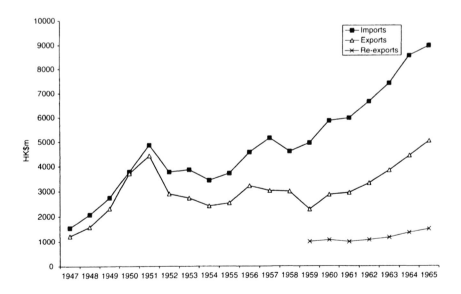

Figure 1.2 Hong Kong's merchandise trade.

the US and then by the United Nations in 1950/1 caused stagnation. Imports (mainly food and raw materials) recovered rather sooner, fuelled by industrial expansion and the swelling population. As a result, Hong Kong maintained a substantial and increasing trade deficit throughout this period, particularly with China as the main source of food and water imports into the colony. The symbiotic economic relationship between China and Hong Kong is discussed in a separate section below.

Hong Kong's port facilities were the initial and lasting source of the colony's strategic and economic status. The deep, 10-mile-long harbour hosted larger shipping as well as the traditional small lighters and junks, which made the port an ideal link between European/American ports and smaller Asian destinations. From the nineteenth century, goods from East and Southeast Asia were brought to Hong Kong in small vessels and transferred to ocean-going ships. In turn, Western goods were redistributed throughout Asia. After the war, the port facilities were quickly restored. By 1949, two oil companies provided direct bunkering facilities and the government supplied 39 buoys for ocean-going vessels ranging from 300 to 600 feet in length. Vessels drawing up to 32 feet could berth directly on the port's wharves. Three companies dominated the supply of wharves and storage, of which the largest was the Hongkong & Kowloon Wharf & Godown Company. In 1949, it operated over 100 godowns and provided storage for about 750,000 tons of cargo, with berths for 10 ocean-going vessels up to 750 feet in length. These facilities attracted the members of 11 freight conferences representing 80 shipping companies. The speed with which goods were transhipped through Hong Kong was not only faster and more efficient than most other Asian ports, but also exceeded those in the UK, the USA and Australia.[29] Having established Hong Kong's commercial links, the next section explores the international monetary links of Hong Kong.

Hong Kong in the international monetary system

It is a major premise of this book that Hong Kong was profoundly affected by the unique position it occupied in the international monetary system during the postwar period. The two decades after the war were characterised by restrictions on trade and payments that persisted into the 1970s, and by the crumbling of the international monetary system in the 1960s. During the war, the Americans and British planned for a more closely regulated international economy based on freer trade and payments than had existed in the inter-war period. The Bretton Woods agreement of 1944, which established the International Monetary Fund and the World Bank, was supposed to usher in their vision of a world of stable fixed exchange rates and freer trade and capital flows. In the economic chaos of the immediate post-war period, however, fixed exchange rates had to be protected by tight restrictions on trade and payments by almost all countries. Liberalisation was only possible on a piecemeal basis and within selected groups of countries such as Western Europe, and the sterling area. As a member of the British empire, Hong Kong was part of the sterling area group of countries that agreed to fix their exchange rates to sterling, pool their foreign exchange earnings, and trade more freely amongst themselves than with the rest of the world. These countries included the UK, all the members of the Commonwealth and colonies as well as oil-producing states in the Persian Gulf, Libya and Iraq.[30]

Currency stability was assured by the colonial monetary system. In the absence of a central bank, the Hong Kong dollar was issued by three commercial banks – primarily the Hong Kong and Shanghai Banking Corporation[31] – and was backed by an Exchange Fund of sterling assets held by the Hong Kong government. Authorised banks sold sterling to purchase claims on this fund in respect of cover for their note issue. These claims took the form of non-interest-bearing Certificates of Indebtedness so the interest earned by the currency reserve accrued to the Exchange Fund, not to the issuing banks. The profits of the fund were re-invested in securities so that the actual cover for the local currency was greater than 100 per cent.[32] Under this quasi-currency board system, the Hong Kong government had little monetary policy autonomy because changes in the money supply were automatically determined by the balance of payments. Confidence in the HK dollar had been established before the war when the exchange rate of the HK dollar with sterling had maintained at 1s3d from 1935 to 1939. After the war, the exchange rate of the HK dollar was pegged to sterling at HK$16 to £1, reflecting the official sterling cross rate of US$4.06. This peg was maintained until the devaluation of sterling in 1967.

Many writers have commented on the importance of the colonial legacy of stable government and a well-developed legal system for Hong Kong's commercial success.[33] Less well understood is the fact that Hong Kong's colonial status also offered important privileges in the increasingly regulated international economic system which emerged after 1945. The sterling area affiliation conferred stability to the monetary system and demand for Hong Kong's goods and services. Hong Kong benefited from an absence of exchange controls on capital flows between Hong Kong and the rest of the sterling area, as well as preferred access to goods markets because of its colonial status. The Hong Kong currency was pegged to sterling in line with all other colonial currencies and Britain was obligated to support its foreign exchange requirements, as for all other colonies.

Hong Kong's financial system was profoundly affected by the freely floating exchange market for US dollar which the colony needed in order to function as a trade entrepot. The official fixed exchange rates of the HK dollar to sterling and to the US dollar co-existed with a parallel free market exchange rate set by demand and supply. Local Chinese banks and moneychangers exchanged currencies at rates set freely in response to supply and demand, while larger banks operated at the official fixed exchange rate. Residents of other countries of the sterling area (such as the UK) had access to this floating exchange market because of the limited exchange control within the sterling area.[34] This free market facilitated capital flows as well as trade in goods and specie through Hong Kong.

During the crucial period from 1945 to 1965, when Hong Kong was rocked by a succession of political and economic shocks, Hong Kong's regulatory system fell into the cracks between the tightly controlled sterling area arrangements and the free markets which persisted in Asian trade. The result was that Hong Kong attracted customers from the West as well as elsewhere in Asia. These investors and merchants sought to maximise their profits by exploiting the opportunities for trade and arbitrage which were offered by the free markets in Hong Kong. It was this combination of being a British colony and an Asian entrepot that was the foundation for Hong Kong's emergence as an international financial centre in these early decades.

Despite a persistent and growing overall trade deficit, Hong Kong's foreign exchange reserves increased from HK$1 billion in 1950 to HK$3.7 billion by 1963. This reflected a substantial inflow on the capital and invisibles account. Szczepanik reports that 'fairly uniform opinion prevailing in the Colony' put the annual inflow of capital in the region of HK$300–600 million in the mid-1950s, and considerably more in the period 1948–50. He estimated invisible earnings at HK$1billion p.a. in the mid-1950s.[35] The Hong Kong government estimated that external trade in services earned a surplus of HK$1.5–2 billion p.a. from 1961 to 1965.[36] In 1967 a World Bank mission to Hong Kong estimated that the balance on the capital account was a surplus of HK$1 billion in 1960, rising to HK$2 billion by 1965.[37] Given the lack of direct evidence, no precise conclusions can be drawn except to note that these estimates accord with anecdotal evidence that there was a substantial and increasing inflow of foreign capital on both short term and long term into Hong Kong throughout this period. The inflow of capital was partly for investment in industry, the stock market, and property, and partly for deposit in Hong Kong banks, which were seen as a safe haven for the savings of overseas Chinese in neighbouring territories. During the political instability of these volatile decades, Hong Kong was recognised as a stable target for flight capital, first because of its relative political stability, and second because the absences of exchange controls meant that savings could be repatriated at any time.

Hong Kong and China 1949–65

The prosperity of Hong Kong has always been closely linked to events in China. The relationship was strained by China's internal political and social turbulence, and efforts at self-sufficiency, but since the 'Open Door Policy' announced by Deng Xiao Ping in 1978, the integration of Hong Kong with China has developed rapidly, culminating in the creation of Hong Kong as a Special Administrative Region of China in July 1997. This section reviews the course of Hong Kong's relations with China as a background to the more specific analysis of Hong Kong's international financial links with China which are dealt with in greater detail in Chapter 2.

At the end of the war, Hong Kong's relations with China was an important aspect of Britain's strategic and commercial policy. In 1941, it was estimated that the value of UK investment and property in China amounted to about £200–300 million.[38] This compares to a British estimate of about £350 million invested in Hong Kong in 1949.[39] In order to protect these commercial interests, Britain sought to maintain commercial links with China despite the change in regime after 1949. This policy, however, met with increasing resistance from the new People's Republic of China (PRC).

Initially, the PRC tolerated foreign business because economic recovery was vital to the stability of the new regime. However, in order to preserve China's scarce resources the government was quick to begin to take over the administration of foreign exchange and trade. The banking system was also centralised during the early 1950s. Private merchants (both foreign and Chinese) were gradually squeezed out as the state exerted control over trade in essential materials and began to ration foreign exchange. During 1950, the Chinese government established a variety of trading agencies in Hong Kong whose purpose was to coordinate trade and to make contacts with Western suppliers and markets. These agencies in Hong Kong were directly linked to the various state trading authorities, some of which represented regions while others specialised in particular products.[40]

In the first half of 1950, the optimistic view in London and Hong Kong of the future prospects of trade between China and Hong Kong seemed justified by the re-stocking boom in China's trade. After China entered the Korean War in October 1950, however, the US reinforced its trade embargo and froze Chinese US dollar assets. As a result, China relied more heavily on the Eastern Bloc as a source of supply, effectively cutting Hong Kong out of China's import trade.[41] In May 1951, the UN finally imposed a general embargo on trade in strategic goods with China. In September 1952, state trading in the PRC was further consolidated by the new Ministry of Foreign Trade, which restricted trade mainly to barter and reoriented markets toward the Eastern Bloc. The proportion of trade conducted by state companies increased from 66 per cent in 1950 to 93 per cent by 1952 and 99 per cent by 1955.[42] As a result of these developments, the share of Hong Kong in China's total trade declined from 32 per cent in 1951 to 5 per cent in 1959.

In 1957 and again in 1958, Britain reduced the list of products that were subject to embargo.[43] This relaxation allowed China to import more machinery, helping to fuel the production of light manufactures for export. The domestic economy was thrown into disarray, however, by a series of political purges that disrupted society and the economy. In 1958, China embarked on the Great Leap Forward in an attempt to accelerate the development of heavy industry. The policy ended in disaster with widespread famine and inefficiency crippling the economy and sending a flood of refugees into Hong Kong. In 1960, relations between China and the Soviet Union broke down, further threatening the sustainability of the Chinese economy since it was heavily dependent on Soviet aid and industrial products. The domestic social and political crisis peaked in 1966–9 when Mao embarked on the historically tragic Cultural Revolution, which was to push China into internal turmoil until the 1970s.

Despite the increasing xenophobia of the PRC and the growing madness of its central policies in the Mao period, China maintained its external trade links with Hong Kong. Table C in the Appendix shows that Hong Kong ran a persistent trade deficit with China, except during the re-stocking boom in 1950 and 1951. Exports to China tailed off due to external embargoes and the nationalisation of Chinese trade, but imports continued to increase. Hong Kong's deficit with China grew from HK$310 million in 1952 to HK$2 billion by 1965. In the early 1960s, China's exports to Hong Kong began to recover, lifting Hong Kong's share in China's trade back to 12 per cent in 1964. The nature of the trade between Hong Kong and China also changed. Between 1955 and 1965, the value of Hong Kong's imports of Chinese manufactures quadrupled, growing from 25 per cent to 41 per cent of Hong Kong's total imports from China. The shift to manufactured goods was largely responsible for the doubling of the value of Hong Kong's imports from China between 1960 and 1965. Over the same period, the proportion of China's total exports that were bound for Hong Kong doubled from 10 per cent to 20 per cent by value.

A good proportion of Chinese manufactured goods arriving in Hong Kong were no doubt destined for re-export, mainly to other developing countries in Asia. No statistics are available for the first half of the 1960s, but in 1966 22.5 per cent of imports from China (HK$627 million) were re-exported, making up over one third of Hong Kong's total re-export trade in that year.[44] The traditional story that Hong Kong's entrepot trade with China disappeared after 1951 is certainly not sustained by these figures. Indeed, goods flowing from China to Hong Kong increased their share in both countries' trade in the first half of the 1960s.

Despite these changes in commodity composition of trade, by 1965 almost half of Hong Kong's imports from China were food products. Hong Kong's dependence on this supply is evident in that close to half of all its imported food came from China throughout the decade. From 1961 Hong Kong also began to import water from China at a cost of HK$10 million by 1965. The proportion of total water coming from China increased sharply, rising from 15 per cent of Hong Kong's water supply in 1965 to 40 per cent in 1967. Jao and others suggest that the supply of cheap food-stuffs from China was an important contributor to Hong Kong's successful labour-intensive industrialisation, because it kept the cost of living lower in Hong Kong than otherwise.[45]

Hong Kong's dependence on Chinese imports had important implications for its relationship with China. On the one hand, the threat that China would cut Hong Kong off from these vital supplies was raised from time to time as a possibility should China's relations with the UK deteriorate, although the threat was seldom a serious one. On the other hand, the trade surplus China earned from Hong Kong was its most valuable source of foreign exchange, since these exports earned convertible HK dollars. The co-dependence of Hong Kong and China was not eliminated by China's trade autarky, nor by Hong Kong's industrialisation in these decades.

The main financial link between Hong Kong and China after 1951 was through remittances.[46] The bulk of remittances from overseas Chinese to their relatives in China went through Hong Kong banks. There are no firm figures on the total value, but a variety of estimates are presented in Table 1.3.

The figures for the Bank of China in Hong Kong are cited in two contemporary publications (one Chinese and one Japanese) and by Taipei's Overseas Chinese Affairs Commission. It is assumed that the other China state banks in Hong Kong together handled an amount of remittance business equal to the Bank of China. The final column of Table 1.3 includes US$2–4 million of remittances from Singapore and Malaysia each year, investment by overseas Chinese in the state-operated Overseas Chinese Investment Corporations, and the proceeds of food parcels to China. The estimates for 1961–7 are even more speculative than those for the 1950s, being based on a variety of contemporary newspaper reports.[47]

Table 1.3 Remittances to China through Hong Kong (US$m)

	Remittances through Hong Kong			Total remittances
	Bank of China	Other banks	Total	
1950	44.38	44.38	88.76	91.1
1951	48.37	48.37	96.74	101.7
1952	49.45	49.45	98.9	103.3
1953	35.93	35.93	71.86	77.3
1954	33.3	33.3	66.6	69.7
1955	30.7	30.7	61.4	70.8
1956	25.43	25.43	50.86	63.2
1957	18.05	18.05	36.1	49.7
1958	17.26	17.26	34.52	42.7
1959	12.06	12.06	24.12	33.7
1960	15.82	15.82	31.64	42.6
1961			30	62.7
1962			30	63.8
1963			40	62
1964			50	64.3
1965			67	67

Sources: F.-H. Mah, *The Foreign Trade of Mainland China*, Edinburgh, University of Edinburgh Press, 1972, pp. 238–45.

Some insight into the nature of this business is possible from archival records. In 1950, the Hongkong Bank in Beijing complained about losing remittance business to the Shanghai Commercial Bank (also Hong Kong registered). The latter had received over 300 inward remittances from Hong Kong compared with eight (of which seven were in HK dollars) to the Hongkong Bank. The bank's compradore in Hong Kong was instructed to encourage the native banks and moneychangers to put more of this business through the Hongkong Bank.[48] This correspondence confirms that the remittances flowed in to local Chinese-controlled banks from elsewhere in East and Southeast Asia. The small banks then used larger banks as intermediaries to transfer the remittances to China. The correspondence also confirms that Western banks were gradually squeezed out of this traffic. In October 1951, the Bank of China required that cover for all remittances should be handed over to the Bank of China in the territory where the remittances emanated.[49] After the centralisation of banking control in China during 1952, the proportion of remittances coming through banks other than the Bank of China probably fell further. By 1955, it might be assumed that most cash remittances ultimately went via the China state controlled banks in Hong Kong, even if they were initially transferred from overseas to a different Hong Kong bank.

This section has highlighted the continuity in Hong Kong's economic relationship with China, which persisted despite the exile of China from the international community. Chapter 2 examines the political and economic friction that resulted from the clash of regime between Hong Kong and China that underlay the working relationship between the two economies. The resolution of these conflicts paved the way for the relatively stable economic relations that followed. Chapter 4 will show that China's trade surplus with Hong Kong created a demand for sterling among Hong Kong banks that linked them to foreign exchange markets in New York and London, and created arbitrage opportunities for international investors. In this way, the China connection was a vital ingredient in the international financial operations of institutions in Hong Kong even before the open-door policy in 1979 ushered in direct investment links.

Government policy and the 'laissez-faire' myth

The post-war period in Britain was characterised by a deliberate increase in the role of government in the economy, typified by the establishment of the Welfare State. In Hong Kong, by contrast, the liberal tenets of the nineteenth century continued to prevail. Perhaps the most famous aspect of the economic development of Hong Kong has been the apparent success of strictly 'laissez-faire' government economic policy.[50] Owen described Hong Kong as 'unique in its correspondence to the classical economist's dream world which existed in the golden age before 1914'.[51] The caricature of the 1950s and 1960s is that successive governors of Hong Kong allowed the forces of capitalism to reign freely, facilitating the dramatic restructuring of the economy from entrepot to manufacturing power-house based on small-scale, competitive producers. Low taxes, lax employment laws, absence of government debt, and free trade are all pillars of the Hong Kong 'model'. Alternatively, the government's attitude has been described as 'positive non-interventionism' to reflect that it was a deliberate and active policy choice rather than merely an absence of policy.[52] Recently, the deliberate nature of government policy has been confirmed by Ngo in his critique of the state's neglect of industry.[53]

In fact, of course, the reality was much different than the myth. First, there were considerable constraints on the potential effectiveness of any government economic policy in the early 1950s. A large and uncontrollable influx of Chinese into Hong Kong made economic planning virtually impossible. On top of this, the US and UN trade embargoes distorted traditional markets. The changing emphasis of the economy from trading to manufacturing was thus significantly determined by external forces on labour and trade, whose impact was largely beyond the control of the Hong Kong government. On the other hand, the government was more active in the economy than is generally recognised. After the war, the government held a monopoly on the purchase and distribution of vital food and raw materials including rice and cotton yarn. Price controls were not eliminated until 1953. The state's programmes of public housing, land reclamation and infrastructure investment were ambitious. From 1953, new industrial towns in Kwun Tong and Tsuen Wan were built to house immigrants, provide employment and aid industry.[54] The Kai Tak Airport (built partly from British investment) was vital to the international links that formed the basis of Hong Kong's manufacturing. Spending on education and public health also increased in this period, from 9 per cent of government expenditure to 11 per cent between 1950 and 1965, representing an increase from HK$16 million to HK$164 million. In 1957, the Hong Kong Tourist Association was created to promote a new and growing sector of the economy. As a result of these programmes, government expenditure grew steadily from 6.5 per cent of GDP in 1950/1 to a peak of 14.3 per cent in 1961/2, before declining gradually to 11.5 per cent by 1969/70.[55] While these changes in spending were quite dramatic, the overall level remained low compared with other countries. In 1961/2, the share of government spending in GDP was less than half that of the USA or the UK.[56]

The one sector where there seems to have been a true adherence to 'positive non-interventionism' is in finance. Exchange controls were limited to a few imposed by the UK, and there were no controls on international flows of capital. There was no central bank and therefore no monetary policy. The government was stubbornly resistant to regulating the banking system, the stock market, or the gold market despite pressure both from within and from outside Hong Kong. Manufacturers consistently complained about a shortage of investment at reasonable rates; the banks warned of the instability caused by the lack of regulation; the UK and Chinese governments protested that the Hong Kong free markets were disrupting their own controls.

The resistance of the Hong Kong government to these pressures to intervene in financial and monetary markets owes much to the resolution of the successive governors of Hong Kong: Sir Alexander Grantham (1947–57) and Robert (Robin) Black (1958–64). Of sometimes greater importance were the Financial Secretaries, A.G. Clarke (1951–61) and especially J.J. Cowperthwaite (1961–71). Clarke presided over a doubling of the share of public expenditure in GDP, but his successor was more conservative, reducing the share of the public sector in almost every year of his tenure. Nevertheless, Clarke and Grantham preserved and defended the liberal focus of Hong Kong's financial markets during the period of greatest external pressure for regulation. The following chapters will show that Cowperthwaite certainly earned his reputation for conservative and liberal attitudes to markets in the 1960s, although these views were not always shared by the market participants.[57] In general, the analysis of the historical development of Hong Kong's financial institutions will reveal a more complicated picture of the relationship between the state and the market in Hong Kong than the 'free market' stereotype.

Outline of the book

The following chapters capture the post-war recovery and later development of Hong Kong's international financial institutions in the first two decades after the war. First, the key relationship with China is addressed. The conflict generated by the juxtaposition of Hong Kong's free markets and China's tight regulatory framework was fundamental to establishing the working relationship between China and Hong Kong for the subsequent two decades. This chapter also explores the development of Hong Kong's place in Britain's China policy in these key years. The following three chapters explore the different institutions which comprised the financial services offered in the colony. The major themes of these chapters are the development of the regulatory framework, the impact of the international monetary system and regional politics, the views of the private sector expressed in archives and the media, and the inter-relationship among the individual markets. The limited data available prevents a detailed accounting of the importance of the financial sector to Hong Kong, or indeed relative to other centres. Nevertheless, the penultimate chapter assesses Hong Kong's position in the international financial system, and the interaction between the international financial sector and the domestic economy. A final chapter offers an epilogue and general conclusions.

Appendix

Table A Hong Kong GDP 1948–67 (HK$m)

Year	GDP			GDP per capita			Real GDP p.c.	Retail price index
	A	B	C	A	B	C		March 1947 = 100
1948	1,564	2,050		869	1,138		1,237	92
1949	1,775	2,700		954	1,452		1,296	112
1950	2,330	3,230		1,040	1,442		1,335	108
1951	2,800	3,305		1,386	1,636		1,363	120
1952	2,800	3,055		1,315	1,434		1,215	118
1953	3,200	3,205		1,422	1,430		1,144	125
1954	3,600	3,440		1,525	1,451		1,262	115
1955	4,000	3,780		1,600	1,512		1,315	115
1956		4,160			1,600		1,333	120
1957		4,465			1,653		1,476	112
1958		4,735			1,661		1,408	118
1959		5,190			1,769		1,487	119
1960		6,045			1,965		1,665	118
1961		6,885	7,434		2,169	2,347	1,808	120
1962		7,745	8,656 (16.4)		2,314	2,619 (11.6)	1,928	120
1963		8,830	10,393 (20.1)		2,523	3,038 (16.0)	2,035	124
1964		10,000	11,853 (14.0)		2,782	3,382 (11.3)	2,191	127
1965		11,212	13,911 (17.5)		3,114	3,866 (14.3)	3,044	131
1966			14,234 (2.3)			3,921 (1.4)	2,926	134
1967			15,427 (8.4)			4,144 (5.7)	2,800	148

Note: Growth rates in parentheses. A = Szczepanik, B = Chou, C = Hong Kong Government. Real GDP p.c. based on RPI and using Chou 1948–60, Hong Kong Government 1961–67.

Sources: Chou and Szczepanik from J. Riedel, *The Industrialization of Hong Kong*, J. C. B. Mohr, Tubingen, 1974, p. 18. Hong Kong Government expenditure based estimates from *Estimates of Gross Domestic Product 1961–1994*, Hong Kong, Census and Statistics Department, 1995.

Table B Hong Kong's merchandise trade

Year	Imports	Exports	Re-exports	Trade balance
1947	1,550	1,217	n.a.	− 333
1948	2,077	1,583	n.a.	− 494
1949	2,750	2,319	n.a.	− 431
1950	3,788	3,715	n.a.	− 73
1951	4,870	4,433	n.a.	− 437
1952	3,779	2,899	n.a.	− 880
1953	3,872	2,734	n.a.	− 1,138
1954	3,435	2,417	n.a.	− 1,018
1955	3,719	2,534	n.a.	− 1,185
1956	4,566	3,210	n.a.	− 1,356
1957	5,150	3,016	n.a.	− 2,134
1958	4,594	2,989	n.a.	− 1,605
1959	4,949	2,282	996	− 1,671
1960	5,864	2,867	1,070	− 1,927
1961	5,970	2,939	991	− 2,040
1962	6,657	3,318	1,070	− 2,269
1963	7,412	3,831	1,160	− 2,421
1964	8,550	4,428	1,356	− 2,766
1965	8,965	5,027	1,502	− 2,436

Source: *Hong Kong Statistics 1947–1967*, Hong Kong, Census and Statistics Department, 1969.

Table C Hong Kong's trade with China (HK$m)

	Imports	Exports	Re-exports	Trade balance	Deficit with China/ total deficit (%)
1947	382	267		− 115	34.5
1948	431	280		− 151	30.5
1949	593	585		− 8	1.8
1950	782	1,260		478	—
1951	863	1,604		741	—
1952	830	520		− 310	35.2
1953	857	540		− 317	27.9
1954	692	391		− 301	29.6
1955	898	182		− 716	60.4
1956	1,038	136		− 902	66.5
1957	1,131	123		− 1,008	47.2
1958	1,397	156		− 1,241	77.3
1959	1,034	9	105	− 920	55.0
1960	1,186	13	107	− 1,066	55.3
1961	1,028	8	91	− 929	45.5
1962	1,213	8	77	− 1,128	49.7
1963	1,487	8	62	− 1,417	58.5
1964	1,970	13	47	− 1,910	69.0
1965	2,322	78	54	− 2,190	89.9

Source: *Hong Kong Statistics 1947–1967*, Hong Kong, Census and Statistics Department, 1969.

2 Hong Kong and China 1945–51

It was argued in Chapter 1 that the wider international political and economic environment in which Hong Kong emerged in the post-war period was instrumental in determining the financial relations of the colony. This chapter seeks to position Hong Kong in the Asian economy of the immediate post-war period by examining in detail the turbulent relationship with China, culminating in the withdrawal of China from the international economy in the 1950s. The Civil War and the subsequent Communist government in China had profound effects on international trade and payments in Hong Kong. Through the 1960s and 1970s, China was separated from most international economic contact partly by excluding itself and partly by being shunned by the West, but it maintained banking and trade links with Hong Kong. The pragmatic and low-profile relationship of these later decades was forged out of the chaos and conflict of the immediate post-war period. The events of these years exposed the opportunities as well as the difficulties presented by the close operation of two distinct economic regimes, and the impossibility of completely separating Hong Kong from the Chinese economy.

The usual interpretation of this period is that the war years and subsequent immigration threatened the political and economic future of Hong Kong, and the interruption of trade with China after 1949 forced Hong Kong entrepreneurs to look for other ways to sustain themselves. This marked the beginning of labour-intensive manufacturing, which was the foundation for Hong Kong's economic 'miracle'.[1] This chapter offers a more positive interpretation of the turbulent years immediately after the war, based on more detailed analysis of the various obstacles that Hong Kong faced. The disruption of relations with China marked a change in some aspects of Hong Kong's relations with China, but there were also fundamental elements of continuity with the pre-war period. The financial services available in Hong Kong, combined with loose regulatory control, allowed traders to take advantage of opportunities as well as respond to problems. The ability of Hong Kong to weather the trials of this period did much to establish its reputation for flexibility and resilience, and confirmed the centrality of Hong Kong's financial institutions to the future prosperity of the colony, as well as their importance to the economic survival of China.

Unlike the political events, the economic and financial history of these years has attracted relatively little attention from historians.[2] Within the economic history, most attention has focused on commerce and the impact of the UN trade embargo rather than the important financial relations between Hong Kong and China.[3] However, financial relations are important for understanding the subsequent position of Hong Kong in the economic policy of both China and Britain. The ways in which Hong Kong's government and institutions responded to the political and economic crises of these years laid the foundations for the emergence and development of Hong Kong as an international financial centre.

Nationalist chaos and Hong Kong's recovery

The prolonged collapse of the Nationalist regime in China in the five years after the Second World War was accompanied by economic and financial chaos. Poor fiscal control, rampant corruption, and rising military costs prompted monetary expansion, generated inflation, and drained China's scarce foreign exchange reserves. Massive immigration, inflation, and the interruption of internal trade also dislocated the traditional activities of Shanghai as the major entrepot for Chinese production. After the Japanese occupation, the port facilities were left in poor condition, making the goal of re-establishing the prominence of Shanghai more difficult.[4] The influx of refugees and the separation of Shanghai from its hinterland by the post-1945 Civil War sent the city into a downward spiral of inflation, speculation and stagnation, reliant on US aid for its livelihood.[5]

In contrast, the port of Hong Kong seemed ideal to replace the former international settlements in Shanghai. With relative political stability and a local financial and transport infrastructure, Hong Kong was a haven for flight capital and for entrepreneurs fleeing from the Civil War. A UK Trade Mission to China in 1947 reported that 'there is hardly a British firm in Shanghai which has not since the war transferred its principal office in that part of the world from Shanghai to Hong Kong. Many Chinese foreign firms had done the same, and this movement is not confined to commerce but applies also, though with less force, to industry.'[6] Up to the middle of October 1946, 193 British companies operating in China (representing the bulk of such 'China Companies') had registered at the Registrar of Companies, Hong Kong Supreme Court,[7] and by November 1946, 100–150 prominent Shanghai businessmen had moved to Hong Kong.[8]

Commercial spheres of influence had been fairly clearly distinguished before the war, with Shanghai dominating the trade of North and Central China while Hong Kong acted as an entrepot for South China. After the war, however, Hong Kong became the primary centre for regional merchants and threatened Shanghai as an important entrepot for Chinese tung oil and other products from North China. The Colonial Office Annual Report for Hong Kong in 1947 noted that due to the unsettled conditions in China, 'quantities of goods originally destined for China were diverted to Hong Kong and then re-exported elsewhere, while many firms, finding business conditions in Shanghai too difficult, moved to Hong Kong and brought with them their experience and business connections'.[9] In the same year, the China Association, which represented British business interests in China, advised the Secretary of State for the colonies that 'Hong Kong is now a far more important place than it was before the war, as its functions as an entrepot and port of transhipment for the foreign trade of China have greatly increased owing to the conditions prevailing in Shanghai and elsewhere in China.'[10]

The implications of this rivalry were not lost to the Chinese. In March 1947, a Shanghai observer (believed to be an adviser to the Central Bank of China) noted that 'Hongkong, following on the abolition of extraterritoriality in China, is rapidly stepping into the shoes of the former foreign Settlements at Shanghai ... the more this is allowed to develop, the bigger the bone of contention and the greater the problems which will ultimately arise.'[11] Lance, of the UK embassy in Shanghai, noted that China's export trade had become distorted during the Japanese occupation and that 'it has been the Chinese contention that this distortion has been prolonged into the post-war period because of premiums offered in Hong Kong by open markets in both Chinese national and United States dollars'.[12] In general, the lack of regulation in Hong Kong was seen by China as a 'thorn in the side' of the Nationalist government's attempts to stabilise the Chinese economy.[13] The Chinese often charged that 'by continuing to allow the constant stream of smuggling to cross the border, Hong Kong were undermining China's efforts to restore her economic and financial stability'.[14]

In contrast to Shanghai, the Hong Kong authorities encouraged a free market in foreign exchange to allow the prices of currencies to be competitive enough to allow trade at a profit.[15] Shanghai hosted a black market in foreign exchange but the Chinese made strenuous and often successful attempts to suppress it because it siphoned scarce foreign exchange away from the state.[16] Hong Kong merchants, however, were allowed to retain three quarters of the US dollar proceeds of their exports while surrendering 25 per cent at the official rate which undervalued the US dollar. They could use their retained US dollars to import goods to be sold at a profit (thus covering any losses on their exports or surrender of exchange) or they could sell these US dollars on the free market at a premium. The free market was vital to the entrepot trade of Hong Kong because other centres such as Macao and the Philippines also operated foreign exchange markets at a discount. If Hong Kong traders were forced to operate at the fixed official exchange rate, they could not offer as competitive prices as their rivals and the entrepot business would merely go elsewhere.

The Nationalist government made several efforts to forestall the shift of economic power to Hong Kong. China Customs required that exports transhipped at Hong Kong but destined to be returned to other Chinese ports were subject to export and import duty on the same basis as foreign goods. In addition, only Chinese shipping could be involved in the coastal trade between Chinese ports. These combined to limit the usefulness of Hong Kong as an entrepot for China and also hindered British shipping based in Hong Kong. In 1947 L.H. Lamb of the British embassy in Nanjing asserted that the restrictions on foreign shipping were 'clearly designed to be retaliatory against Hong Kong for the island's favourable geographical position as a free trade entrepot'.[17] The regulations were also reported to be a salve to the powerful shipowners of Shanghai, even though they hindered the trade of China as a whole.[18] Despite these constraints, there was considerable diversion of China's trade through Hong Kong. At the beginning of 1946, the value of trade through Shanghai was about half the value in the same period of 1941.[19] About one third of China's exports were declared to be destined for Hong Kong, which was about twice as much as before the war.[20]

Among the greatest obstacles inhibiting the recovery of China's trade were the tight trade controls and exchange rate policy enforced by the Nationalist government in an effort to shore up the crumbling economy. From February 1946, all exporters had to surrender their foreign exchange to the state at the overvalued official exchange rate. This ensured that exports were much more profitable if the proceeds were sold instead on the free market in Hong Kong, where the US dollar traded at a premium of about 40 per cent above the official rate.[21] At the end of 1946, for example, traders were able to take a loss of about 10–15 per cent on exports of Chinese products to the USA because the dollars they earned could be sold on the open market at a profit of 20–30 per cent over the official exchange rate.[22] In November 1946, the Nationalist government imposed quantitative controls on imports in order to conserve foreign exchange, and also established a state monopoly on exports of some minerals and produce. It was reported that the November regulations generated 'an influx of Shanghai merchants into the colony where they freely drew on the US dollar open funds resources of Hongkong'.[23] The regulations generated a shortage of foreign goods, which ensured large profits on contraband imports as well as exports. Furthermore, the import controls were very complex which inhibited legitimate trade to the point that it was cheaper to evade them.[24]

Between February 1946 and February 1947, the foreign exchange and specie holdings of the Central Bank of China fell by almost US$500 million to US$347 million.[25] At the official exchange rate of CNC$3,320 per US dollar set in August 1946, exports were virtually impossible and so traders were driven to smuggle through Hong Kong in order to use the free dollar market there. The overvaluation of the CNC dollar also encouraged capital flight. Chinese sold CNC dollar in Shanghai for US dollar at the overvalued official rate of CNC$12,000 per US dollar and then sold the proceeds at a premium for HK dollar or sterling in Hong Kong. The profits could then be used for imports or converted to CNC dollar on the free market. Briefly, the overvalued official exchange rate for the Chinese currency and the operation of a free market in Hong Kong were important incentives to engage in smuggling for Chinese exporters and deprived the Nationalist government of a significant proportion of potential foreign exchange earnings.

On 16 April 1947, the *Far Eastern Economic Review* estimated the value of the smuggling trade for 1946.[26] The results are presented in Table 2.1. These estimates must be treated with caution, but the *Far Eastern Economic Review* was privy to market information not always available to the authorities.[27] The data were calculated from the difference between the Chinese and Hong Kong trade returns plus 80 per cent of Macao's trade with Hong Kong, which was believed to comprise smuggling to and from China. Smuggled exports were about 22 per cent of official exports, while smuggled imports were about 7–8 per cent of total imports.[28] Table 2.1 also presents estimates made on a similar basis by the Central Bank of China for

Table 2.1 Estimates of smuggled trade with China: 1946 and 1947
(US$m)

	1946	1947
China imports		
from Hong Kong	40	
from Macao	3	
Total	43	65.2
China exports		
to Hong Kong	30	
to Macao	7	
Total	37	21.5
Balance of merchandise trade	− 6	− 43.7
China exports of silver to Hong Kong	4	
Balance of payment of smuggled trade	− 2	

Sources: For 1946, *Far Eastern Economic Review*. For 1947, Chang, *Inflationary Spiral*.

1947, showing that smuggled imports via Hong Kong and Macao had reached US$65.2 million or 13.6 per cent of official recorded Chinese imports. Exports smuggled to Hong Kong were estimated to amount to US$21.5 million or 9 per cent of official Chinese exports.[29]

The rise in the value of smuggled imports in 1947 reflects the imposition of quantitative import controls in November 1946, which were further tightened in February 1947. The fall in the share of smuggled exports in total trade may be due to the adjustments in the official exchange rate during 1947. With each devaluation of the official rate, exports through official channels expanded. Expectations of devaluation in the official rate may have encouraged exporters to hold back their goods until official devaluation and then release the goods through official channels at a profit.[30] A further consideration is that winter was the peak period for exports from China, and through the second half of 1947 the official exchange rate shadowed the black market rate. This reduced the gap between the two rates, lessening the gains from smuggling during the peak exporting months.

In November 1946, the Chinese Premier T.V. Soong sent a representative of the customs service to Hong Kong to discuss ways in which to stem smuggling. In December, the drain of foreign exchange from China due to the attractions of the free market in Hong Kong for traders and capital flight prompted the Chinese to request a Financial Agreement to impose exchange control on China–Hong Kong trade and payments.[31] This was followed in February 1947 by a visit of Pei Tsu-yee, Governor of the Chinese Central Bank, to discuss controlling Hong Kong's free market in Chinese currency. The result of these consultations was a Draft Customs Agreement and a Draft Agreement on Control of Chinese Currency Sales and US$ Operations. The Customs Agreement provided for Chinese officials to be stationed in Hong Kong to patrol the waters between Guangdong and Hong Kong. The Financial Agreement proposed that Hong Kong's US dollar earnings should be shared between China and Hong Kong, according to a formula that would return to China the US dollar proceeds of her exports through Hong Kong. British representatives in Nanjing urged their government in London to accept both agreements, despite the disadvantage for Hong Kong. They were under pressure from Soong, and they agreed with him that stability of China's economy was in Britain's interest by helping the KMT resist Communist forces.[32] Despite this advice, the British authorities were worried about the impact on Hong Kong and the decision was delayed.

At the beginning of March 1947, Pei Tsu-yee was replaced by Chang Kia-ngau as head of the Central Bank. By this time, the gap between the market and official rates in Shanghai had begun to widen again and the emergency regulations of February were shown to be inadequate, making smuggling become more profitable than ever. On 18 April, Chang visited H.H. Thomas, UK Financial Controller in Shanghai, and threatened that if the Customs Agreement fell through, China would blockade trade with Hong Kong by vigorously checking cargo and licences.[33] Chang also suggested new provisions for the Financial Agreement including the control of all currency movements between Hong Kong and China in order to constrain the illegal outflow of capital to Hong Kong. Hong Kong responded that it could not agree to impose currency controls, because they could not be made effective given the porous geographical barrier between China and Hong Kong. On the other hand, if the controls were effective, they would ruin Hong Kong's transit trade.[34] Furthermore, the welfare of Hong Kong relied on food imports from South China that were paid for in HK dollars. Between 50 and 60 per cent of Hong Kong's imports from South China was food in 1946–8.[35]

As the Chinese economy deteriorated, the longer-term impact on the Hong Kong economy began to occupy the colonial authorities. The Governor of Hong Kong (Sir Mark Young) worried that China intended to starve Hong Kong of legitimate trade. At the end of May 1947, Young tried to use the Financial Agreement to try to wring guarantees of support from Britain for Hong Kong's entrepot role.[36] The Bank of England advised against any such commitment as it might quickly become a large claim on the central reserves if Hong Kong's position deteriorated.[37] The Hong Kong authorities continued to pursue this angle, however. In July, the Head of the Department of Trade, Industry and Supplies in Hong Kong complained that

> it is fairly obvious that for political reasons we are about to commit economic suicide for there is now no money available from any source to finance the entrepot trade on which we depend for our complete existence.[38]

Thomson, therefore, asked the UK to agree to subsidise the transit trade up to US$0.5–1.0 million per month for the next two to three months until trade conditions improved.[39] The Colonial Office supported this proposal (up to a total of US$12 million) to 'save' Hong Kong.[40] The Bank of England disagreed, asserting that 'once we open the US dollar tap there, it is going to be very difficult to turn off',[41] and the Hong Kong authorities were turned down.

Meanwhile, the frustration felt by the Chinese authorities over the continued drain through Hong Kong reached new levels. In June and again in December 1947, Chiang Kai-Shek expressed his desire either to introduce armed forces along the South China coast to stop smuggling through Hong Kong, or to close Hong Kong off entirely from Chinese trade.[42] In the end, Hong Kong bowed to this pressure and accepted the Customs and Financial Agreements, but warned that if smuggling through Macao increased or Chinese exports from Hong Kong decreased then Hong Kong would withdraw.[43] Hong Kong also retained its US dollar free market as long as China operated a flexible exchange rate. There was some further haggling but H.H. Thomas was finally able to report that 'at long last after much labour and several false alarms the Sino-Hong Kong Financial Agreement (a somewhat puny infant perhaps, not the robust child of its first conception last August) saw the light of day on January 5 1948'.[44]

Events quickly overran the agreements as the Chinese economy disintegrated under the pressure of spiralling inflation. From February 1948, the black market rate for CNC dollar depreciated sharply against the official rate and generated a substantial capital inflow into Hong Kong.[45] In April, the Bank of England estimated that about US$20 million per month was being deposited in native banks' US dollar accounts in Hong Kong, representing the revenue from Chinese exports, flight capital and remittances.[46] At the same time, the Financial Counsellor in Shanghai reported that 'From both Shanghai and Canton funds have poured into Hong Kong, not only in the form of T/T and drafts, but, it is popularly reported, in the form of notes by the shipload.'[47] In June, press reports in the *North China Daily News* (published in Shanghai) implied that the independent status of Hong Kong was under threat if the flight of capital from Shanghai to Hong Kong was not stemmed.[48] In March[49] and again in June 1948,[50] in response to new exchange regulations, China urged Hong Kong to eliminate the black market in CNC dollar in Hong Kong to stem the capital outflow. Hong Kong responded that they wanted the gap between the black market and official rates in Shanghai to be closed before they would implement any further aspects of the Financial Agreement. Hong Kong was particularly unwilling to introduce new restrictions on its merchants that would prove unenforceable.[51] Meanwhile, in Shanghai rigorous police measures succeeded in driving the black market deep underground, if not eliminating it.[52]

Through the second half of 1948, conditions deteriorated as the Communist forces advanced. In August 1948, the Nationalist government tried to break the cycle by introducing a new currency, the Gold Yuan (GY), and declaring illegal all use of foreign currency. In October, it was reported that GY5 million was remitted from Tianjin to Shanghai each day. Travellers from Shanghai to Canton were subjected to restrictions on the amount of cash they could carry with them to contain the flow of capital to Hong Kong.[53] Remittances from overseas Chinese also decreased. In 1948, China's Vice Minister of Finance reported that the total overseas remittances in 1945/6 had been US$32 million and in 1947 US$30 million[54] compared with US$100–150 million before the war. By August 1948, remittances were running at less than US$0.5 million per month.[55]

Exports continued to be smuggled out of China on such a scale that it has been estimated that 40 per cent should be added to official statistics of Chinese exports in 1948 and 15 per cent to statistics of imports.[56] The disintegration of the Chinese economy made it impossible to get proof of origin or destination of foreign exchange used in trade with China, and banditry and smuggling accelerated. In March 1949, W.P. Montgomery, UK Trade Commissioner in Hong Kong, reported that piracy was disrupting trade with South China due to the disintegration of the Nationalist forces.[57] Meanwhile, the Nationalist government itself was believed to be dealing on the Hong Kong black market.[58] On 28 August 1949, Grantham asked to be allowed to terminate the Financial Agreement before the Communists took complete control of China.[59] It was finally terminated at the end of October 1949 by W.Y. Lin of the Central Bank of China.

During the Civil War in China, financiers, merchants and industrialists found the attractions of Hong Kong much preferable to the chaos of Shanghai. However, the attractions of Hong Kong as a free market centre prompted political as well as economic tensions. In this period, Britain, Hong Kong and China grappled with the impact of the contrasting systems on markets in China and Hong Kong. The efforts of the KMT government to conclude financial and customs agreements with Hong Kong reveal the extent of arbitrage between China and Hong Kong in goods and currency, and the difficulties of controlling the porous economic frontier between the colony and South China. The gradual collapse of China's external trade and finance was merely compounded by the exchange and trade controls imposed by the KMT government to contain the crisis. The next section examines the impact of these controls on the monetary links between the two territories.

The Hong Kong dollar in China

An unusual aspect of Hong Kong's influence in Asia in the late 1940s was the circulation of HK dollars in neighbouring territories. This was a result of close trade integration, instability of local currencies, and the convertibility of the HK dollar provided by the free dollar market. In China, the inflation, the depreciating exchange rate of the Nationalist currencies, and political instability provided the perfect context for currency substitution.[60] As Young, Governor of Hong Kong, noted in February 1947, the 'fact is that if good currency and bad currency are close neighbours people will go to any lengths to obtain good currency'.[61]

Two aspects of the China–Hong Kong relationship – the openness of the South China border with Hong Kong, and the stability of the Hong Kong currency – made the HK dollar the perfect candidate for substitution in China. First, the geography of the region made it impossible to police the movement of people, goods and currency between Hong Kong and China, especially given the reluctance of the Hong Kong authorities to threaten their entrepot status by imposing controls. Second, unlike the CNC dollar, the note issue in Hong Kong was strictly linked to foreign exchange reserves. Prices in Hong Kong were remarkably stable until the second half of 1949, and even then they did not approximate the hyperinflation of the Chinese economy.[62]

The KMT believed that the circulation of HK dollars in China undermined the credibility of the CNC dollar and frustrated their attempts to stabilise the currency. On the other hand, the circulation of a stable and liquid means of exchange sustained trade between Hong Kong and China. From Hong Kong's point of view, the circulation of its currency also facilitated capital flows. In May 1946, Sir Arthur Morse, manager of the Hongkong and Shanghai Bank (hereafter the Hongkong Bank) which was the main issuing bank of Hong Kong currency, reported that

> In my opinion the freedom of movement of Hongkong Dollar Notes does not lead to any abuses to the disadvantage of the Colony, and rather than leading to export of capital makes the currency more attractive and tends to bring money into the Colony. Of the new accounts opened by the Hongkong & Shanghai Bank since re-occupation, Chinese alone have deposited over $25 million.[63]

During the war Hong Kong notes were hoarded, and in the economic confusion after 1945 the circulation expanded. Immediately after Shanghai was liberated from Japanese occupation, the officials of the Hongkong Bank reported that 'there is a lot of speculative buying of Hongkong Dollar notes going on' with preferential rates for notes with 'old' dates of issue which were considered more likely to be honoured by the bank.[64] By late September 1945, Adamson reported that 'this place [Shanghai] is lousy with Hong Kong Dollar notes, mostly big denominations'.[65] The large denominations suggest that the HK dollar was held as a store of value in this turbulent period. Evidence of the HK dollar as a means of exchange is more difficult to establish, but Jamieson of the Hongkong Bank in Canton observed in July 1947 that

> The value of property is almost always quoted in Hong Kong currency and it is not unusual for the better class of shopkeepers (curio and silverware shops) as well as professional men (doctors, dentists etc.) to request payment in Hongkong dollars.[66]

At the same time he noted that 'it is said that in the Canton Black Market alone notes to the value of HK$1.5 millions change hands daily'.[67] He advised that the demand for HK dollar was due to native Chinese banks covering remittances between Shanghai and Hong Kong, merchants paying for their imports in HK dollars, and hoarders of foreign currencies. The supply was chiefly from overseas Chinese remittances to their families in China through Hong Kong, and from organised smugglers. The use of HK dollar in Canton, therefore, resulted from the balance of payments surplus that the region earned from Hong Kong.

The rush to print currency in Hong Kong during the post-war years gives an indication of the demand for HK dollar notes in China. Between 1945 and 1947, the Hongkong Bank note issue increased from HK$320 million to HK$618 million. Some of this increase was obviously in response to wartime inflation in Hong Kong, but the officials of the Hongkong Bank were convinced that most of the excess demand was from mainland China. In effect, Hong Kong was providing currency for southern China. In July 1947, Adamson wrote to the Canton office of the

Hongkong Bank that

> our Note Issue is still steadily increasing. Everything points to this being due to the greater demand for our notes from South China owing to the depreciation in the value of the C.N. Dollar. We have no means of forming an accurate estimate of what proportion of our total issue is held in China, but it must be very large.[68]

In September 1947, the British Treasury estimated that the circulation of HK dollars in China amounted to HK$300 million,[69] an increase of HK$200 million on the pre-war level. This evidence suggests that about two thirds of the increase in the note issue from 1945 to 1947 was destined for China. On the basis of these estimates, the circulation of HK dollar notes in China amounted to about 16 per cent of the total circulation of CNC dollars at the end of 1947.[70] Since the use of the HK dollar was concentrated in coastal areas and Canton, the ratio in these regions would be higher. By 1949 it was estimated that HK$400–500 million or half of the total HK dollar notes in circulation were in China, an increase of HK$300 million on the pre-war level.[71] This was equivalent to about US$112.5 million or GY23,062,500 million compared to a note issue in China of GY2,037,105.7 million at the end of April.

As the Communists gradually took control of more territory, they introduced the People's Bank Dollar (RMB) to replace the Nationalist currency in the regions they conquered. The Foreign Office was not optimistic about its prospects, advising that

> The future of this new currency must be dubious in the extreme, and one can presumably expect that the Communist authorities will have the greatest difficulty in establishing a stable currency, particularly as the Central Government have removed large quantities of gold from China to Formosa.[72]

Nevertheless, in January 1949 the introduction of the RMB in the northern city of Tianjin was reportedly a success, with 272 exchange stations crowded with customers to convert their Gold Yuan to RMB at a rate of GY6 and then GY8 per RMB.[73] It took several months, however, for the RMB to establish itself further south. In May 1949, in Shanghai the exchange rate with the HK dollar was set at RMB138, but it quickly depreciated.[74] At the beginning of July, the British embassy in Shanghai reported that

> Recent reports through foreign firms indicate a serious widespread distrust on the part of the Chinese merchants and traders, with whom they are associated, of the new currency which appears to be based both on economic and political grounds.[75]

Figure 2.1 shows the official exchange rate of the RMB against the HK dollar between November 1949 (once the Communist takeover of China was complete) and May 1950. This shows that the RMB depreciated rapidly through the end of 1949. From the beginning of 1950, however, the depreciation slowed and the currency was relatively stable through the first half of 1950 at RMB6,000 = HK$1 before beginning to appreciate.

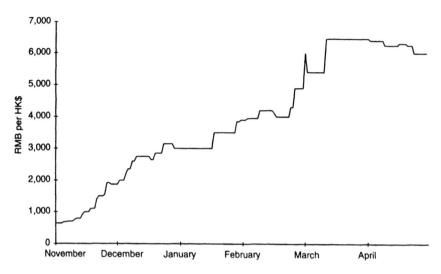

Figure 2.1 Official daily exchange rate 1 November 1949–1 May 1950.

The new Communist regime took strong measures to stabilise the value of their currency. The RMB was backed by a reserve of commodities held by the state that could be sold on the market to affect the price level. Such government dumping stemmed inflation in mid-June 1949. Parity Deposit Units (PDUs) were introduced in mid-June 1949 to reduce the currency in circulation, increase confidence, and maintain the purchasing power of savings. PDUs had a fixed value in terms of a basket of basic consumer commodities, and they became the medium for wage payments.[76] This established a store of value separate from the currency. Despite these stabilisation measures, however, the HK dollar continued to be in demand, especially in the south. At the end of 1949, W.P. Montgomery, UK Trade Commissioner in Hong Kong, reported that

> Indications are that the general public in the Canton area is offering a marked resistance in accepting People's Notes in exchange for HK$ and that in the majority of business trade continues on a HK$ basis. The requests of the Authorities have so far been ignored.[77]

The Communist regime resented the circulation of HK dollars in China. The official organ of the party, the *Renminribao* (People's Daily), reported in May 1950 that the circulation of HK dollars in Canton 'was not only a tool of British imperialism to seize huge supplies of the Kwangtung people but also a means of bandits and special service agents and depraved merchants in their speculative operations'.[78] A report by the Canton branch of the Chinese People's Association for Foreign Cultural Relations in 1959 asserted that by the late 1940s 'the market was flooded and stifled by foreign currency' which helped to make Canton 'the slave of

Hongkong and Macao'.[79] Currency substitution was seen, therefore, as an avenue for foreign intervention in the affairs of China. After the painful economic chaos under the KMT, part of the success of the Communist regime relied on the introduction of a viable national currency. A national currency would not only help to stabilise prices, but would also represent an important symbol of national unity.[80]

Over the course of March 1950, the Communist authorities finally succeeded in stabilising prices and the exchange rate. The value of the PDU in terms of RMB actually fell 7 per cent in Shanghai during this month.[81] The official reason for this turnaround was the centralisation of financial control in State Treasuries and the rationalisation of food distribution. British representatives reported, however, that the view of 'the average businessman' in Shanghai was that money was so tight after heavy taxation and enforced purchase of Victory Bonds that few could afford to buy anything.[82] The deflation of March proved to be a turning point for the RMB.

The exchange of foreign currency for RMB was reported in the local newspaper for March and April 1950. This reported that the Shanghai office of the Bank of China concluded 7,182 transactions exchanging RMB for foreign currency in March and 35,600 in April.[83] The East China branch of the People's Bank estimated that about 75 per cent of people were using the RMB by the end of May 1950 compared with one third at the end of February.[84] At this point, the Communist authorities cheerfully reported that 'ever since the latter part of March, banks have been crowded with people exchanging Hongkong dollars for People's Currency – a phenomenal development'.[85] After the RMB started to appreciate on the official market in August 1950, it increased in popularity and deposits denominated in PDU were phased out in favour of RMB deposits.[86] At the beginning of 1951, Yoxall of the Hongkong Bank in Shanghai reported to Head Office that 'by price fixing, heavy taxation, and strict control of credit, the People's Government has stabilised the currency, an achievement previously considered impossible'.[87]

By October 1950, the Governor of Hong Kong estimated that the volume of Hong Kong currency circulating in China, Macao and Formosa combined had been reduced to about HK$200 million or about half of the level at the beginning of the year.[88] Grantham expected that the repatriation of Hong Kong notes would continue gradually, although 'in view of past experience of recurring currency depreciation, there must be many among the more educated classes of the community who will be reluctant to part with any reserves of foreign currency which they have accumulated'.[89] This was not the end of currency substitution in China (the HK dollar still circulates in South China) but it marked the end of the extreme conditions experienced after the war.

The prevalence of currency substitution between Hong Kong and China emphasised the close economic and monetary integration of the region. This is in direct contrast with the growing ideological gulf between free market capitalism in Hong Kong and the interventionist regimes in China. The KMT resented the presence of HK dollar because it undermined their efforts to stabilise the CNC dollar. Their Communist successors also resented the circulation of HK dollar as an infringement of their sovereignty, portraying currency substitution as an imperialist tool to exploit the Chinese people. In order to sustain their political credibility, both regimes were intent on insulating their economies from the free markets in Hong Kong. The Hong Kong authorities resisted this pressure from the KMT, but acquiesced to the new regime after 1949. The Western powers added to the isolation of China through their commercial and financial policies, as the following sections show. It will be seen below, however, that the economic frontier between Hong Kong and China was never completely closed. Before moving to a discussion of Western embargoes, the impact on Hong Kong of the KMT blockade will be addressed.

The Nationalist blockade

The Communist takeover of China moved gradually from the north to the south during 1949. Trade with Communist-occupied North China was initially disrupted by the uncertainty associated with the changeover of political control. Trade was conducted either on a barter basis or using privately supplied foreign exchange. Towards the end of March 1949, three steamers chartered by local Chinese merchants departed from Hong Kong to Tianjin to engage in barter.[90] The Communist authorities restricted imports to essentials in order to conserve foreign exchange, resulting in losses for Hong Kong merchants who had held contracts dated from before the liberation. The Commodities Exchange Bureau in North China ports went so far as to order inessential goods to be returned to Hong Kong. The ensuing congestion and uncertainty brought trade with Hong Kong to a virtual halt by mid-May 1949.[91]

Conditions eased through June, but the bombing of the *Anchises* in Shanghai and the announcement by the KMT on 26 June that Communist-held ports were to be blockaded forestalled the resumption of trade. The blockade included air and sea attacks, and the mining of the Yangtse River. After the fall of Canton to Communist forces at the end of October 1949, the blockade was extended to the Pearl River, further disrupting shipping from Hong Kong.[92] Despite protests of the British and the Americans,[93] the blockade was formally lifted only in late May 1950.[94]

The blockade was initially effective all the way up the Chinese coast, but in the first part of July the KMT lost control of islands off Taku which made any blockade of Tianjin or Qingdao impossible. From mid-July, the KMT concentrated their attention on blockading the port of Shanghai and so ships destined for ports further north (Qingdao, Tianjin, Yingkou) were left relatively unmolested.[95] The profits to be made from running the blockade tempted both foreign and local shipping. Jardine, Matheson and Co., and Butterfield and Swire ran 30,000 tons of cargo to North China from August to mid-October 1949.[96] In September 1949, these two companies were agents for five out of the 15 sailings from Hong Kong to Tianjin.[97]

The northern ports of China recovered quickly.[98] Given the potential for profit, traders found ways to transport their goods through ports other than Shanghai, and between July and mid-September an estimated 130,000 tons of cargo were shipped from Hong Kong to Chinese ports.[99] The main commodities shipped to China were steel bars, chemicals, rubber tyres, petrol, kerosene, vehicles, copper wiring, medical supplies and bulk paper. On their return voyage, the ships carried bean curd/cakes and food items. The Shanghai manager of the Hongkong Bank reported that during the blockade, 'certain small coasters, run by local mushroom companies, have traded between Hong Kong and Shanghai but their high freight rates and uncertain services inspired little confidence, and most traders preferred the train routes to Tientsin and Tsingtao'.[100] In September 1949, total imports into Tianjin doubled and exports increased 50 per cent over August, exceeding the pre-war level. While about 90 per cent of Shanghai's trade was conducted by Chinese state trading companies, they were responsible for only about one third of the trade of Tianjin. Of the other two thirds, foreign merchants accounted for 21 per cent of exports and 5 per cent of imports. Just over half of exports from Tianjin were destined for the USA and 41 per cent for Hong Kong.[101]

There were a total of 97 departures from Hong Kong to China and North Korea in October and November 1949.[102] Ships flying the British flag accounted for just over half of the total sailings. Butterfield and Swire were the most prominent agents, contracting 19 departures, mainly to Tianjin. Panamanian ships were the next most common, accounting for 18 departures, half of which were destined for North Korean ports. By contrast, only seven vessels set sail for Shanghai in September and October and most were intercepted by the Nationalist Navy and charged 'squeeze' before being allowed to continue their journey. For example, the American ship *Flying Trader* of the Isbrandtsen Line reached Shanghai on 3 October with freight worth HK$100 per ton and paid HK$25 per ton in bribes.[103] It carried cigarette paper and machinery from New York, cotton from Karachi, rubber from Colombo and Singapore, and a wide selection of industrial goods from Hong Kong including chemicals, dyes, pharmaceuticals and oil.[104] Of 13 ships which left Hong Kong for Shanghai after 23 October, only four succeeded in completing the round trip, returning with varying degrees of risk, delay and damage.[105] Another Isbrandtsen ship, the *Sir John Franklin*, was heavily shelled and unable to leave Shanghai, prompting a public protest from the US State Department. In November only four vessels entered Shanghai and six were able to clear the port. The next month, no ships were able to enter and only one ship cleared.[106] In November, by contrast, 49 ships entered Tianjin and 28 entered Qingdao (of which 16 were from Hong Kong). In the same month 42 ships cleared Tianjin and 24 cleared Qingdao (of which 13 were destined for Hong Kong).[107]

Because the world's trade with China focused on Hong Kong for transhipment, the main impact of the blockade on Hong Kong was the accumulation of goods that had been imported for re-export to China via Shanghai. Through bills of lading were difficult to contract, and goods were left in Hong Kong awaiting charters willing to run the blockade. This built up to a critical congestion of merchandise and shipping through the second half of 1949.[108] By July 1949, for example, 50,000 bales of raw cotton were stored in Hong Kong awaiting export to Shanghai.[109] Banks operating in China and Hong Kong were put under increasing pressure as merchants incurred large losses, and letters of credit had to be extended. From early November 1949, there was a queue of at least six ships waiting in Hong Kong to run through the Nationalist guard ships at the mouth of the Yangtse River. Some returned to Hong Kong or were diverted to ports further north.[110]

After the fall of Canton to the Communists in October 1949, the Nationalist blockade was extended south. At first, motor junk traffic with the southern port of Swatow thrived on the shortages of goods in China. Junks charged an extra fee for running the blockade which amounted to about HK$20 per 100 catties of commodities, so that a medium-sized junk could earn HK$10,000 for each trip. The main commodities in this trade were evaporated milk and kerosene.[111] Larger ships began to trade with Amoy (Xiamen) and Swatow in November. At the beginning of the month, however, two British ships, the *Sin King* and the *Cloverlock*, were bombed during daylight in Swatow so that ships in future loaded at night and were left unattended during the day.[112] The UK Trade Commissioner in Hong Kong advised in December 1949 that 'the blockade in the mouths of the Yangtze and the Pearl Rivers continued to be regarded as dangerous'.[113]

All but junk traffic was excluded by November 1949 after KMT destroyers intercepted the SS *Kwai Wah*.[114] Junks were small enough to evade Nationalist guards by negotiating shallow rivers, often running via Macao. Air transport was also used to evade the blockade, and to compensate for the disruption of rail and road transport due to the war.[115] Motor junk traffic was initially irregular and subject to interception, claims for ransom, and confiscation of cargo. After the loss of Sam Chau Island, KMT naval vessels retreated to Lin Tin Island and the rewards for blockade running tempted more traffic into the trade. The continuation of the trade in essential commodities prevented shortages and kept prices from rising excessively in both Hong Kong and Canton. The most lucrative commodities were flour, industrial chemicals, dyestuffs, medicines and sugar.[116]

The overall impact of the blockade on the trade of Hong Kong is difficult to determine. Figures 2.2 and 2.3 show that the total value of trade between Hong Kong and China increased during 1949 despite the blockade. This was particularly true for exports, which increased both in terms of value and also as a percentage of total Hong Kong exports. Part of this increase, of course, was due to rises in the price of traded goods due to shortages, and because of the extra cost of shipping.[117] Because of the decline of Shanghai, Hong Kong's trade had already shifted toward ports in North China and away from South China before the blockade was imposed. Hong Kong's exports to North China comprised only 8–9 per cent of total exports to China in the late 1920s compared with 21 per cent in 1947 and 42 per cent in 1948. Eighty per cent of Hong Kong's exports to China went to South China in the late 1920s compared with 63 per cent in 1947 and 37 per cent in 1948. In any case, the disruption tended to be short-term as new trade routes were found to Shanghai overland via Tianjin or by rail or air to South China and then to Hong Kong either directly or via Macao. The Pearl River blockade was even more short-lived as the KMT forces were weakened by the time the embargo began there. In the longer term, trade was distorted not only by the blockades but also by the uncertainty and administrative changes associated with the war with Japan since 1937, the Civil War in China, and then the establishment of the Communist regime. Perhaps the most important conclusion is that the blockade tested the ingenuity of the Chinese merchants and their Western partners in evading these

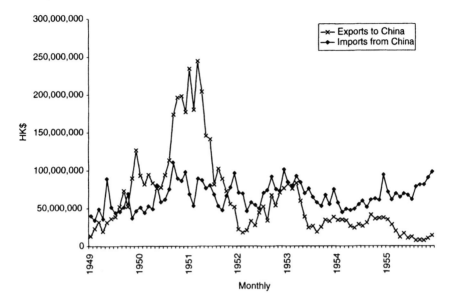

Figure 2.2 Hong Kong's trade with China 1949–55.

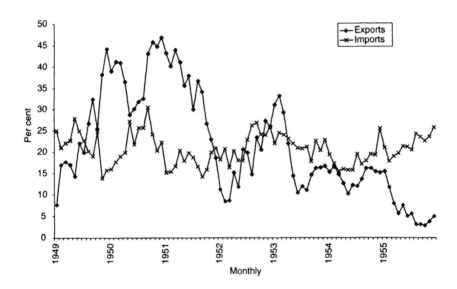

Figure 2.3 Hong Kong's trade with China as a percentage of total trade.

obstacles. The financial and commercial sanctions imposed by the West were to prove even more challenging for Hong Kong's merchants.

The US dollar freezing order

A further blow to the recovery of Hong Kong's relations with China was the freezing order issued by the American government on 16 December 1950. This froze all Chinese-owned US dollar assets and had far-reaching implications for foreign banks still operating in China. Hong Kong bank accounts were not frozen, but all transactions involving a Chinese name had to be vouched for to establish that there was no Communist connection.[118] Hong Kong branches of Chinese companies were considered to be 'tainted' and had their US dollar assets frozen.[119] Most importantly, the freezing order encouraged the movement toward barter trade organised by Chinese official trading organisations.

As early as June 1949, the manager of the Citibank in Shanghai warned the Hongkong Bank that the State Department intended to freeze Chinese US dollar assets.[120] This prompted the Foreign Office to ask the US Treasury directly if this was their intention.[121] The US Treasury denied any such plans and suggested that this was a proposal from the Citibank itself.[122] Nevertheless, from the beginning of 1950 the Hongkong Bank anticipated the freezing of Chinese dollar accounts. In mid-1950, Dunkley of the Tianjin branch enquired whether they could shift funds from account of the Bank of China to a special Hongkong Bank account to protect the funds from any action by the USA. Raikes, of the New York branch, replied that due to increased hostility of the US government toward the Communist regime, 'it would be a dangerous policy for us to try in any way to cover up in our books funds held here which we know are an account of the [Bank of China]'. He concluded that 'Should a freezing order be put in force there is no doubt that our books would be closely inspected and all funds held in Special Accounts for our China Agencies would have to be fully explained.'[123] By 13 December, days before the freezing order, the Bank of China account in the New York branch of the Hongkong Bank was closed, although the New York branch's Tianjin account held US dollars for account of the Bank of China which were used to finance trade.[124]

The Chinese authorities also anticipated the freezing of US dollar accounts. In January 1950, the Shanghai manager of the Hongkong Bank reported that, in anticipation of a freezing of Chinese assets, US dollar credits of six banks that acted in foreign exchange for the Bank of China had been transferred to Russian account in the USA.[125] The Chinese also shifted their US dollars to Swiss bank accounts that they hoped to conceal from the American Treasury. In March 1950, Hongkong Bank and Chartered Bank received instructions to open accounts in their own names in New York for the Bank of China and to receive US$3 million each from the Chemical Bank Trust Co. The Bank of China then instructed them to transfer these funds less US$100,000 in each case to the Swiss Banking Corporation New York for account of the Societe de Banque de Suisse in Zurich.[126] In the event, the US dollars secreted in Switzerland proved difficult to use and provoked a serious conflict between the Hongkong Bank and the Bank of China which dragged on through 1951 and 1952, complicating the closure of the Shanghai branch of the Hongkong Bank.

The freezing order generated suspicion and ill-feeling on the part of the Chinese toward foreign business, and encouraged the shift of all trade to a strict barter basis. In February 1951, Russell of Arnhold Trading Company called on Yao Lai-an, chief buyer of the Chinese National Import Corporation, and was told that the CNIC would conduct business almost entirely on a barter basis due to fears of further freezing orders. If trade on this basis was not forthcoming, then the Chinese were willing to look to become self-sufficient.[127]

The February regulations required that no goods were to leave China until imports of an equal value (or foreign exchange) had arrived in China.[128] This would avoid outstanding contracts that might be captured by future freezing orders. In March, a Barter Exchange was established in Shanghai to connect importers and exporters and applicants for foreign exchange.[129] Since most foreign traders and banks could not accept the shipment of goods without payment in advance, or by tying the sale of their goods to sales of Chinese products elsewhere, trade with China through private foreign interests was drastically reduced. Hong Kong was in a convenient position and retained some business by virtue of the speed of the turnover of trade through the port (essential in barter trade). Nevertheless, the freezing order contributed to the difficulties in Hong Kong, as the US and UN trade embargoes began to affect Hong Kong's trade.

Development of embargo policies in the USA and UK

In November 1949, the USA imposed an embargo on exports of strategic goods to China. This was followed by more general restrictions on trade in December. In May 1951, the United Nations imposed an embargo on trade with China. These trade embargoes are more deeply researched in the existing literature than the blockade or financial controls discussed above.[130] Despite the importance for the future prospects of Hong Kong, however, there has been relatively little detailed research on the role of Hong Kong in the development of the embargo policy.[131] This section will first identify the importance of Hong Kong to the Anglo-American deliberations over trade restrictions. The next section will examine the impact of the embargo on Hong Kong's trade. This account draws on Bank of England and US State Department sources as well as the more commonly used UK Foreign Office and Treasury files.

From the outset, the positions of the US and the UK on the approach to the new Communist regime in China were very different, culminating in Britain's recognition of the People's Republic of China in January 1950. The British hoped to maintain the status quo as far as possible, and to encourage the continuation of political influence through commercial links. The importance of China to the prosperity of Hong Kong (now a strategically as well as economically important British outpost) was of considerable influence in this policy. For the Americans, political rather than economic considerations were most influential, and the changeover in China fell into the Cold War ethos of American foreign policy. The Americans were much more active in supporting the Nationalist cause and more determined to resist the legitimacy of the Communist regime.

In early 1949, once the Communists had gained control of parts of North China, the Americans began to plan their embargo against Communist China. From the start, it was obvious that British cooperation was essential because of the importance of Hong Kong as the pivot of China's international trade.[132] The official American position was that 'British co-operation, with particular reference to the entrepot centre of Hongkong, would be essential to the effectiveness of US controls' over strategic exports to China.[133]

Groves, of the British embassy in Washington, was called into the State Department in February 1949 to be questioned about the possibility of imposing controls on Hong Kong's trade with China in order to prevent Chinese supplies reaching the USSR.[134] Groves was reluctant to engage the Americans on this issue, but he was subsequently informed that the State Department had developed a scheme for control of trade in Hong Kong and he was invited to view it.[135] Groves initially demurred, but finally saw the State Department plans at the end of March. Groves insisted on what was to become the British line on such trade restrictions: that restricting the trade of Hong Kong alone would not suffice. Other ports in Asia (including American-occupied Japan) would need to be included to prevent the entrepot business merely shifting away from Hong Kong and to another centre.[136] The American response was that Hong Kong was the only really active port in the area and was the only one to be considered. They agreed, however, that an embargo would require the cooperation of the UK, SCAP and possibly other European states.[137]

The UK was asked formally for their opinion on 21 April 1949.[138] They stalled, unwilling to act against the interests of Hong Kong despite increased pressure from the State Department after the fall of Shanghai. Opinion was split between the Foreign Office, Treasury, Colonial Office and Board of Trade, but provisional views were finally given to the State Department at the end of May. Control of exports from the UK to China posed no problem, although they could not guarantee the support of the rest of Europe. The problem was that Britain would also have to impose controls on exports to its colonies such as Hong Kong, Singapore and Malaya. Even these controls would be ineffective without restrictions on trade elsewhere in the Far East such as Japan and Manila. Otherwise, trade would merely be diverted away from British colonies to their detriment. In conclusion, the Foreign Office solicited from the Americans specific proposals that could be discussed at a technical level in London.[139]

American officials duly arrived in London on 20 June 1949. The American plan was to control exports to China of arms and strategic goods that were currently restricted in trade with Eastern Europe (known as 1A goods). In addition, however, they wished to add certain other goods such as oil and petroleum products, mining and steel making equipment, transport and power generating equipment, which were important to the Chinese economy (known as 1B goods).[140] They suggested that the embargo should start with the UK, USA, Hong Kong and Singapore, and that only afterwards should efforts be made to attract other participants.[141] The British position was that new controls would be administratively and politically difficult to impose, and in general they doubted the effectiveness of trade controls as a political tool. Furthermore, the embargo would threaten British interests in China and, finally, there would be considerable damage to entrepots such as Singapore and Hong Kong if the embargo were not geographically complete.[142]

The British Ministerial position was not established until the end of July 1949, at which time it was agreed that the UK would not extend existing control on transhipments to Hong Kong and Singapore until the Belgian, French and Dutch had agreed to do the same in their territories. Importantly for the Americans, Ministers also insisted that Japan should conform to the embargo.[143] Once these other countries had agreed to participate, the UK would control the first category of goods, i.e. arms and strategic material, but they were not willing to extend control to the industrial products put forward by the Americans. They suggested instead that British, American and Dutch oil companies should be asked not to sell oil to China in excess of China's domestic civilian requirements.[144]

Not surprisingly, the Hong Kong Governor (Sir Alexander Grantham) was strongly opposed to any further control on transhipments in Hong Kong.[145] He argued that this would merely divert trade elsewhere, and that such controls would be impossible to enforce because smuggling was rife in the waters around Hong Kong. If controls had to be imposed, they should be initiated at source rather than in Hong Kong. He also noted that three US oil companies were actively selling oil to China on barter terms; indeed a Caltex tanker had been sent to Shanghai as soon as the port opened and was only stopped by the Nationalist blockade. This smacked of inconsistency between the American government and US business. There was also a danger that China would react by cutting off essential food exports from Canton to Hong Kong.[146] The Governor, therefore, supported the British policy of resisting American overtures. British embassy officials in Nanjing agreed that any repercussions from China over the embargo would be aimed at Hong Kong. Furthermore, an embargo on industrial goods would merely push China towards autarky, which would generate suffering for the Chinese people and undermine UK business interests.[147]

At the beginning of August, the Americans formally expressed their disappointment in the British response, suggesting that this cast doubt about the possibility of a joint approach to Communism in Asia. They insisted on the importance of an embargo on industrial goods and asked for talks with the UK to be resumed.[148] In an internal memo, Dening expressed the British position (agreed in London by the Secretary of State):

> At the moment we are concerned only with the survival of our business interests in China. If they do not survive, then we shall have lost the trading machinery with the aid of which we hope, in due course, to convince Mao Tse-tung and his boys that there is some advantage in playing with the West. We should also lose all our contacts with China, and the Communists would recede still further into the arms of Moscow.[149]

The response to the Americans was couched somewhat differently. It asserted that the basis of the disagreement was whether export controls would influence Chinese political policy, since Communist governments tended not to link trade with politics. Secondarily, it was noted that the UK believed that a continued commercial presence in China was desirable to exert pressure and influence where possible.[150]

Toward the end of 1950, the British began to reconsider the possibility of joining the USA in an economic embargo on China, perhaps by including controls on financial transactions as well as commercial trade. The Bank of England was not optimistic about the effectiveness of such a policy. At the beginning of December, Graffety-Smith advised that 'My guess would be that any economic blockade would be fairly useless in view of the long coastline, the neighbouring countries and the innate qualities of smuggler which are present in every Chinese.'[151] The bank's advice was that a trade blockade would have to be extended to Hong Kong, Indo-China, Burma and Siam, and would kill off Hong Kong's entrepot trade and local industry if all leaks were closed.

On the financial side, there was the possibility that Chinese-owned assets held in Hong Kong could be blocked or controlled. Exchange controls would be very difficult to impose, however, since it was difficult to distinguish a Chinese resident from a Hong Kong resident. This complication was to be a long-running obstacle for those who sought to control capital flows in Hong Kong. Echoing the negotiations with the KMT in 1946/7, it was also noted that exchange controls would make Hong Kong's entrepot business more difficult. Finally, since food imports from China were bought with HK dollars, it was impossible to prohibit the flow of HK dollars to the mainland without causing hardship in Hong Kong. Heasman concluded that 'As long as Hong Kong continues on anything like the present basis it may be possible to stop some of the gaps but I am doubtful if all of them could ever be completely closed.'[152] Unlike the USA with its US dollar freezing order, the UK could not impose a complete exchange control between itself and its colony. The integration of the Hong Kong and Chinese economies was too entrenched to be overridden for political reasons.

In late January 1951, an inter-departmental Working Party on Economic Sanctions Against China was set up to prepare for a joint Anglo-US study group.[153] The advice of the Working Party was that existing controls on the export of strategic materials from the UK could be enhanced. A total embargo, however, would need to be extended to neighbouring states (including Hong Kong and Malaya), and would also need the cooperation of India and Pakistan, which was unlikely to be forthcoming. Restrictions on shipping would require the cooperation of all UN members including India, Panama and South Africa, who might not join. Such a move would also hurt UK shipping companies. A naval blockade would be an extreme measure that would invite retaliation and hostility from other members of the Commonwealth, such as India. An embargo would thus threaten Commonwealth solidarity, especially with India and Pakistan. Financial measures would not be sufficient on their own to stop trade and they would bring sterling into disrepute.

Finally, the repercussions of an embargo on the UK and on Hong Kong were assessed. The trade loss to the UK was not expected to be very significant. UK companies were already reducing their presence in China, although they could still be confiscated by the Chinese, putting British citizens at risk. The repercussions for

Hong Kong were, of course, more serious. There was a potential loss of 45 per cent of exports, the loss of essential imports of food and raw materials, and a rise in unemployment. If Hong Kong were no longer an entrepot, its value to China would be reduced which paradoxically might encourage the Chinese to attack, generating a loss of British prestige in the East. If made effective, therefore, a total embargo could lead to the loss of Hong Kong to China. The Working Party concluded that a selective embargo could be recommended but that shipping and financial controls should be used only if necessary to make such an embargo effective. Accordingly, on 18 May 1951 the British joined the UN Additional Measures Resolution to impose an embargo on exports of strategic materials to China and North Korea.[154] Among the abstentions were the Commonwealth countries of India, Pakistan and Burma.

Impact of the embargo on Hong Kong

Export controls were first imposed in Hong Kong in the second half of 1949 to conform to Britain's policy to restrict strategic goods reaching China. Export licences were also implemented (on petroleum exports for example) in order to ensure that dollar area imports into Hong Kong generated US dollar earnings for Hong Kong exporters to China. These early controls, however, did not affect trade significantly because of the narrow range of goods to which they were applied, and the relaxed attitude to licensing.[155]

Instead, in the months leading up to the Korean War in the summer of 1950, Hong Kong benefited substantially from China's re-stocking boom when both prices and volumes of exports to China soared.[156] Rationalisation of China's trading policy and the resurrection of communications also revived trade. The Hongkong Bank reported that in 1950, 'The development of interior collecting centres through the Government Trading Organisations, better transport, and unification of the country, released larger quantities of export commodities than have been available for many years. Many small exporters dropped out, but the larger and more experienced ones, both foreign and Chinese, had generally a successful year.'[157] Figure 2.3 shows that Hong Kong's exports to China soared from 15–20 per cent of total exports in 1949 to 40–45 per cent in the first half of 1951.

Gradually, American trade restrictions began to affect Hong Kong's commerce. In April 1951, J.F. Nicoll, Colonial Secretary in Hong Kong, wrote to the Colonial Office to complain that the American consulate was threatening non-US firms in Hong Kong with the loss of licences to import US branded goods if they happened to be exporters to China.[158] The Colonial Office agreed that this was objectionable, but that the American consulate should not be challenged since the State Department appeared to believe that Hong Kong's trade controls were very firm when in fact they were quite ineffective. The policy was to avoid rocking the boat. The Foreign Office minuted that 'we had ourselves noticed elsewhere the State Department's optimism about Hong Kong's controls. The Colonial Office at any rate are apparently under no illusions.'[159]

The UN embargo declared in May 1951 threatened more serious consequences for Hong Kong. From June, Hong Kong imposed more widespread controls on trade

with China, in particular on exports of pharmaceuticals, cotton and rubber.[160] Figures
2.2 and 2.3 show that the drop in exports in the second half of 1951 is sharp indeed,
but in part represented a return to the levels that had prevailed in the late 1940s
before the Korean War boom.[161] Meyer goes further to note that the slump after 1951
merely represented a return to the trend in Hong Kong's trade from the 1920s. He
argues that Hong Kong's trade with China would probably not have increased much
even without the embargo because China remained poor and underdeveloped.[162]

Most analyses of the impact of the embargoes are on the basis of recorded trade
and ignore the evasion for which the Hong Kong market was renowned.[163] Goods
could be smuggled directly to mainland China or exported to Macao for re-ship-
ment to China. Macao did not operate effective controls on trade with China
because of the nature of the local administration and the vulnerability to Chinese
retaliation. Although statistics are by definition impossible to collect, some indication of the volume of such trade is available.

From 1949 to the end of 1951, Hong Kong's recorded exports to Macao were
very volatile. There was a substantial increase toward the end of 1949 and through
the first few months of 1950, which then subsided until the first half of 1951 (after
the tightening of the US embargo). In the wake of export restrictions in the second
half of 1951, trade declined to a relatively stable level of HK$5–10 million per
month through to the end of 1955. Since almost all exports from Hong Kong to
Macao were destined ultimately for China, this increases the total value of exports
bound for China by HK$60–120 million per year during the UN embargo.

In October 1951, the US State Department observed that

> since the imposition of embargoes on strategic goods exported to Communist
> China, the Chinese Communists have utilised Macau both as a transhipment
> point for the physical movement of strategic materials and as a place to contact
> and make deals with business agents from other countries who can operate in
> Macau with a minimum risk of government surveillance and interference.[164]

In addition to recorded trade, State Department intelligence indicated that 'there is
a substantial volume of exports of strategic goods from Macao to Communist
China which have been imported into Macao through various channels, such as
smuggling from Hongkong'. In particular, it was believed that 2,000–2,500 tons of
petroleum products were exported to China each month.[165]

Evidence on smuggling activities is necessarily patchy and anecdotal. In
September 1951, the US Chief of Naval Operations reported that the UN embargo
'has had no apparent effect on the China trade' and that China's imports continued
to be mainly strategic materials related to the war effort.[166] Furthermore, 'The main
transhipping point continues to be Hong Kong, however, India and Burma are
becoming increasingly important in this capacity.' Banks in Hong Kong were
reported to be involved in financing Burmese overland exports of rubber and cotton. The report concluded that 'all evidence indicates that smuggling activities are
increasing very rapidly ... smuggling is carried on chiefly between HK, Macao,
Kowloon, and Canton; even shipments from Okinawa have been noted. The largest

volume of smuggling seems to be in petroleum products, but large quantities of pharmaceuticals, rubber, and tires also find their way into China by this means.'

In 1952–4 there was a short-lived attempt to compile balance of payments statistics for Hong Kong that included estimates for smuggling. These were compiled by 'a competent Chinese official' whose appointment was prompted by a visit to Hong Kong by a representative of the Bank of England.[167] These put smuggled merchandise exports at £6 million (HK$96 million) in 1952 and £4 million (HK$64 million) in 1953 based on information about seizures which were believed to be a fairly consistent proportion of total trade.

In 1955, the *Far Eastern Economic Review* reported that

> Many smuggling organisations handle the delivery of strategic goods to Mainland China for local traders. They often deposit 100% of the value of the goods with the local exporter. On delivery of the goods at destination, the firm in China confirms the receipt by cable or by other prearranged methods. The exporter here refunds the deposit plus a bonus of 30% to 50% to the smuggling agents. This arrangement has been so well accepted by all parties that Chinese authorities grant an adequate amount of foreign exchange for smuggling expenses in addition to the cif value.[168]

The US State Department believed that the main impact of existing controls on Hong Kong by 1952 was to reduce business profits rather than increase unemployment.[169] They recognised, however, that any further controls would affect employment adversely, and consumption standards would fall if imports of food from China were stopped. Hong Kong imported about 80 per cent of its meat from China and about one half of its vegetables in amounts that were equivalent to about US$30 million p.a. Indeed, recorded trade of meat imports was believed to underestimate actual imports by about one half, based on comparing recorded imports with actual slaughters in 1950 and 1951.[170] The prospects for increasing Hong Kong's trade with other countries were not considered very bright given the large efforts already made in this direction and the imminent return of Japan as a competitor in shipping and port facilities.

It is important to recognise, therefore, that the embargoes did not sever the economic links between China and Hong Kong. Cotton was imported from Pakistan and Egypt and rubber was imported from Ceylon, but most other products came from Hong Kong either directly or via Macao. Together, these five territories comprised 90 per cent of China's imports from non-Communist countries in 1952.[171] In this sense, Hong Kong became a more important trading partner for China after the embargo than it had been before. This was especially true for goods that could not be imported from the Eastern Bloc including pharmaceuticals (antibiotics and sulpha drugs), machinery and dyes.

Although Hong Kong's recorded exports to China fell substantially both in absolute terms and as a percentage of Hong Kong's total trade after 1951, imports from China remained a stable proportion of total imports. This generated a trade deficit with China, so that Hong Kong remained the most important source of foreign exchange for mainland China. Hong Kong currency was convertible to most other currencies through the free exchange markets in Hong Kong, making this surplus particularly valuable for China.

The pressure on Hong Kong was alleviated by a relaxation on American exports to Hong Kong in March 1952, but the trade recession from 1952 to 1954 did constrain the growth of prosperity in the colony. The post-Korean War slump hit most developing countries in the world, but there is little doubt that Hong Kong was particularly affected. Tsang has asserted that the Chinese trading community in Hong Kong was disproportionately affected by the recession of 1952–4 because of the small margins on which they operated and their greater exposure to the China trade.[172] It should also be remembered that Hong Kong's trade with China was affected by factors other than trade embargoes. Political campaigns in China, such as the Five-Anti Campaign of early 1952, would have disrupted Hong Kong's trade even in the absence of an embargo.

Conclusion

This chapter has addressed the complicated relationship between the economies of Hong Kong and China in the period 1945–51. The trade embargoes are widely discussed in existing literature, but less attention has been paid to the importance of the Nationalist blockade of 1949/50 and the freezing of Chinese-owned US dollar balances at the end of 1950. These two measures had important implications for Sino-Hong Kong relations that aggravated the impact of the Western trade embargo. The blockade prolonged the disruption of trade that was caused by the changeover of administrative control and the attempt to stabilise the Chinese economy after years of inflation and civil war. The freezing order was arguably as important as the embargoes in encouraging the move to autarky by the Chinese government, because it destroyed confidence in the use of foreign exchange. The discussion of the monetary link between Hong Kong and China emphasises the high level of integration of the region. When examining the relationship between Hong Kong and mainland China in these critical years, all these aspects of the nature of Hong Kong's economic links with China need to be considered.

China's attitude to Hong Kong evolved during these immediate post-war years. On the one hand, China benefited from the monetary stability in the colony and from the balance of payments surplus earned from Hong Kong. On the other hand, however, the clash of ideology generated frictions that threatened the relatively peaceful relations between the two territories. By 1951, the benefits of continuing the economic links with Hong Kong outweighed the costs. The new Communist regime had succeeded in stabilising the economy and had moved resolutely toward self-reliance in most of its economic relations with the world. Hong Kong, however, remained an important source of foreign exchange, and the colony continued to act as the international financial centre for China, processing remittances and operating its foreign exchange market.

These early years after the war also confirmed the importance of Hong Kong in British policy. First, as a military outpost in East Asia, Hong Kong was important for Britain's global strategy. Second, British commercial interests in Hong Kong were influential in shaping British policy. The commercial and strategic priorities coincided in the recognition that Hong Kong had to be allowed to prosper economically in order to maintain its political integrity. If Hong Kong's economic prospects were dashed, the Communists would have an easier task in taking control of the colony. The paradox that at a time of great economic challenge on the mainland, China would be less willing to take on Hong Kong if it were fundamentally weakened, did not shake the commitment to the twin goals of economic and political stability. This commitment formed the basis of the British attitude to Hong Kong's financial markets for the next two decades. This chapter has also described how and why Hong Kong took over many of the commercial and financial activities that had flourished in Shanghai before the war, including banking, foreign exchange, the stock market and insurance. The following chapters will address the evolution and maturing of these institutions.

3 The banking system

Over the course of the period 1945–65, the banking system of Hong Kong was profoundly changed by pressures within and outwith Hong Kong. In these years, the restructuring of the Hong Kong economy and the general expansion of international banking created new demands for banking services. The immediate post-war uncertainty provided profit opportunities for smaller banks, in particular, and they greatly increased their capital. The slump of the early 1950s then weeded out many of the weaker institutions that had expanded too rapidly. After 1954, the economic prospects for the colony brightened, and increased wealth and greater political stability combined to tempt large amounts of hoarded cash and gold into bank deposits. In the absence of specialised property lenders, the building boom offered almost irresistible opportunities for speculative profits by banks, prompting an aggressive search for deposits. Political instability elsewhere, and the growth of the domestic export industry, increased the demand for the international commercial and financial activities of the colony, and enhanced the competitiveness of Hong Kong.

Structure of the banking system

The banking system in Hong Kong was divided into various classes of institutions, although the classifications were not watertight. They included modern, native, foreign, and Chinese state banks. The 'modern' banks were usually Hong Kong incorporated and offered the usual banking services (deposits, loans, foreign exchange) and included the 'authorised banks', which operated the official exchange market. The local or native banks were generally smaller and some did not take deposits from the public. They operated the free market in foreign exchange, and most were members of the Gold and Silver Exchange Association. Branches of foreign banks in Hong Kong serviced the international trade requirements for their home country and provided brokering services for international stock markets. The final group was the China state banks, which financed trade with China and transferred remittances. All categories of bank were engaged in international transactions at some level.

At the beginning of the period, commercial banking was dominated by a small number of British-linked banks that focused almost exclusively on the overseas commercial activities of the colony. Parallel to this sector was the large number of small, unincorporated institutions that collected deposits, offered unsecured loans, and channelled remittances. The use of conventional banking services by the public was generally quite limited. By the end of the period, however, the banking system was much more homogeneous and competitive, offering a wider range of services to a broader spectrum of customers. Still, the financial system remained dominated by commercial banks. In 1960 the Hongkong Bank established the first dedicated hire purchase institution, Wayfoong Finance, but until the 1970s there were no specialised building societies, or merchant banks. The lack of specialised institutions was partly due to weak banking regulation that allowed banks to engage in a variety of wholesale and retail activities, including merchant banking, real estate lending, insurance and brokering.[1] In this way, the larger Hong Kong banks more closely resembled the mixed banks of continental Europe rather than the British model of specialised commercial banks.

The banking system was notoriously unregulated in the 1950s. In the immediate post-war period, a rash of banks sprouted up to service the swelling population and to manage the flood of flight capital. In November 1946, the American journalist J.W. Powell remarked that 'Chinese banks are opening Hongkong "branches" at the rate of several a week.'[2] A year later, it was estimated that about 250 institutions offered banking services; these included 14 European/American banks, 32 Chinese commercial banks (double the number prior to the war), 120 native banks (about the same number as before the war), 76 exchange shops and 20 others, including insurance companies.[3] At this point, the Financial Secretary became concerned that some of the banking institutions that had emerged since the war were taking advantage of the unstable economic and political climate in China to engage in smuggling and/or destabilising speculation.[4] This prompted the Banking Ordinance of January 1948, which remained in force until 1965.

The ordinance defined what constituted a bank very loosely, including many small institutions that performed only a limited range of financial activities including money-changing or remittances.[5] There were no reserve requirements, nor statutory liquidity ratios, and no requirement to publish or even to prepare complete balance sheets. So long as the HK$5,000 licence fee could be raised, individuals or groups were free to attract deposits and operate as banks. Special provisions were included to allow the native Chinese banks to operate within the ordinance, paying a smaller licence fee of HK$500 to act as money-changers. The 1948 Ordinance also established a Banking Advisory Committee that operated the regulations and granted licences. The Committee was comprised of the Financial Secretary, the Accountant General, representatives of two banks (Hongkong Bank and the Bank of East Asia) and an accountant.[6] When the 1948 Ordinance was due to be replaced, it was noted by the Financial Secretary, J.J. Cowperthwaite, that

> its purpose was not so much control of banking as control of the growth of small exchange shops which were then assisting speculation against the Chinese currency. The Ordinance is of little practical use for the protection either of depositors or of the general financial security of the Colony.[7]

In 1948, 131 banks were licensed under the regulations, including 13 European/American banks, 8 Chinese state banks, 32 Chinese-owned commercial banks and trust companies and 78 native banks, gold and silver dealers. This total soon declined as small banks suffered from the interruption of commerce with China. By 1954 there were 92 licensed banks, and this number fell to 82 by 1959.

While the overall number of licensed banks decreased, the number of authorised banks increased from 23 in 1950 to 42 in 1959. The Exchange Control designated 'authorised' banks allowed to deal in official foreign exchange. They comprised the Exchange Banks' Association, which set the official exchange margins and rates for merchanting business. They tended to be the larger and more modern institutions, including almost all the foreign banks.[8] Becoming an authorised bank was not necessarily linked to any considerable economic advantage (indeed the 'authority' precluded the bank from engaging directly in the free exchange market), but the label was considered an important status symbol.[9] Authorised banks could, of course, instruct non-authorised banks to act in the free market for them. Among the authorised banks were the note-issuing banks: the Hongkong Bank, Chartered Bank and Mercantile Bank.

The various categories of bank in Hong Kong did not act completely independently. Indeed, they were often in direct competition or arranged cooperative relationships.[10] Most banks held balances with each other and they were consolidated into groups within the Clearing House. Until 1962 this was restricted to 25 authorised banks that also acted as clearing agents for non-members. In May 1962, in response to recommendations by R.F. Chatham, the system was streamlined to comprise 16 full members who acted for other authorised banks.[11] Unauthorised banks of good standing could join the system on the recommendation of existing members. In this way, a hierarchy of banks developed with the Hongkong Bank at the pinnacle. Of the 69 member banks in 1962, the Hongkong Bank was the primary clearer for 28 foreign and domestic banks. The Chartered Bank was the next most prominent clearer, acting for eight banks.

The banking groups were also linked by the call money market that emerged in 1959. By 1962, five authorised brokers intermediated among exchange banks while 10 other money brokers served the unauthorised banks. The demand for call money usually came from foreign banks who did not hold large balances in Hong Kong, but who had intermittent need for liquidity for trade finance. Surplus funds were usually found in the local Chinese banks. Call money rates reflected demand and supply conditions in Hong Kong, but also conformed to money market rates in London since most large banks had access to funds there.

The Chartered Bank offers an example of the nature of inter-bank deposits. Between 1960 and 1965, money at call with other banks increased from 14 per cent to 30 per cent of the Chartered Bank's total balance sheet assets.[12] In 1960 Chartered's cash at call amounted to HK$13.5 million, of which $7.5 million was at Bank of Tokyo, HK$4 million at Banque Belge pour L'Etranger, and HK$2 million at United Commercial Bank Ltd (registered in India). By 1965 the total was HK$30 million, distributed among 14 banks, all but two of which were foreign banks. In addition, the bank held substantial current account deposits, primarily for other Hong Kong banks. These, too, increased dramatically during the period, from HK$4.5 million on account of some 30 banks in 1956, to HK$80 million on account of 53 banks in 1965. Chartered's only deposit at another bank was its cash balance at the Hongkong Bank. The Chartered Bank also made loans to several Hong Kong and foreign banks, including import credit loan accounts.

Modern local banks

The modern banks adopted conservative lending practices, often preferring self-liquidating loans. Many were members of the Hong Kong Exchange Banks' Association and all were part of the Hong Kong Clearing House. The Bank of East Asia was the largest Chinese-controlled modern bank in Hong Kong and was one of only two banks listed on the Hong Kong Stock Exchange.[13] Along with the Bank of Canton, Shanghai Commercial Bank and Chekiang First Bank, it pursued a particularly cautious strategy with respect to lending and branch networks throughout this period, allowing it to weather the storms of crisis which drove other less prudent banks out of business in the early 1960s.[14] Until the mid-1950s, the Bank of East Asia was also extraordinarily restrictive with respect to deposits. Initial deposits had to amount to at least HK$30,000 and be accompanied by letters of recommendation from two existing depositors.[15] Despite these restrictions, deposits grew steadily from HK$5 million to HK$10 million between 1948 and 1956. After the restrictions were relaxed, deposits grew more quickly from HK$11 million in 1958 to HK$250 million in 1964. Nevertheless, the Bank of East Asia's share of total deposits in Hong Kong fell from 8 per cent in 1956 to 4 per cent by 1964. With the exception of one year (1959), the Bank of East Asia maintained a liquidity ratio above 70 per cent between 1953 and 1964.[16] The Shanghai Commercial Bank's deposits remained at about HK$5 million from 1951 to 1957, and then doubled from 1957 to 1962, and doubled again by 1966. Again, despite this dramatic increase, the bank's share of overall deposits fell from 5 per cent in 1955 to 2.5 per cent by 1966.

Several local modern banks had overseas branches that they used to collect deposits and to develop their trade and remittance business. The Hongkong Bank had the largest international branch network of any local bank, covering 17 countries as well as a wholly owned subsidiary in California, opened in 1955.[17] By purchasing the controlling interest in Mercantile Bank and the British Bank of the Middle East in 1959/60, the Hongkong Bank became a truly global institution, and dominated the local banking system. Registered in Hong Kong, it was run by British expatriates and was deeply embedded in the commercial and industrial activity of the colony.

The rationale for multinational banking attracted academic interest in the 1980s as the world banking system adjusted to the globalisation of financial markets. The identification of economic factors that prompt banks to branch follows the literature on multinational corporate expansion more generally.[18] These include regulation, changes in technology, and exploitation of firm specific advantages. In the first half of the 1960s, British and British overseas banks were forced into defensive strategies of expansion to counteract the aggressive policies of American banks.[19]

This pattern is reflected in the case of the Hongkong Bank, which sought to counteract increasing competition in existing markets and to prevent other banks taking advantage of acquisition opportunities. The Hongkong Bank rarely actively sought the acquisitions; instead it was offered the option to purchase the banks. Another factor was the risk of political and economic instability in Asia, which encouraged greater geographical spread. As Perry-Aldworth of the London Committee of the Bank explained to the Bank of England in January 1959,

> we are having our toes well trodden on by all the [UK] Clearing Banks, who are impinging on our preserves abroad, and also by the rising generation of indigenous banks, so that quite apart from the dangers inherent in the East we must move to meet increasing competition.[20]

The Chairman described the Mercantile deal in the bank's 1958 Annual Report,

> Early in 1957 an indication reached us from the holder of a large block of shares that he was looking for a purchaser and he wondered whether we would be interested. This approach came at a time when it was becoming more and more clear that, in British exchange banking as in many other activities, the tendency must be for consolidation, not only because larger units tend to become stronger and can operate more effectively, but also because they are less vulnerable to take-over bids from parties who wish to make a profit by obtaining control of large liquid assets.[21]

At the time, Chase Manhattan Bank was interested in gaining control of Mercantile, and the Hongkong Bank wanted to prevent an American bank gaining this foothold in its markets.[22] Negotiations between Hongkong Bank and Mercantile were initially broken off in July 1957 because Mercantile could not reveal its hidden reserves. Talks resumed over a year later after a reorganisation of capital, and the takeover was agreed in December 1958.

In the first quarter of 1959, the London Committee of the Hongkong Bank put considerable pressure on the Hong Kong Board of Directors to accept an invitation to take over the British Bank of the Middle East (BBME) and National and Grindlays Bank.[23] The motivation again was to expand Hongkong Bank's global interests and to prevent an American bank taking control of these British banks. The Hong Kong board resisted on the basis that the deal did not offer immediate benefits for shareholders, there were negative tax implications, and the Mercantile Bank was still being 'digested'.[24] By June 1959, however, the Bank of England had resolved the tax issue, and the Hong Kong board was convinced of the benefits of acquiring BBME (although they did not take up the offer of National and Grindlays[25]). Ninety-nine per cent of the shares of BBME were acquired in the first quarter of 1960.

With a few exceptions, the Chinese-controlled banks tended not to open offices abroad. The Bank of Canton had branches in Thailand and Singapore, and the Chiyu Bank had an office in China. By 1977, the Liu Chong Hing Bank and the Shanghai Commercial Bank each had one branch overseas, and the Overseas Trust Bank had four. While cautious in its domestic banking, the Bank of East Asia had a more aggressive international policy and maintained branches in Singapore, Shanghai and Saigon. The Saigon and Shanghai offices had been established before the war and resumed business shortly afterward. Unlike the branches of European banks, the Bank of East Asia (along with the Chiyu Bank) was permitted to continue independent operations in China, mainly related to commerce. The Saigon branch was also constrained by political events, but it continued limited operations, returning to profit in 1963, mainly due to its involvement in US dollar transactions for the American government and army.[26] The Singapore branch was the most consistently prosperous, and grew out of an informal relationship with Singapore's Lee Wah Bank.[27] The Bank of East Asia had sent personnel from Hong Kong to lead Lee Wah's foreign exchange business, and then opened its own office in 1952.

The fact that most Chinese banks did not open branches abroad suggests that their international activities could be performed more efficiently through correspondent relationships with foreign banks in Hong Kong and abroad. The facilities of the Hongkong Bank, the Chartered Bank and the Mercantile in major financial centres like New York and London were used regularly by other banks in Hong Kong. As Casson describes, 'links with well-established territories whose trade is dominated by linkages with other locations will tend to be handled by correspondent arrangements'.[28] Correspondent relationships were used to transfer funds for local and international clients related to trade and investment, but in most cases the volume of business with a particular centre did not justify the expenditure involved in opening a branch office.

Correspondent relationships were considered important assets. It was not worth jeopardising these arrangements by becoming too competitive in the home markets of correspondent partners. In 1962, J.A.H. Saunders of the Hongkong Bank noted with respect to expansion in Europe:

> we hold the view that as far as trade with the East is concerned opening in Brussels or Rome, either on our own or through subsidiaries, must cause the loss of valuable correspondent business. This supposition applies particularly to Belgium, where competitors of the Societe Generale do business with us rather than the Belgian Bank, which is so widely represented where we operate.[29]

Perhaps more importantly, the increasingly nationalistic regulatory environment elsewhere in East and South Asia was a disincentive to regional expansion. This will be discussed further in Chapter 6. The freer regulatory environment goes far to explain why Hong Kong was attractive to foreign banks, who became keen competitors in the provision of increasingly complex international financial transactions.

Foreign banks

Figure 3.1 shows the source country of the 29 foreign banks operating in Hong Kong as of 1965. From this it is clear that the predominant source was elsewhere in Asia. Those from Southeast Asia were primarily the overseas Chinese banks with head offices in Singapore, Malaysia, the Philippines and Thailand. Of the foreign

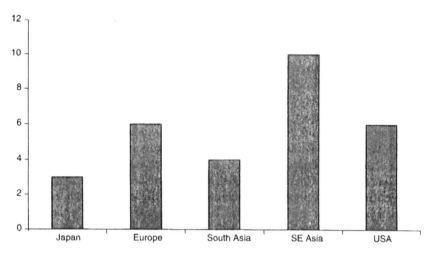

Figure 3.1 Source of foreign banks in Hong Kong 1965.

banks, nine were established before 1939 (including the Chartered and the Mercantile). Almost all the foreign banks operating in China in 1946 had well-established branches in Hong Kong to facilitate their trade.[30] After 1949, they maintained their branches in Hong Kong while extricating themselves gradually from China. A further six foreign banks arrived in Hong Kong from 1948 to 1957 and roughly two per year opened offices until 1965.

About half of the foreign banks opened additional branches beginning in 1959, so that by 1965 there were 46 branches of foreign banks in Hong Kong, plus 17 local branches of the Chartered Bank. After the Chartered Bank, Banque Belge pour L'Etranger had the most aggressive branching policy. It opened its first branch in Hong Kong in 1935, its second in 1960, and had a total of five offices by 1965. The French BNCI, Bangkok Bank and Bank of America each had three branches, while a further nine foreign banks had two branches by 1965. The branching activity of the foreign banks suggests that they were using the colony as a funding centre as well as merely financing trade. No direct evidence is available about the deposits of these banks other than for the Chartered Bank. Deposits at the Chartered Bank in Hong Kong increased from HK$70.5 million in 1955 (6.2 per cent of total deposits) to HK$731.8 million (10 per cent of total deposits) in 1965.[31] In 1964, the 27 largest Hong Kong banks, plus the Chartered Bank, held about half of the total deposits in the colony. The Hongkong Bank probably accounted for a further 35 per cent, leaving perhaps 15 per cent of deposits for other foreign banks.[32]

The influx of American banks into Hong Kong was symptomatic of a worldwide expansion of American financial institutions in this period.[33] This was caused by restrictions on international banking in the USA, and the demand for services from American multinational corporations located in Europe and Asia. Initially, US banks in Hong Kong were constrained by restrictions imposed in 1950 on US dollar transactions, and the American embargo on trade with China. These obstacles prompted the Chase Bank to close its office in Hong Kong in January 1951, and it did not return until 1963.[34] Remaining US banks soon found ways around the restrictions, however. The Bank of East Asia, for example, acted as an intermediator between American banks and the Bank of China for foreign exchange in these difficult years.[35]

One of the longest-standing US banks in Hong Kong was Citibank (formerly International Banking Corporation, then First National City Bank).[36] It opened for business in Hong Kong in 1902 and engaged primarily in remittances from the USA and Canada, as well as servicing American clients. Because many employees spent the war in Macao, Citibank was able to reopen on 15 October 1945, quickly after the Japanese surrender. After the US dollar freezing order in December 1950, the bank was forced to conduct all business on a 100 per cent margin basis, which put them at a considerable disadvantage vis-à-vis other banks in Hong Kong. Once the US Treasury restrictions were lifted, they rebuilt their business quickly. Nevertheless, Head Office rejected local plans to expand the branch in 1960, citing fears of political instability. They changed their mind as the economy of Hong Kong took off, and the first branch was opened in Nathan Road, Kowloon, in June 1962 followed by the Causeway Bay branch in October 1964. The bank's official history notes that these additional offices were opened because 'business was particularly brisk because of the absence of exchange controls and restrictive banking regulations'.[37]

Foreign banks entered the Hong Kong market through acquisition as well as greenfield investment. In October 1962, the Japanese Dai-Ichi Bank bought one third of Chekiang First Bank's capital stock (an investment of ¥126 million) and appointed two Japanese officers to the bank's Board of Directors. The cooperation was intended to increase local and Southeast Asian foreign exchange operations.[38] In 1963, the Chase Manhattan Bank bought the Hong Kong, Singapore and Bangkok businesses of the Nationale Handelsbank from the Rotterdamsche Bank in a broad expansion into Southeast Asia.[39] Acquisition became more widespread after the government imposed a moratorium on new banking licences in 1965.

As in European financial centres, American banks were keen competitors, attacking cosy markets with aggressive marketing and lending strategies. In 1959, Perry-Aldworth of the London office of the Hongkong Bank noted that 'The Americans are fierce competitors who keep to no rules, and surely it is good policy to make things as expensive and as difficult for them as possible.'[40] In 1964, the Hong Kong manager of the Hongkong Bank reported that 'The amount of travelling that American bankers do in this part of the world is quite staggering. I am afraid there is no doubt that they want to dominate the financial scene in South-east Asia.'[41]

This resentment against the newer foreign banks extended beyond hostility to the aggressive Americans. In 1952, the Hong Kong manager of the Mercantile Bank reported that

> The premises previously occupied by the Bank of China in Queens Road Central just west of our office are being renovated for the United Commercial Bank Ltd who will be opening shortly ... This is unfortunate as no doubt there

will be a margin war on Letters of Credit. These people are well known for their tactics elsewhere and we ourselves will have to look to our defences, especially with the large Indian Firms here.[42]

In the same year, the Mercantile Bank's manager complained that the Nederlandsche Handel-Maatschappij NV Amsterdam bank were 'very strong competitors of ours in the Colony, and are continually trying to get our business'.[43] The influx of foreign banks made the commercial bill market particularly competitive, squeezing the local banks into less liquid assets.[44] H.J. Tomkins of the Bank of England reported considerable resentment against the influx of foreign banks during his visit to Hong Kong in 1961–2, but he dismissed claims that these banks were engaged in 'unfair' competition and rejected calls for restrictions on their activities since 'Hong Kong, which is so dependent on international freedom of trade and payments, would be ill-advised to impose discriminatory restrictions on expatriate banks.'[45]

Not all applications to open branches in Hong Kong were successful. In at least one case, the entry of a foreign bank was played off against reciprocal facilities for Hong Kong banks. In 1962, the Hongkong Bank was prevented from opening a branch in Nagoya Japan, and in response the bank

> prevailed on Government to stop the Sumitomo Bank opening here on the grounds that we have been refused permission to expand in Japan. I now want to show that we are very willing to play ball and allow Sumitomo in as a quid pro quo for the Japanese authorities' change of mind about Nagoya.[46]

Sumitomo subsequently opened in Hong Kong in December 1962, an event which the Director described as realising 'a 10-year dream to set up an office in the economic centre of South East Asia'.[47] In 1960, Lombard Banking Ltd lobbied the Chartered Bank to ask for sponsorship to open a bank and a hire purchase company in Hong Kong, but the Chartered Bank refused to help and in the end the application did not go forward.[48]

In addition to the foreign banks licensed to operate in Hong Kong, several others advertised their services without maintaining an office. By 1962, these included Lombard Banking, Isle of Man Bank Ltd and Westminster Credit Finance Ltd, the last of which found clients primarily among expatriate civil servants.[49] By 1965, Hong Kong also hosted representative offices of a further eight international banks.[50]

The number of foreign banks in Hong Kong is an important indicator of the nature of international financial and commercial business that attracted them to open offices. That the foreign bank presence increased through the 1950s, despite the interruption of the traditional entrepot trade, shows that the financial centre was not reliant on the relationship with China. Instead, banks were attracted by Hong Kong's growing domestic prosperity, the freedom to finance Asian trade from Hong Kong, and the expansion of domestic exports in the 1950s. As in other centres, they also came to service their nationals who established businesses in Asia.

Between 1957 and 1965, 364 foreign companies registered in Hong Kong, bringing the total number to 570.[51]

China state banks

After 1945, several banks controlled by the Chinese government operated branches in Hong Kong to administer to international trade and remittances. By 1949, there were nine such banks controlled by either the Chinese government or by provincial governments.[52] The local employees all pledged their support to the People's Republic of China (PRC), and most were allowed to continue operations under the direct control of the Communist government. By 1960, there were 10 Beijing registered China state banks, as well as two registered in Hong Kong: Nanyang Commercial Bank and Po Sang Bank. Of these 12 China state banks, nine were authorised exchange banks, while the Po Sang Bank dealt in bullion and was sometimes classified as a native bank.

The Bank of China, which dominated this group, had been formally established in 1912 (although its origins traced back at least a decade earlier). From 1928, it specialised in international money transfers and other foreign exchange, and after 1949 it became the official foreign exchange bank of the PRC. The Hong Kong branch was the major financial link between China and the rest of the world.[53] In the 1960s, the bank was a major purchaser of sterling to build up reserves as well as to finance imports. From 1955 to 1965, the Hongkong Bank sold close to £550 million to the Bank of China to finance China's purchases from the sterling area. The other official banks specialised in trade and remittances. Again, this group contributed to the range of international financial services provided in Hong Kong. The published accounts of the Hong Kong registered China state banks show a high level of liquidity, which reflects their specialisation in remittances and trade finance rather than local loans.[54]

Native Chinese banks

The 'native' or local banks were identified by their membership of the Chinese Gold and Silver Exchange, their closer and more traditional relationships with their customers (including longer opening hours), and a greater tendency to lend against real estate.[55] Most exploited place-of-origin networks, including Shanghai, Cantonese and Fujian groups. They ranged from large, incorporated institutions to small sole-proprietorships or unincorporated partnerships. When H.J. Tomkins arrived in Hong Kong from the Bank of England in 1962, he remarked that 'there are certainly some funny banks here'.[56] The main activity of native banks was money-changing, transferring remittances, and financing trade, all of which involved them in close correspondent links with banks in the USA and elsewhere. In the mid-1950s, the slump in the gold market decreased their number and those that survived diversified into moneylending and real estate speculation.

The service offered by the smaller banks was reinforced by the accessibility of managers to their customers, which provided 'an atmosphere in which banking customers feel that they are well looked after and their problems sympathetically considered'.[57] This personalised and flexible service was a source of competitive advantage over the larger commercial banks. As will be seen, this advantage eroded through the first half of the 1960s, as other banks opened branches in the growing residential areas outside Hong Kong Island.

In the prosperous years of the late 1940s, six banks emerged as the leaders of this sector: Hang Seng, Dao Hang, Wing Lung, Wing Tai, Wing Hang, Kwong On and Hang Loong. In May 1948, the *Far Eastern Economic Review* reported that 'their considerable reserves, the acumen proved by their managers, the good reputation enjoyed among Chinese and European clients have further tended to increase the volume and scope of these native banks' businesses'.[58] In 1947, only 20 of the 200 native banks made losses, while the rest posted profits ranging from HK$100,000 to Hang Seng's HK$6 million.[59]

As the opportunity to make quick profits by exploiting exchange controls between China and Hong Kong ended, there was a consolidation of banking activity in this sector. Some went out of business or adapted their activities to become trading companies. By 1959, three large native banks dominated the rest; these were Hang Seng, Wing Lung and Kwong On (the last became an authorised exchange bank in November 1959), who together accounted for about one half of the capital and reserves of the group.[60] The larger native banks acted as correspondents for the smaller banks, collecting their foreign exchange proceeds for transfer to accounts abroad. The larger banks operated closely in line with the formal commercial bank sector, but the others operated on a more risky basis, tending to be undercapitalised and heavily engaged in property speculation.

The differentiated market for native banks compared with 'modern' commercial banks was reflected in the spread of interest rates. In a scramble for funds to take part in the financial boom of the late 1940s, native banks offered interest on deposits ranging from 6 to 10 per cent p.a. compared with 1–2 per cent obtainable from commercial banks. In turn, they offered loans against gold or US dollars valued at free market rates, collateral which was not acceptable to the commercial banks, and then charged higher interest for such facilities. The increased competition which small local banks faced from the aggressive branching activity of the mainstream banks forced them to continue to offer higher rates to attract deposits. By 1963, some banks offered as much as 7.5 per cent p.a. on three-month deposits, compared to 4 per cent p.a. paid by the larger banks.[61] Higher deposit rates in turn forced them to lend at greater risk, but for higher nominal return. Despite the fact that the close relationship between native banks and their customers helped to reduce risk, high interest rates of around 16–24 per cent p.a. for loans were usual in the 1950s, compared with 6–8 per cent p.a. at modern banks. The insecurity that resulted from this strategy (evident in periodic bank failures) then made it more difficult for these institutions to attract deposits, widening the gulf even further.

The high interest rates charged to borrowers also reflected the alternative investments available. Much of the activity of these banks was related to speculation in real estate, the stock market and the gold market. During the 1950s and early

1960s, there were spectacular profits to be made in these markets, especially in real estate. In 1958, the average yield from portfolio investments by native banks was about 10 per cent, while the profit on foreign exchange dealing was about 15 per cent. Interest on forward gold transactions was about 5–10 per cent p.a. in 1952–4. These investments had the added benefit of greater liquidity than loans, which were usually made for six months.

A fourth factor in the higher rates charged by native banks was the lack of competition from the mainstream banks for personal loans, since the collateral was often not adequate for modern banks. The fact that there was a market for the loans offered at such high rates by native banks shows there was considerable demand for such credit among the Chinese community. Commercial lending (related to international trade) was much more competitive, however, and so the native banks charged only 5–6 per cent p.a. on trade credit. Loans secured against stocks and shares were also available from the modern banks, which meant that the native banks had to keep their rates in line. Borrowers using share collateral were charged a lower rate of 0.6–0.8 per cent per month, and loans were regularly made up to 80 per cent of the market value of the collateral (compared with 50–70 per cent of the value of real estate collateral).

In evidence to the UK Radcliffe Committee on the Working of the Monetary System in February 1958, Perry-Aldworth, London manager of the Hongkong Bank, remarked that 'a good deal of the business done by indigenous banks would not be handled by us at any rate of interest'. He explained that this was due to 'the nature of the business and the impossibility of controlling many orientals'.[62] The large banks preferred shorter-term and more liquid loans, and they lacked the personal contact with many Chinese borrowers that helped smaller institutions manage risk.

Table 3.1 shows the combined balance sheet of 10 native banks compiled by Ng Kwok-Leung in 1960.[63] As noted above, Hang Seng, Wing Lung and Kwong On together accounted for about one half of capital and reserves of the group and 60 per cent of deposit liabilities. The high volume of cash assets (21 per cent compared with 2 per cent for the banking system as a whole[64]) was due to the foreign exchange business of these banks. Commercial advances were about one third of other loans. About two thirds of loans were against real estate on terms of six months, and earned interest of 1–1.2 per cent per month. Investments in shares and real estate accounted for about 9 per cent of total assets of these banks, compared with less than 3.6 per cent for all Hong Kong banks.

As with the China state banks, the native banks were clearly involved in significant international financial transactions as intermediaries between overseas and domestic customers in the service of remittances, as well as packing loans and trade bills to facilitate international trade. In the 1940s, most had branches in major cities in China to facilitate remittances, and some operated formal or informal branches elsewhere in Southeast Asia. Many were closely associated with Macao banks and gold dealers. The Hang Seng Bank, for example, was linked with the leading Macao native bank, Tai Fung Bank, which was run by the gold dealer Fu Tak-yam. Chiu Tai Bank was owned by a son of Ko Ho-ning, a wealthy Hong Kong resident who originated in Macao.[65]

Table 3.1 Estimated combined balance sheet of 10 native banks (HK$m)

Liabilities		Assets	
Capital	40	Cash	50
Deposits	167	Bankers' acceptances	5
Foreign credits and guarantees on behalf of customers	30	Bills receivable	35
		Loans	90
		Shares	6
		Real Estate	15
		Bank premises and equipment	6
		Liabilities of customers in respect of foreign credits and guarantees	30
Total	237	Total	237

Source: Ng, K.-L., 'The Native Banks: Their Structure and Interest Rates', *Far Eastern Economic Review*, 11 February 1960, p. 309.

Hang Seng was the leading operator in the Hong Kong free exchange market, and the founder and manager of Hang Seng Bank was Chairman of the Gold and Silver Exchange Society from 1946 to 1949. The bank was established in 1933 and incorporated in 1952 with a paid-up capital of HK$5 million.[66] By 1954, it had deposits of HK$21 million and total assets of HK$32 million. Ten years later, total deposits amounted to almost three times those at the Bank of East Asia (and 80 per cent more deposits than the Chartered Bank). By this time it was the largest Chinese-controlled bank incorporated in Hong Kong, and the second largest deposit-holder after the Hongkong Bank.

The Foreign Division of Hang Seng was engaged in inward and outward remittances, sales of travellers cheques (for First National City Bank, Bank of America, American Express, Midland, Australia and New Zealand Bank), issuing travellers' letters of credit as agents for Manufacturers Hanover Trust Co., NY, collecting clean bills drawn on banks abroad, and money-changing.[67] At the end of March 1965, Hang Seng's foreign currency accounts showed a balance of matching assets and liabilities of US$9.5 million plus £3.8 million in sterling.[68] Among the largest items were US$3.8 million in deposits balanced by US$2.5 million in Hang Seng accounts with local and foreign banks and money at call. Most of the accounts were associated with the finance of international trade. Table 3.2 shows the sources of supply and demand for US funds in 1965.

In addition, Hang Seng received constant offers of discounted security or 'switch' sterling from firms and banks in London, Zurich and New York, which it bought for US funds from the free market. The sterling was credited to Hang Seng's No. 2 accounts with banks in London and was used to finance inward bills or sold to other banks in Hong Kong at inter-bank rates. Hang Seng did not charge commission on inward remittances denominated in US dollars or Cdn dollars that were payable in the original currency or in HK dollars bought through the free market. The bank noted that 'this is definitely to the advantage of the payees and therefore many of them request their friends and relatives abroad to route the remittances through us'.[69]

Table 3.2 Hang Seng US$ account

Sources of US funds
Proceeds of US$ export bills
Purchases from banks, exchange houses and firms in HK
Inward remittances and drafts drawn on Hang Seng
Drafts and money orders purchased over the counter
Proceeds of sales of the Philippine peso and Cdn$ transfers to correspondents abroad
Proceeds of sales of banknotes to foreign correspondents

Demand for US funds
Reimbursement for negotiations under import Letters of Credit
Drafts and travellers cheques sold by Hang Seng
Outward remittances
Purchases of banknotes from banks abroad
Sales to banks, exchange houses and firms in HK
Switch sterling and other arbitrage operations
Sales to gold merchants

Source: Hang Seng Report of Foreign Division, April 1965, GHO322, HSBC.

With respect to trade finance, the Exchange Control allowed Hang Seng to deal directly with correspondents in the sterling area and with Hong Kong's regional trading partners, although all other transactions had to go through an authorised bank. Hang Seng had correspondents in all these territories except for Burma, India and Pakistan, where they used the Hongkong Bank. In the USA, the bank's correspondents included Irving Trust Co., NY, Manufacturers Hanover Trust Co., NY, Chemical Bank NY Trust Co., Bank of America, and Crocker-Citizens National Bank, San Francisco. The Hang Seng reported in 1965 that 'To these depositories we often mail approximately 4,000 drafts, cheques, etc. totalling about US$250,000 on each despatch. Upon receipt of the shipment they credit the entire amount to our account prior to clearing.'[70] Full use was made of Bank of America's affiliates in Europe, Japan, the Philippines and Singapore.[71] The bank reported that its outward bills business had doubled in the year from March 1964, due in part to the finance of silver exports to the UK. As well as import letters of credit, inward bill loans, and shipping letters of guarantee, they also offered credit to small retailers to take partial delivery of shipments which 'add[s] much to the smooth operation of many firms in the Chinese community'.[72]

Hang Seng's commitment to international contacts was fostered by personal visits of the bank's leading officers. In 1950–2 S.H. Ho (founder and manager) and Q.W. Lee (later Chairman) travelled to 17 cities in nine countries on four continents to learn about different banking practices and to build up international contacts. In 1964, Lee again set out to drum up international business, visiting Chinese communities in Singapore, Australia, New Zealand, Tahiti, Honolulu and Japan. The following year, Ho Tim (General Manager) 'embarked on a round-the-world-tour to visit Chinese communities in an effort to strengthen ties and encourage their investment in Hong Kong'.[73] Hang Seng is an extraordinary example of the local or native banks since it was so much larger than most others, but its activities and growth show the international character of banking activity in Hong Kong where a large proportion of transactions were related to international commerce or finance.

The persistence of small, unincorporated banks alongside very large banks was one of the unusual aspects of the Hong Kong banking scene. This dual structure can be explained partly by reference to the limited economies of scale available in some bank activities. These include the wide range of speculative opportunities available for investing deposits including the gold market, real estate and the stock market, all of which had small entry costs and correspondingly limited economies of scale. In addition, the small scale of manufacturing in Hong Kong and the importance of family control and personal connections preserved a place for small lending institutions. The native banks also received government support because they were seen as serving the local trader and small depositor in ways that the British banks and even the large Hong Kong Chinese banks were not. The link between the financial sector and industry will be dealt with in greater detail in Chapter 6. Despite the apparent over-supply of banks, there were very few mergers and most banks were still closely associated with the prominent men who had founded them.

By the early 1960s, the native banks and the modern banks had become closer competitors, as the former adopted more Western banking practices and the latter engaged in more domestic lending. The share of Hong Kong's external trade that went through the inward and outward bills department of the Hongkong Bank increased from 1958 to 1963, peaking at about one quarter of Hong Kong's trade in 1963, but then the share started to decline, falling to less than one fifth by 1965.[74] In 1963, the bank attributed the beginning of this decline to 'the aggressive measures adopted by one or two local Chinese banks and although we may not be losing business to these competitors we have without doubt fallen behind them in attracting new business'.[75] The Hongkong Bank's share of total advances was higher than for trade finance, but it too fell from 46 per cent at the end of 1958 to 34 per cent by March 1962, while the share of deposits fell from almost 50 per cent to 37 per cent in the same period.[76] By June 1966, the bank's share in total advances had fallen further to 30.6 per cent.[77] The changing competitive environment for banking in Hong Kong is the subject of the next section.

Domestic banking: Expansion, crisis and new regulation

The dramatic increase in banking activity in Hong Kong during the 1950s and 1960s is apparent in the statistics of deposits and advances. Figure 3.2 shows the expansion in deposits, especially time deposits, from 1959. Bank deposits as a proportion of GDP increased from about 41 per cent to 70 per cent between 1959 and 1964. Until 1961, only the authorised exchange banks were included in these statistics, and from then only banks with a minimum level of capital resources. Since the excluded banks were generally very small, it can be assumed that their gradual inclusion accounts for only a small part of the increase in recorded deposits. The addition of 10 banks from June to September 1961 was responsible for an increase of only $200 million.[78]

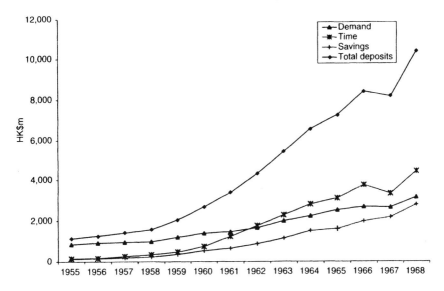

Figure 3.2 Deposits in reporting Hong Kong banks 1955–68.

The banking boom was caused by inflows of capital, increased prosperity, immigration, and aggressive marketing by banks as they sought liquidity to participate in the economic development of the colony, as well as to speculate in shares and property. It has been estimated that half of the deposits in banks in Hong Kong in the 1950s were hot money from Southeast Asia.[79] The depositors were predominantly overseas Chinese who faced uncertainty in the volatile political and economic climate of countries such as Indonesia, Vietnam and the Philippines. Hong Kong's low taxation, price stability, and the relaxed exchange control (which facilitated repatriation) were important attractions.

The competitive atmosphere of the late 1950s also led to rising interest rates that attracted depositors from overseas and at home. The threshold above which tax was payable on interest earned from savings accounts was raised from 2 to 2.5 per cent in early 1960 and then to 3 per cent in September 1960. This allowed higher rates to be offered on these accounts. The fastest growing type of account, however, was time deposits. Figure 3.3 shows movements in three-month deposit rates for a leading authorised bank and for a leading unauthorised bank. This shows that from mid-1960 to 1963 the rate offered on time deposits increased substantially, exceeding the increases in the London bank rate. It should also be noted that about a quarter of time deposits were government funds, mainly held at the Hongkong Bank.

The increase in deposits accompanied a rapid extension of bank offices, which spread the 'banking habit' in Hong Kong. From 1960, the Banking Advisory Committee became concerned that this trend would generate increased instability, so they took administrative action to limit the number of new licences. Successful

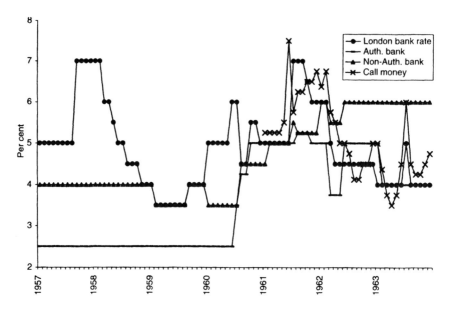

Figure 3.3 Interest rate comparison.

applicants were unofficially required to have a minimum capital of HK$5 million and demonstrate that they had adequate trained staff to operate as a bank.[80] The Committee was powerless, however, to restrain the branching activities of banks that already had a licence, and by 1961 it was considered that Hong Kong had too many banks. The Tomkins Report claimed that excessive competition had driven some less experienced bankers to overextend themselves, offering unsupportable rates to attract deposits with which to speculate for short-term gain.[81]

Figure 3.4 shows that the number of licensed banks declined slightly in the decade before the 1964 Banking Ordinance, but the number of branch offices expanded sharply from 1960. Whereas in 1960 banks were almost exclusively located in the Central district and Sheung Wan, by 1965 many banks had extended into the growing population centres on the north coast of Hong Kong Island, as well as in the Kowloon peninsula and the New Territories.

Table 3.3 shows the impact of branching on banking density in Hong Kong. After falling slightly in the period 1954–8 due to the closure of some smaller banks and an inflow of immigrants, the ratio of banking offices to population doubled from 1959 to 1963, almost completely due to branch expansion. Table 3.4 shows the number of branches of prominent banks by the end of 1966.[82] Of the 49 Hongkong Bank branches, 41 were opened after 1959, while all but one of the Chartered Bank branches opened after 1959. It was only after 1967 that the approval of the Banking Commissioner was required to open a new branch.[83]

The extensive network of the Hongkong Bank reflected its policy of embedding itself deeply in the commercial and industrial expansion of the colony, and the need

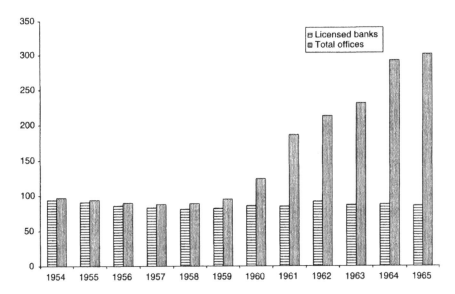

Figure 3.4 Banks expansion 1954–65

Table 3.3 Banking density in Hong Kong

	Bank offices per 10,000 people
1954	0.42
1955	0.40
1956	0.36
1957	0.33
1958	0.32
1959	0.33
1960	0.42
1961	0.58
1962	0.64
1963	0.66
1964	0.81
1965	0.82

Source: Jao, *Banking and Currency in Hong Kong*, p. 21.

to acquire deposits to allow it to do so. The first branch, opened in Mongkok in 1948, was established to service the growing garment industry in this area.[84] It was so successful in attracting accounts that it moved to a large new eight-storey building in 1954. In 1962, it was noted that '[T]he deposits which these offices [Hong Kong branches] obtained were extremely useful to the main office' although most of these branches initially operated at a loss.[85] The Hongkong Bank increased its share of total bank offices from 8.5 per cent in 1961 to 15.4 per cent in 1966 (excluding branches of Mercantile and Hang Seng).[86]

Table 3.4 Branch banking in Hong Kong 1966

	Number of branches
Hongkong Bank	49
Chartered Bank	17
Far East Bank	13
Hang Seng Bank	11
Overseas Trust Bank	11
United Chinese Bank	9
Liu Chong Hing	8
Foreign banks	38
Other	162
Total	318

Source: *Far Eastern Economic Review*, 27 April 1967, p. 182.

Of the branches of the Chartered Bank, the Kowloon office was the largest and most profitable. By 1965, deposits at this branch amounted to one fifth of those at the Hong Kong head office, while total assets in Kowloon were 13 per cent of the Hong Kong office. Kowloon turned its first profit in 1963 (two years after opening) and by 1965 contributed 10 per cent of the net profit of all the Chartered Bank's offices in Hong Kong.[87] The Kowloon branch specialised in overdrafts to local retailers and industry, and engaged in less direct trade finance than the Hong Kong office.

The extraordinary growth of small banks in Hong Kong is exemplified in the experience of the Wing Hang Bank Ltd. This bank was founded in 1937 as the Wing Hang Cheong Kee Bank by Y.K. Fung to engage in money-changing, and he remained Chairman until 1984. At the end of the war, Fung relocated to Bonham Strand East with a paid-up capital of HK$300,000 and a staff of 19. The bank was registered as a limited company and granted a full banking licence in May 1960, by which time it had a paid-up capital of HK$2.5 million and deposits of HK$6.8 million. In the prosperity of the early 1960s, the bank moved to new headquarters in Queens Road Central in 1963 and opened its first branches at Yaumati and Nathan Road Kowloon in 1964. In 1973, Irving Trust Co. NY (later the Bank of New York) bought a majority interest in the Wing Hang, by which time deposits totalled over HK$200 million and total assets amounted to HK$274.5 million.[88] This story is typical of many Hong Kong banks that began as small family concerns before or immediately after the war, expanded rapidly in the period 1955–65 while maintaining family control, and were subsequently bought out partly or wholly by foreign banks in the early 1970s.

The rapid expansion of small banks on the strength of the booms in shares and property in 1959/61 contributed to the banking crisis of 1961. In 1948, Liu Po Shan established the Liu Chong Hing Savings Bank in the western district of Hong Kong to collect savings and small deposits of the Chinese community. It was incorporated in 1955 as the Liu Chong Hing Bank with a registered share capital of HK$5 million, of which HK$4 million was fully paid up. Three years later, the registered share capital was expanded to HK$20 million of which HK$10 million was paid up, and the first branch was opened in Mongkok. In 1960 alone, the bank opened further branches in Causeway Bay, Kowloon City and Sham Shui Po.[89]

In June 1961, there was a run on the bank after it ran into difficulties as a result of property speculation and the liquidity squeeze that accompanied the stock market boom. The Liu Chong Hing Bank reported that 'depositors were misguided by malicious rumours'[90] that the police were investigating the bank and that its General Manager had been asked to leave Hong Kong. The Hongkong Bank and the Chartered Bank were asked to support Liu Chong Hing, and in the end a debenture was taken with a specific charge on certain properties. Eventually the run was ended after the press and radio announced that the Hongkong Bank and the Chartered Bank were offering support.[91] In fact, the problem was one of liquidity rather than solvency, but it was indicative of some of the risky banking strategies that were being employed during the boom period. Investigation by Tomkins of the Bank of England revealed that

> the trouble was caused by the [Liu Chong Hing] Bank getting too deep into property (they have come out very much on the right side now) for its own account and for account of the former Managing Director Liu Po Shan who has since died. Shan dipped into the till to the extent of HK$8m leaving his cheque in the safe in place of the cash i.e. 'borrowing' and not 'stealing'. The bank in its returns counted Shan's cheque as cash![92]

Liu Chong Hing Bank was allowed to continue trading with a reconstituted Board of Directors (including four members of the Liu family), but this did not resolve the general banking situation.[93]

The crisis of Liu Chong Hing fulfilled the gloomy predictions of the authorities. A year earlier, the Financial Secretary A.G. Clarke had told a visiting Bank of England official that 'control over banks was quite ineffective and there was a need to enjoin stricter standards if the risk of serious failure by some of the Chinese banks was to be avoided'.[94] At this time, Clarke used the weakness of banking regulation as an argument for the establishment of a central bank. His successor, J.J. Cowperthwaite, was to take a very different approach. The banking establishment agreed with Clarke. After having to support the Liu Chong Hing, the incoming General Manager of the Hongkong Bank told the Bank of England that he was 'strongly in favour of inspection as a means of securing proper standards in commercial banking practice since many Chinese banks were dangerously illiquid'.[95]

The Bank of England routinely advised colonies and the Commonwealth on central banking issues.[96] Initially, the Bank of England felt it lacked sufficient local expertise to advise the Hong Kong government on whether stricter banking control was desirable or necessary. Also, it was possible that a more comprehensive banking law would be unenforceable, or might have negative political repercussions if new legislation was interpreted as being biased against native Chinese banks. Along with these difficulties, the Hong Kong government was also concerned that if it were required by law to intervene in the activities of a bank, this would involve the government in responsibility to the depositors.[97] It was decided that any advice from the Bank of England could wait until the next scheduled visit of a bank representative to Hong Kong in the spring of 1963.

The local banking establishment, however, continued to press for new legislation. In August 1961, Pullen of the Chartered Bank told a Bank of England representative in London that 'Chartered Bank were very disturbed about the illiquid position of some of the Chinese banks in HK and he thought that if a run started on any of these institutions it might have serious repercussions throughout the banking system as a whole.'[98] This prompted a change of heart by the Bank of England,[99] and in December the Hong Kong government formally invited a Bank of England representative to study the banking ordinance. In February 1962, H.J. Tomkins arrived in Hong Kong to prepare new banking legislation.

The Bank of England's change of heart was no doubt influenced by the news that Oliphant (manager of the Hongkong Bank) had begun to draft a new ordinance, which was diplomatically described to Tomkins by the new Financial Secretary Cowperthwaite as 'only a cockshy, and while most of the principles on which it is based found favour with our banking advisory committee some parts of it did not and, of course, it needs a great deal of tidying up in detail'.[100]

Tomkins' draft ordinance was completed by the beginning of March 1962, and was 'a blend of Oliphant's draft and the penultimate draft of the North Borneo Banking Ordinance'.[101] It departed from similar colonial legislation by including details of the procedure to be followed if a bank should get into difficulties, as well as the usual provisions for the protection of depositors. Interestingly, the Bank of England asked Tomkins to include some provision for disappointed licence applicants to air their grievances to keep the law from seeming 'undemocratic'.[102] Tomkins replied that this suggestion had come too late since the document had already gone before the Banking Advisory Committee.[103] Disappointed applicants would only be able to appeal to the Governor, although this would at least give them some public forum.

Tomkins' draft departed from Oliphant's on several important details.[104] First, unincorporated native banks were excluded completely from the Tomkins' draft ordinance rather than allowed exemptions from parts of it, since they were not 'banks' under the new definition of soliciting deposits 'from the general public'. Tomkins believed that if these institutions could not advertise themselves as banks, they would be unable to attract a significant number of depositors needing statutory protection. This definition also permitted other institutions, such as trading companies or manufacturers, which collected deposits from a limited range of associates, friends or relatives, to operate outside the ordinance. Such deposits were in effect loans, and it was assumed that these depositors would be lending their money fully aware of possible risks. However, in the final version of the legislation the native banks were again included, but were exempted from most of the provisions of the new law on the condition that they did not use the title 'bank' and did not accept deposits in excess of HK$2 million. This met political objections that the new law would eliminate most of the native bank sector.

Secondly, Oliphant had included provisions regulating hours of business, interest rates and lending policy, but Tomkins preferred to leave these details to be decided by a new association of bankers on which all banks would be represented. Tomkins believed that an inclusive bankers' association would have the added advantage of promoting a greater sense of professionalism amongst bankers. In April 1962, Tomkins reported that a working party was considering such an association[105] but, in the end, this was not fully accomplished until 1980 when the Hong Kong Association of Banks replaced the Exchange Banks' Association. In the meantime, the Exchange Banks' Association negotiated an interest rate agreement, which will be discussed below.

Tomkins did not want the Financial Secretary to have responsibility for regulating terms of lending and interest rates, since his duties would then approach those of a central bank. Nor were these powers within the desire or capabilities of Cowperthwaite at the time. Tomkins described him as possessing 'near doctrinaire "laissez-faire"' principles.[106] Oliphant's draft also gave the Financial Secretary discretion to vary the minimum ratio of specified liquid assets, which was rejected by Tomkins for the same reasons. He reflected that 'I was reluctant to leave a lot of taps and levers lying around for inexperienced hands to twiddle.'[107] Interestingly, Tomkins found considerable support for a central bank among Chinese banks in Hong Kong. He noted that

> during my enquiries S.H. Ho and Q.W. Lee of the Hang Seng and Poon of the Ming Tak all advocated a central bank or at least some sort of mutual support association. Y.H. Kan of the Bank of East Asia favoured the former while Y.N. Lee of the Canton Trust and Commercial Bank, and Lamson Kwok of the Wing On Bank advocated the latter.[108]

The issue of a central bank was contentious, but had no support from the government. In 1963, it was suggested that the Bank of England, the Hong Kong government and the Hongkong Bank were hostile to a central bank, that most expatriate banks were indifferent, and that the bulk of local banks wanted one.[109] A call for a central bank by the Wah Kiu Yat Po in 1966 noted the need for bank supervision, an independent note issue, and lender of last resort.[110]

Oliphant also included several clauses that discriminated between local and foreign banks, which Tomkins avoided. As a 'genuflexion to the local Chinese banks who complained that foreign banks were parasites who brought no money to Hong Kong', Tomkins included an amended form of Oliphant's provisions for minimum local capital in relation to local liabilities.[111] This required that the Hong Kong branches of foreign banks should be considered separate entities for the purposes of the calculation of the ratio. In practice, however, foreign banks could borrow from or re-lend to their head offices to comply with the requirements.

Finally, Tomkins provided for a new banking commissioner (responsible to the Financial Secretary) to implement the ordinance. This new post was unpopular with both the Hongkong Bank and with the Financial Secretary.[112] The Banking Advisory Committee was restricted to discussing matters of policy and advising the Governor. One final item worth noting is that Oliphant suggested that all banks use only English for their accounts. Tomkins included an exemption for banks that had operated under the 1948 Ordinance using Chinese or any other language, remarking that 'Oliphant's suggestion of a flat injunction to use English seemed unreasonably over-bearing.'[113] Tomkins' draft banking ordinance was published in April 1962, and was then subject to further debate and negotiation with the banks to produce a bill for the Legislative Council. Final legislation was delayed by disagreements over the details, a lack of enthusiasm on the part of the Hong Kong government,[114] and finally a volte-face by the banks after they had agreed to the first version of the bill put before council in June 1963.

The main bones of contention were rules that constrained unsecured lending to cronies, and speculation in shares and real estate, both of which had contributed to the banking crisis of 1961. The Chinese banks objected strongly to Tomkins' requirement that the value of investment in real estate and shares should not exceed 25 per cent of paid-up capital and reserves.[115] He also restricted unsecured loans to businesses in which the Directors of a bank had an interest, a position which particularly exercised the Hongkong Bank since their Directors were on the boards of over 100 companies.[116] Initially, Tomkins had restricted unsecured loans to such businesses to HK$5,000 per loan, but he relented under pressure from the Hongkong Bank, and his final draft restricted such loans to 1 per cent of paid-up capital and reserves or $250,000, whichever was the smaller amount. Before publishing his draft ordinance, Tomkins reported that 'Saunders [Hongkong Bank] was not very happy but reluctantly said that I must, of course, recommend what I thought fit.'[117]

After the Tomkins Report was published, Oliphant petitioned the Financial Secretary to try to get this part amended so that it either applied only to banks with paid-up capital and reserves of less than HK$250 million, or exempted the Hongkong Bank on the basis that it was established under special ordinance of the laws of Hong Kong.[118] Both suggestions were refused and the debate simmered for the next two years. In the end, these unsecured advances were grouped with investment in real estate and shares as a group of assets that could not exceed 55 per cent of capital and reserves with an individual limit of 25 per cent for any one element of the group.[119] The new bill was submitted to the Legislative Council in September 1964 and came into force in December 1964, with a 12-month grace period to allow banks to conform to the requirement to keep a minimum liquidity ratio of 25 per cent against deposit liabilities.

The Liu Hong Ching affair prompted moves for self-regulation as well as government regulation. It was believed by many inside and outside the banking system that aggressive deposit-taking was primarily responsible for the 1961 crisis.[120] The heightened competitive atmosphere of 1959–61 had tempted smaller banks to offer extraordinarily high interest rates to attract deposits, which then required them to engage in high return but also risky investments. The general rise in interest rates was also deemed unfavourable to local industry since it inflated the rates on loans.[121] In September 1961, the Hongkong Bank precipitated an interest rate war by raising the deposit rate at the Wayfoong Finance Co. from 6 per cent to 7 per cent, and their own rates up to 6.5 per cent. Other banks soon followed, and the Exchange Banks' Association initiated talks among authorised and unauthorised banks to contain interest rate competition. An initial proposal of graduated rates within a range of 1 per cent was presented in October but was rejected by the unauthorised banks, who wanted a wider spread. Subsequent proposals were also rejected, but in December the unauthorised banks agreed voluntarily to reduce their fixed deposit rates to a maximum of 6.5 per cent. In March 1962, the authorised banks also agreed to lower their rates temporarily.

The unauthorised banks were not the only obstacle to an agreement. Some smaller foreign banks were not satisfied with the competitive edge enjoyed by the Chinese banks under the scheme.[122] The large number of banks involved also prolonged the negotiations. At the end of April 1964, Oliphant reported that

> The agreement on interest rates appeared to be nearing signature, when Hang Seng who had been negotiating as representative of many smaller banks, announced that they had no power to commit the others and had not kept them informed of the progress of the talks, so the final outcome is still in doubt.[123]

The agreement was also opposed by Hong Kong's Financial Secretary on the grounds that it unwisely hampered free competition. Oliphant noted that

> Cowperthwaite seems to be strongly opposed to the whole idea, largely for such reasons as that '87 individual decisions are more likely to be right than one central decision' etc. We have removed his misapprehension that coercion was being used to get people to join in.[124]

In the end, a scheme was finally agreed in April 1964 and came into force in July. It established a ladder with 'basic' interest rates offered by foreign banks and the leading Hong Kong banks, and a graduated scale for other categories of banks stepping up by 0.5 per cent on the basic rate. The 'foreign' category included the Hongkong Bank but excluded the Chinese state banks, and banks registered in Malaysia, which made up the A1 group. The system was designed to enable smaller banks to compete for deposits with the larger banks, but at the same time to constrain such competition to avoid upward drift in interest rates. All banks paid 4 per cent on seven-day deposits, and then were allocated a rate for three-month deposits depending on the nature of the bank. Rates on 6- and 12-month deposits were 0.25 per cent and 0.5 per cent higher respectively. There were no restrictions on deposits over 12 months. The terms of the agreement are shown in Table 3.5.

The agreement continued to be controversial. As an uncharacteristically large Chinese bank, Hang Seng was asked to quote a rate between the foreign and local banks but they refused.[125] Once the Hongkong Bank had control of Hang Seng in April 1965, however, their rates were lowered to the foreign bank level

> in the hopes that this would facilitate an agreement to reduce the differentials between the various categories of banks. This was unsuccessful. An approach was then made to the Group A1 banks to voluntarily agree to quote below their

permitted maximum and it was made clear that if this was not possible we reserved the right to increase Hang Seng's rates to those permitted for their category.[126]

The manager of Hang Seng, Q.W. Lee, objected strongly to the new rate, complaining that

> As to the interest rate, I am quite sure you understand this is a matter of survival of the Hang Seng Bank and I wish to put on record our strong dissent of having to quote the same rate as the Hongkong Bank.[127]

In May 1965, three European banks threatened to drop out of the agreement and thereby managed to get the spread of rates between the Chinese and foreign banks narrowed in July. In March 1966, it was agreed that the advantages enjoyed by the largest local banks was unfair, and Hang Seng, Bank of China, Bank of East Asia, Nanyang Commercial Bank and the Bank of Canton were identified as a 'special category' of banks that offered 0.25 per cent above the foreign banks and 0.25 per cent below other Chinese banks. These changes in categories reflect the increasing competition between the various classes of bank. The growth of some local Chinese banks in the early 1960s had brought them much closer to the modern commercial banks. As will be seen below, however, the accounts of the Hang Seng Bank at the time of its takeover in 1965 show the very different lending practices of this bank compared to 'British' and foreign banks in Hong Kong.

Before the 1964 Banking Ordinance could be fully implemented, a second banking crisis in early 1965 again revealed the fragility of the banking system. Near the end of 1964, property prices began to fall after a spurt of speculative building in the first half of 1963 when builders had rushed to initiate projects before the introduction of a new Building Ordinance. The market was also depressed by banks' sale of property assets to conform to the new Banking Ordinance.[128] This left many banks (especially Chinese banks) overexposed as the demand for funds associated with the Chinese New Year approached.

At the end of January 1965, the Ming Tak Bank (with two branches) was found to be insolvent and was closed by the Banking Commissioner.[129] This was followed a couple of weeks later by a two-day run on deposits of the Canton Trust and Commercial Bank (with 25 branches) which was also heavily involved in the property market. The Hongkong Bank agreed to lend Canton Trust HK$25 million, but

Table 3.5 Interest rate agreement

	Three-month deposit rates (% p.a.)					
	Foreign	*Special*	*A1*	*A2*	*B1*	*B2*
1 July 1964	4.5	—	5.25	5.75	6	6.25
July 1965	4.5	—	5.25	5.75	6	—
March 1966	5.5	5.75	6	6.375	6.75	—

believed that the general crisis was caused by 'Government reluctance to take firm action in the case of Liu Chong Hing or to limit the number of banks'.[130] Despite this support, the Canton Trust nevertheless suspended business on 8 February.[131] Worried depositors then began to draw on other Chinese banks, including Hang Seng, Kwong On, Dao Hang and Wing Lung. The runs were halted temporarily by the news that the Hongkong Bank and the Chartered Bank were willing to act as lenders of last resort, and by the introduction of a government restriction on cash withdrawals to HK$100 per day as of 9 February.[132] In addition, sterling was declared a temporary parallel legal tender to forestall the crisis from creating a currency short-age. The ensuing relaxation of pressure proved to be only a lull in the crisis.

On 9 April, rumours were published in Chinese newspapers suggesting that the police were interviewing the Chairman of Hang Seng and a run began on this, the largest local Chinese bank. By the end of the day, savings and current account deposits were half the level they had been at the end of 1964. Negotiations were hastily convened and the takeover of Hang Seng by the Hongkong Bank was announced the following day.[133] Subsequent investigations revealed that the ratio of specified liquid assets to deposit liabilities had fallen from 31 per cent at the end of 1964 to 16 per cent by the end of March and then to 7 per cent by the time Hang Seng was taken over.[134] The rumours about the security of the bank obviously had some basis in fact. In May 1965, 90 per cent of all Hang Seng's secured advances were against landed property, and this had left them in a particularly illiquid position.[135]

Figure 3.5 shows the movement in deposits of banks that had at least a 10 per cent change between 1964 and 1965. A quick glance shows that the crisis resulted in a redistribution of deposits away from some Chinese banks and in favour of the Chartered Bank, Hongkong Bank, its hire-purchase subsidiary Wayfoong Finance Co., the China state Nanyang Commercial Bank, and the famously cautious Bank of East Asia.[136] The crisis resulted in the Chartered Bank increasing its share of the

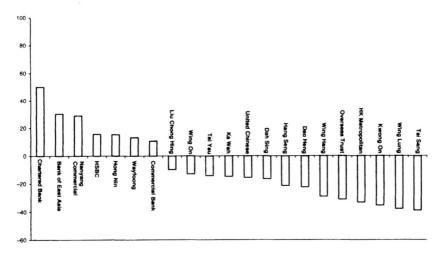

Figure 3.5 Percentage change in deposits 1964–5.

colony's deposits from 6 to 8.2 per cent. The Hang Seng Bank reported the largest absolute decline of HK$150 million, but the largest proportionate declines were declared by the Tai Sang and Wing Lung banks, both of which lost about 38 per cent of their deposits. Tai Sang Bank was so small that this only amounted to HK$5.9 million, but the losses of the Wing Lung Bank amounted to HK$43 million.

The banking crisis did not prompt a flight of capital from the banking system; total deposits increased by HK$800 million during 1965. Hong Kong residents' deposits in banks in the USA increased by US$8 million in 1965, but this was smaller than the US$29 million increase in 1964. In 1967, local disturbances and exchange rate instability had a much greater impact on the Hong Kong banking system. In that year, Hong Kong deposits in US banks almost doubled to over US$200 million.

Conclusion

This account of the banking system has illuminated several facets of the Hong Kong financial system. First, the lack of effective banking regulation allowed the unrestrained expansion of banking services from the mid-1950s, when international trade recovered and domestic industrialisation gathered pace. The expansion of branches in the period 1959–64 threatened the stability of the entire banking system and prompted both government regulation and self-regulation by the banks. Although the banks pleaded for greater supervision, the Financial Secretary resisted intervening in the market. The tension between the banks and the government resulted in a piecemeal and gradual introduction of regulation, which left the banking system liable to periodic crises but able to pursue business relatively unencumbered by the state. It will be shown in Chapter 6 that this freedom, especially relative to Hong Kong's neighbours, was an important impetus for the growth of international financial services.

Like the interest rate agreement, the 1964 Banking Ordinance suffered from delay due to prolonged negotiation with the banks and it proved inadequate to ensure the stability and prudence of Hong Kong banking. The weaknesses in the system are revealed in the series of amendments necessary in 1967 to shore up the system. They increased the minimum capital from HK$5 million to HK$10 million, excluded balances with other banks from specified liquid assets, strengthened the auditing process, required banks to maintain a provision for bad or doubtful debts, and increased the supervisory powers of the Banking Commissioner as separate from the Financial Secretary. This shows that undercapitalised, illiquid, and even fraudulent banking was not eliminated by the 1964 Ordinance. In 1967, 32 banks still had paid-up capital below HK$10 million, and some were found to have appointed unqualified auditors to certify that their balance sheets were accurate.[137]

This chapter has shown that the weak regulatory framework and plethora of small banks led to banking crises in 1961 and 1965. The failure of the native Hang Lung Bank in 1982/3 sparked off a further series of banking crises in 1983–6, which shows that these problems continued to plague Hong Kong's banking system. Jao blamed the weakness of the banking system in the 1980s on the persistence of family ownership combined with inadequate regulatory control.[138] This prompted further piecemeal regulatory responses throughout the 1980s. As Montes argues, the experience of the banking system highlights the key elements in Hong Kong's development as a financial centre, namely 'the strong lead of the private sector, with regulatory institutions playing catch-up; and the rapid growth punctuated by systemic crises'.[139] In the post-war period, weak regulation allowed the persistence of traditional Chinese banking and the expansion of the modern financial sector, but it came at the cost of instability for the system as a whole.

4   Foreign exchange markets

As Jao has noted, 'the foreign exchange market is widely regarded as an extremely important criterion for evaluating an IFC'.[1] This chapter will show that Hong Kong's free market in foreign exchange was the foundation of its role as a regional and international financial centre in the 1950s. By 1957, the *Far Eastern Economic Review* proudly recorded that

> Hongkong's free exchange market has attracted many operators from foreign countries who have found every reason to be satisfied with the bankers and financiers established here ... Several Chinese banks, erstwhile known as 'native banks', have remarkably increased their international connections and are today able of serving the needs of a global free market and also those markets where controls of some sort prevail ... Possibilities of Hongkong/Far Eastern and Hongkong/Europe free exchange transactions offer many opportunities as enterprising Chinese bankers as well as European financiers are exploring them ever on the look-out for better international service and additional profits.[2]

The importance of the post-war global economic environment to Hong Kong's development as an international financial centre is clearly demonstrated in the case of the foreign exchange markets. Hong Kong's position between the sterling area and the dollar area allowed the territory to offer to investors and traders financial services unrivalled anywhere else in the world. As will be discussed in greater detail below, because of exchange controls existing elsewhere the free market facilitated securities trading, and the settlement of sterling debts among people not resident in Hong Kong.[3]

Structure and operation of the dollar market

After World War Two, Britain restricted the convertibility of sterling with the cooperation of a group of Commonwealth and other countries known as the sterling area. The members of the sterling area enjoyed unrestricted capital flows and current transactions with the UK in return for operating a common exchange control against the rest of the world.[4] Hong Kong was one of two gaps in this control.[5] During the 1950s, Hong Kong officially operated a system of foreign exchange restrictions similar to those operating elsewhere in the sterling area. The exchange rate of the Hong Kong dollar was pegged to sterling and the sale of foreign exchange at this rate was restricted to the purchase designated essential imports, such as cereals, rice, cotton and rayon yarn. Excess demand for foreign exchange generated a parallel exchange market in which the price of HK dollars was determined freely by supply and demand. The US dollar market was the most prominent, since this was the most convertible currency in the 1950s, but free rates were also quoted against a variety of Asian, European and Australian currencies. The free exchange market meant that Hong Kong offered an almost unique level of deregulation in the sterling area system of exchange control, at a time when the colony was still ruled by a series of British governments committed to a high degree of intervention in their own domestic financial system.

The initial rationale for the free exchange market was Hong Kong's entrepot status. The Hong Kong economy in the pre-war and immediate post-war period was dependent on entrepot trade with China, Formosa, Korea and Macao. The HK dollar traditionally served as the trading currency in all five territories, and there were few effective restrictions on movements of individuals or currency within this area. To allow Hong Kong to compete as an entrepot between China and the American market, Britain was obliged to allow Hong Kong to operate a free market in American dollars.[6] As noted in Chapter 2, Hong Kong merchants were allowed to retain three quarters of the US dollar proceeds of their exports but had to surrender the remaining 25 per cent at the official rate, which undervalued the US dollar. These proportions were meant to represent the 25 per cent of value added to re-exports in Hong Kong. The Bank of England believed that Chinese traders generally preferred to deal among themselves rather than through official channels, so that in fact a larger proportion of US dollar earnings found its way to the free market.[7] Traders could use their retained US dollars to import goods to be sold at a profit (thus covering any losses on their exports) or they could sell these US dollars on the free market at a premium. At the end of 1946, for example, traders were able to take a loss of about 10–15 per cent on exports of Chinese products to the USA because the dollars they earned could be sold on the open market at a profit of 20–30 per cent over the official exchange rate.[8] Thus, the free market allowed the continuation and expansion of the entrepot activity of the colony before the UN embargo was imposed in 1951.

The free market in Hong Kong functioned mainly through the leading native banks. They offered a range of products, dealing in cash sales, telegraphic transfers from New York or San Francisco (US$TT) and demand drafts on American banks (US$DD). In 1947, it was reported that the native banks and exchange brokers frequently used illegal radio transmitters to arbitrage between Chinese and other Asian markets.[9] The US dollar market was closely linked to the gold market since overseas buyers sold US dollars to the free dollar market to finance their gold purchases. From 1952, the Gold and Silver Exchange dealt also in US dollar notes, merely operating on separate parts of the floor.[10] The US dollars were also supplied from remittances, and net exports to the dollar area.[11]

Overseas Chinese used the market to exchange US dollars to HK dollars for remittances to their relatives in China and Hong Kong. The native banks in Hong Kong dominated this business, using their branches in Canton and Shanghai before 1949. In 1946, two native banks accounted for 40–50 per cent of the daily turnover in CNC dollar remittances which totalled about CNC$6,000 million per day (HK$60–70 million) at this time.[12] Remittances usually took the form of bankers' drafts on New York or San Francisco banks, which were then mailed to Hong Kong and sold on the free market. The buyer then sent the draft back to their bank account in the USA. A second and more efficient method was to credit the New York or San Francisco account of a Hong Kong resident who then sold the US dollar by telegraphic transfer (US$TT), which fetched a higher price in the local market than demand drafts (US$DD). A third and more cumbersome method was to send parcels of consumer goods that could be sold in Hong Kong at a profit.[13]

Hong Kong was used as a financial entrepot for remittances because of the technical difficulties of sending foreign exchange directly to China, and the favourable rates offered in Hong Kong relative to other Asian free markets. Remittances had a seasonal impact on the market, tending to raise the supply of dollars during Chinese holidays such as New Year and the spring Dragon Festival. Emigrants also tended to send more cash to China during periods of political or military turmoil such as during the Korean War. Once this threat receded, remittances through Hong Kong tailed off and began to go directly through Chinese banks. The volume of remittances is difficult to ascertain, although there have been a variety of estimates which were presented in Chapter 1, which suggested that a total of about US$2 billion passed through Hong Kong between 1950 and 1965. It seems clear that remittances to China increased in the period 1950–2 and then declined. In May 1954, an average of HK$15–20 million per month was reportedly remitted to China through Hong Kong.[14]

In the later 1950s, the decline in remittances from overseas Chinese was partly offset by sales of US dollars by American servicemen on duty in the Far East. By 1956, the supply from US Navy personnel on shore leave was reported to be 'very large'.[15] Table 4.1 shows estimates of the proceeds of different types of ships, provided by the Citibank in Hong Kong.[16] At the end of 1955, Citibank reported that (on a conservative basis) an aircraft carrier, a cruiser, an invasion headquarters ship, 10 destroyers and a submarine had generated US$1.2 million. Hong Kong usually received about two aircraft carriers per month, supplying about US$1 million.

Flight capital also flowed through the free market. In the late 1940s, most came from China, and in particular from wealthy Shanghai business families. Increasing taxation, unprofitable manufacturing, political and legal uncertainty, and police harassment all contributed to the flow. Significant amounts also arrived to take part in speculation and gold smuggling in Hong Kong, or to take advantage of the high

Table 4.1 Shore expenditure (in US$) of US naval personnel, 1956

1 aircraft carrier	500,000
1 heavy cruiser	300,000
1 invasion headquarters ship	150,000
1 destroyer	20,000

Source: Estimate by First National City Bank of New York, Letter from A. Bird to W.G. Pullen, 2 February 1956, BE OV65/4.

interest rates offered by native banks.[17] During the 1950s, the ethnic Chinese communities in various Southeast Asian countries came under threat from local political instability and from increasing ethnic nationalism. Hong Kong banks were a relatively secure haven for their savings, given the comparative political stability and the freedom to repatriate these savings at any time. A variety of estimates shown in Table 6.6 suggest that this inflow from overseas Chinese amounted to about HK$6.3 billion between 1950 and 1965, or about US$1 billion. The Hong Kong market was also a competitive target for other holders of US dollars in Asia. In the second half of 1952, for example, the Tokyo rate for US dollar was about 5 per cent below the Hong Kong rate because of the disposal of surplus US dollars by the Japanese. As a result, arbitrageurs operated between the Hong Kong and Tokyo market, generally increasing the supply of US dollar notes in Hong Kong.[18] Finally, Malaya (alone among sterling area countries) had a special arrangement by which they could use the free market to buy US dollars to import goods from the dollar area up to a limit of the value of such imports in 1950. This amounted to about US$22 million p.a., and was justified on the basis that this was a traditional trade route for Malaya, that it helped to ease Malayan inflationary problems, and that it alleviated calls for Malaya to have its own free market.[19]

The relative importance of the many factors in the market was estimated in 1952 as part of a Bank of England investigation. Total cash sales of US dollar in 1952 were estimated to amount to about US$150 million p.a.[20] P.L. Hogg did a spot survey of three dealers in the dollar market, and these results were supplemented by information at the bank to provide an accounting of official and unofficial supplies of US dollar. These estimates are presented in Tables 4.2 and 4.3.

Table 4.2 Estimates of monthly trading on free dollar market (US$m)

	Autumn 1952	Dealer A	Dealer B	Dealer C
Supply				
Bangkok	7		2	5
Korea/Japan		7		
Philippines		0.75		
Tourists		0.75		
Remittances	3.5	1	2	1.25
Exports	2	2	3	0.25
Arbitrage		3		
Other	1.5			
Total	14.0	14.5	7	6.5
Demand				
Gold	7.5	7	4	4
Imports	4.5	6.5	3	2.5
Hoarding	1	0.5		
Other	1	0.5		
Total	14	14.5	7	6.5

Notes: Autumn 1952 based on a sample survey of dealers by the Hong Kong Exchange Controller. Dealers' returns based on surveys by P.L. Hogg. Personal Report by P.L. Hogg, 11 May 1953, BE OV14/9.

Table 4.3 Hong Kong US$ account 1952 (US$m)

US$m	Total	Free market	Authorised banks
Supply of US$			
Exports (fob)	33.88	24.36	9.52
Gold sales	42.56	42.56	0
Smuggling	1.4	1.4	0
Transport and insurance	5.32	2.24	3.08
Interest, profits, dividends	3.64	3.64	0
Travel	8.12	8.12	0
US Navy	1.12	1.12	0
Consulates	2.52	2.52	0
Charitable donations	1.96	1.96	0
Overseas Chinese remittances	34.44	28	6.44
Dishoarding of US$ notes	10.08	10.08	0
Capital investment	3.36	3.36	0
Errors and omissions	48.16	48.16	0
Total	196.56	178.36	18.2
Expenditure of US$			
Imports	65.52	59.92	5.6
Gold purchases	98	98	0
Transport and insurance	8.4	5.32	3.08
Interest, profits, dividends	2.24	0.56	1.68
Travel	0.56	0.56	0
Film royalties	1.12	0.56	0.56
Other invisibles	1.12	1.12	0
Increase in US$ assets	13.44	13.44	0
Contribution to London reserves	6.16	0	6.16
Total	196.56	178.36	18.2

Source: Hong Kong Working Party, prepared by the Bank of England, April 1954, BE OV14/10.

Table 4.2 suggests that about half of the business was related to the gold market, with trade making up most of the remaining demand for US dollar. The Hong Kong Exchange Control estimated that in 1952 Bangkok sold US$87.6 million to Hong Kong, of which all but US$35.3 million was accountable from gold purchases, remittances and capital investment.[21] The excess explains most of the 'Errors and omissions' on the supply side of Table 4.3. The £3.4 million in exports that went through the authorised banks represented sterling area and European re-exports to the dollar area. Table 4.3 shows the overwhelming dominance of the free market as the route through which dollar transactions took place, and also that Hong Kong was a net earner of dollars rather than a drain on the central reserves. US$6.2 million were contributed to the central reserves in 1952 against an official dollar allocation of US$5.6 million. The UK only had to supply 10 per cent of the foreign exchange required for Hong Kong's imports. Table 4.3 also confirms that the gold trade, visible trade and remittances were the largest factors in the market.

Unfortunately, 1952 was not a typical year for the dollar market. Because of the Korean War, remittances were greater than they were in subsequent years and the gold market was particularly active due to hoarding. The volume of gold traded on the market fell from a weekly average of 30 million taels in 1952 to 15 million taels per week in 1953 and remained close to that level until 1958 except for a period of recovery in 1956 in response to the Suez crisis.[22] Overseas remittances dropped 26 per cent in 1953 and declined steadily every year to 1958.[23] It will be noted below, however, that the volume of security switches accelerated through the decade. Balance of payments statistics for Hong Kong are not available, but between 1953 and 1958 Hong Kong ran an accumulated trade deficit with the dollar area of US$473 million while amassing US$181 million in foreign exchange reserves held as sterling assets. This suggests that the parallel market was able to cover the dollar requirements of Hong Kong throughout the 1950s and, indeed, that Hong Kong generated a foreign exchange surplus for the central reserves in London.

The fluctuations in the sterling cross rate in the Hong Kong market and the volume of transactions are shown in Figures 4.1 and 4.2. Figure 4.1 shows that the premium on the Hong Kong market was significantly reduced after the devaluation of sterling in September 1949. After the rage of speculation in the gold market in the early 1950s, the premium fell further until the run on sterling in the first half of 1957. Figure 4.2 shows that the early 1950s were the most active time in the market, and that by the end of the decade the volume of trade had fallen back to about US$1.5 million per week on average. Telegraphic transfers came to dominate the free market after the mid-1950s in response to the increase in security switches. Broadly, notes tended to be sold by hoarders and traders; drafts (personal or cashiers cheques) were often remittances from overseas Chinese; and telegraphic transfers were used for the gold trade, merchanting, speculation and security switches. Notes

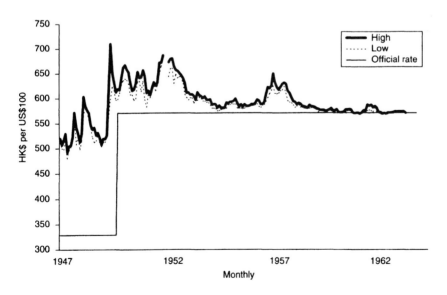

Figure 4.1 Free market exchange rates 1947–63.

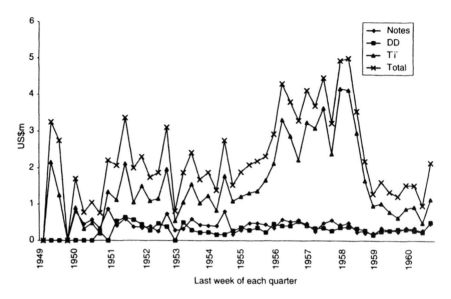

Figure 4.2 Weekly turnover in the US$ market 1949–60.

tended to be bought by native banks, shipped to their accounts in the USA and then sold at a higher rate for US$TT.[24]

Regulating the free dollar market

The existence of the Hong Kong dollar market was reviewed at the time of the sterling devaluation of September 1949. The UK Treasury believed that the premium on dollars was caused by the overvaluation of sterling, so the devaluation was expected to narrow the margin in the free market.[25] The Treasury expected that the superior facilities Hong Kong could offer would attract business from other Far Eastern markets even if the transactions had to take place at the official rate. The Secretary of State for the Colonies informed the Hong Kong Governor that

> we should expect that remitters to China from overseas will prefer the facilities and security of Hong Kong if they are satisfied that the rate they are getting is realistic, rather than fiddle around in the jungles of Macao, Bangkok or elsewhere for only slightly better rates.[26]

The Treasury, therefore, wanted to take this opportunity to close the free market with little cost to Hong Kong. Sir Alexander Grantham, Governor of Hong Kong, protested that there was no guarantee that the superior Hong Kong facilities would retain business at an uncompetitive rate. Furthermore, the transit trade with the USA was averaging HK$44 million (US$8 million) per month, which would have to come out of the central reserves if the free market were closed.[27] Portsmore of the Bank of England agreed with Grantham, and advised the Treasury to abandon their effort to close the free market for the moment.[28] There were also political objections that challenging Hong Kong's entrepot status might undermine confidence in Britain's commitment to support the colony in the wake of the Communist takeover of China.

The Treasury reluctantly accepted the bank's advice and postponed the closure of the free market. However, they remained unconvinced of the importance of the free market to Hong Kong's prosperity. In January 1950, the Chancellor of the Exchequer (Sir Stafford Cripps) wrote to the Secretary of State for the Colonies, reserving the right to abolish the market:

> I have felt great doubt whether HMG ought not to press for the immediate closure of this, the only free market within the sterling area ... I am aware, however, of the arguments, political and other, against taking steps immediately to abolish the free market and I am prepared not to press for this now although we may of course need to reconsider this decision at any time.[29]

Instead, controls were imposed on most current transactions between Hong Kong and the rest of the sterling area through trade licensing and restrictions on debits from sterling accounts in Hong Kong. Controls were considered necessary because it was feared that sterling area residents were transferring sterling to Hong Kong accounts from where it was sold on the free market for US dollars at a discount. In this way, residents of the UK and the rest of the sterling area could evade their national exchange controls to convert sterling to US dollar.

The decision to apply new regulations was taken in January 1950, but Grantham managed to delay the implementation until the end of May by arguing that if it coincided with the withdrawal of Ghurka troops from Hong Kong, confidence in the colony would be seriously affected.[30] Defence (Finance) Regulation 2A was finally enacted on 26 May, which established No. 1 and No. 2 sterling accounts for Hong Kong residents. Authorised banks monitored debits from No. 1 accounts to ensure they were for legitimate transactions. All other accounts were designated No. 2 accounts, and debits were subject to Hong Kong exchange control permission unless they involved payment into a No. 1 account. Credits to Hong Kong accounts were not restricted, so customers outside Hong Kong could still get access to the banking system.

The Treasury and the Bank of England, however, doubted whether these new measures were completely effective.[31] Exchange control in Hong Kong was undertaken by a single representative from the Hongkong Shanghai Bank, who was seconded for a term of two years. A Bank of England delegation found the situation very rudimentary on a visit to Hong Kong in 1953. In March, Hogg reported that R.F. Chandler, Exchange Controller at the time, 'is the only male British official in the Control and it is with the greatest difficulty that he can cope with the mere examining and signing of forms and the answering of innumerable telephone enquiries'.[32] J.G.F. Young of the Colonial Regulation Section of the Bank of England described Chandlers' staff as 'a lady assistant (who also does the typing) and some 12–15 Chinese clerks'. The clerks could be 'entrusted only with the simplest of tasks'.[33] Much of the day-to-day monitoring was delegated to the authorised banks who administered the exchange control and comprised the official exchange market. In May 1954, the Bank of England roundly criticised Defence (Finance) Regulation 2A on the basis that Hong Kong was unable to enforce it due to the inefficiency of the local exchange control and the untrustworthiness of local authorised banks.[34]

In the spring of 1954, the UK Treasury, Bank of England and Colonial Office again considered closing the free market. The deliberations and final report of this Working Party on sterling area free markets reveal what the UK authorities considered to be the benefits and costs of the parallel exchange market in Hong Kong.[35] Closing the free dollar market was rejected on three grounds. First, it was recognised that the dollar market would merely be pushed underground or driven to nearby Macao, thus depriving the Hong Kong dealers of the profits. This corresponds with the traditional justification for parallel exchange markets suggested by Agenor, that the costs of eliminating them may be prohibitive.[36] Given a strong demand from merchants to buy US dollars, and suppliers ready to sell at a discount, the market would merely shift from the unauthorised banks to street corners in Hong Kong or more permanent facilities in Macao. Second, Hong Kong's claim on the central reserves would be vastly increased since the free market supplied about 90 per cent of Hong Kong's dollar requirements. The third objection was the disruption to the remaining entrepot trade of the colony. In the end, no action was taken to curb the free market and it continued to offer important services in East Asia. Hong Kong's Financial Secretary J.J. Cowperthwaite's comments on the report were summed up by Kelvin Stark of the Colonial Office:

> In short Cowperthwaites's comments reinforce what has always been our view that the HK control should be looked at from a wider view and that interference in its detailed working will only tie us and HK up into knots which will serve no useful purpose and will hamper their natural and traditional trade.[37]

Implications of the free market for trade and manufacturing

During the period from 1949 to 1958, Hong Kong emerged from depending primarily on its entrepot status to become a rapidly industrialising country producing exports of its own. In 1952, it is estimated that only 25 per cent of Hong Kong exports were wholly or principally of Hong Kong origin, but by 1958 this proportion had risen to over 40 per cent. The free market in Hong Kong was initially intended to be used almost exclusively for the entrepot trade. This was signalled by the official requirement to surrender part of the export proceeds of Hong Kong manufactures in order to capture the value added in Hong Kong for the official exchange market. This represented a 'tax' on domestic manufacturing, which could have inhibited the incentive for industrialisation. It is uncertain, however, the extent to which the appropriate foreign exchange was actually collected due to the ease of smuggling from the large port in small boats. Furthermore, the Treasury asserted in

1952 that the proportion of export earnings that had to be surrendered at the official exchange rate was varied periodically to keep Hong Kong exports competitive.

In economies such as Hong Kong, where there is a high import content of exports, the foreign exchange lost to the official reserves through the parallel market may be offset by the earnings from the additional exports made possible by imports using the parallel exchange market. The high import content of Hong Kong's exports can hardly be disputed. Determining exactly how much of these imports were purchased using the free market is not possible from Hong Kong's trade statistics, although in 1949 the Governor of Hong Kong estimated that 75 per cent of local factories' raw material needs were financed through the free dollar market.[38] The international competitiveness of Hong Kong's exports also benefited from the devalued exchange rate.

The market also served as an international finance centre for trade that did not touch Hong Kong's ports. Such 'merchanting' transactions were supposed to be referred to British exchange control to ensure that they were legitimate transactions and not a means for foreigners to take advantage of the broken cross rates in the market. In fact, however, it emerged in 1953 that the Exchange Controller did not refer many multilateral transactions to London for approval. These mainly concerned the financing of direct trade between the entrepot area and either Japan or Europe. In May 1952, for example, the Exchange Controller persuaded the Japanese authorities to use banking facilities in Hong Kong to finance direct sterling trade with China. This traffic amounted to up to £7 million at any one time.[39] Another example of how the free market could be used was the complicated business of Siamese rice exports. The Siamese Rice Office insisted on payment in US dollars for all rice exports except glutinous/industrial rice. To get hold of US dollars, European importers bought Siamese rise from Hong Kong merchants against sterling, which was then sold in the free market at a discount for US dollars to pay the Siamese exporter.[40] In this way, the existence of the free market was a major attraction for traders to use the entrepot services of Hong Kong.

It is widely acknowledged that the capital inflow and invisible earnings required to finance Hong Kong's trade deficit and the increase in sterling balances were greatly facilitated by the parallel exchange market.[41] Thus, Jao has asserted that 'the free exchange market...is of crucial significance to Hong Kong's economy'.[42] The parallel market increased the attractiveness of Hong Kong to potential investors because capital could be freely repatriated. This advantage was accentuated by widespread capital controls elsewhere. As King put it, 'US dollars come to the Colony only because they can leave again.'[43] Figure 4.2 shows that the volume of transactions in the parallel market amounted to US$1–5 million per week, which generated invisible earnings for the colony. Finally, the parallel exchange market was essential for the Hong Kong premium gold market, which operated in US dollars. A precise measure of the benefit of the free market to Hong Kong requires statistics of national income and balance of payments that are not available. There can be little doubt, however, that the free market was an important factor in the colony's development. The importance of the market for international capital transactions is the topic of the next section.

The free market and global capital transactions

The unusual position of Hong Kong as a member of the sterling area, and as a host of a free exchange market, attracted customers to the colony from all over the world. The attractions of Hong Kong arose from the complicated exchange controls operating elsewhere. UK residents were prohibited from buying dollar securities from outside the sterling area, since this would generate a drain of US dollars out of the sterling area system. Because demand for US dollar securities was high, however, there was a premium on the price of securities traded among sterling area residents in the London market. A Hong Kong resident could buy dollar securities direct from European or American holders, using free market dollars, and then legally sell them at a premium in the London market against sterling.[44] British residents were allowed to buy these securities legally since Hong Kong was a member of the sterling area. By doing so, British residents effectively converted sterling into dollar securities, which could then be sold for US dollars. In this way, they evaded British exchange control, which aimed to stop the conversion of sterling to US dollar. The profit of such transactions for Hong Kong brokers was equal to the premium in London less the premium paid for the dollars in Hong Kong.

The Hong Kong market was also used by residents of countries outside the sterling area to sell sterling securities against dollars, or for cheap sterling. Unlike visible trade, there were no controls on the source of sterling used to settle invisible debts, so there was a demand for 'cheap' sterling available in a variety of discount markets. Normally, foreign-held sterling securities could only be switched for other sterling securities, or sold for 'security sterling' (also called 'switch sterling') which could then be used only to purchase more sterling securities. This blocked sterling thus traded at a discount on the New York market. Hong Kong brokers could buy sterling securities or switch sterling cheaply in New York for US dollars purchased on the free market. Once in Hong Kong hands, the sterling became 'resident' sterling, which could be used for any type of transaction. It could also be sold to an authorised bank at the higher official rate.

In summary, the Hong Kong Gap (as it became known) allowed Americans and Europeans to sell sterling securities for dollars, which they could not do in London or New York or any other financial centre. Australians, British and other residents of the sterling area could use the market to convert their sterling to US dollar securities within the rules of the exchange control. Again, this was a transaction that was not possible in the usual international financial centres. The opportunity for UK residents to evade their own exchange control in this way was made possible by the demand for sterling in Hong Kong. The magnitude of the drain on the UK reserves was determined by public awareness of the gap (which increased in the 1950s) and the discount on the exchange rate of sterling. Kuwait also operated a free US dollar market based on the US dollar proceeds of its oil revenue, but because Kuwait was not a colony, the UK could not impose its No. 1 and No. 2 account system there so the situation was somewhat different.[45] It will be seen, however, that the two markets were closely related.

The profits on these transactions for Hong Kong dealers depended on arbitrage, so the Hong Kong cross rate between US dollar and sterling was related to the security

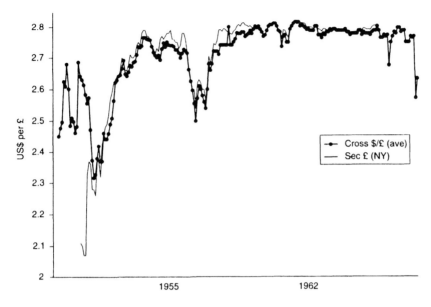

Figure 4.3 Sterling/dollar cross rate in Hong Kong and security sterling rate in New York 1950–65.

sterling rates in New York and to the premium on dollar securities in the London market. Figure 4.3 shows the sterling/dollar cross rate in Hong Kong and the security sterling rate in New York. It is clear that the gap between these rates closed sharply in the early 1950s, and that both rates approached the official rate of US$2.80/£ by the end of the decade.

Security switches began in a small way in 1950 and then accelerated. Up to April 1954, sales of securities by residents outside the sterling area to the UK through Hong Kong amounted to £36 million worth of sterling securities and £10 million of dollar securities.[46] Table 4.4 shows estimates of the volume of security switches through Hong Kong from 1953 to 1957.

In 1953, only four firms dealt in security switches between Hong Kong and London. P.L. Hogg reported that 'When this traffic began they operated on a large scale and made considerable profits. With the hardening of sterling the volume of such transactions contracted sharply.'[47] By February 1956, Morford of the Chartered Bank complained that they were losing business by not engaging in security switches. In addition to the Banque Belge and the Banque de l'Indochine, 'the Hongkong Shanghai Bank, having experienced a similar loss of business, decided some time ago to undertake switch transactions on behalf of customers, and have now got the lion's share of the traffic'. Morford was advised that 'the ban [on authorised banks operating in the free market] is no longer being strictly enforced in so far as switch business is concerned'.[48]

Table 4.4 Security switches through Hong Kong 1953–6 (£m)

	Purchases of $ securities	Purchases of £ securities	Total
1953	6.1	13.7	19.8
1954	5.0	13.5	18.5
1955	4.5	12.0	16.5
1956	12.9	11.5	24.4
Total	28.5	50.7	79.2

Sources: BE EID3/31, EID3/32, EC5/434, EC5/435.

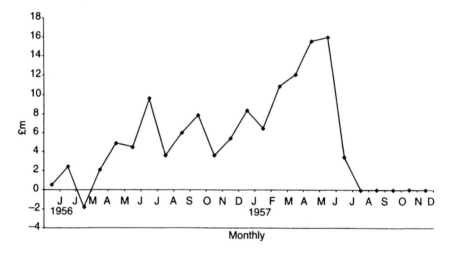

Figure 4.4 US$ security switches through Hong Kong and the Persian Gulf 1956–7.

In the first half of 1957, lack of confidence in the ability of the British govern-ment to arrest inflation generated a capital outflow from the UK. Figure 4.4 shows the acceleration of purchases of dollar securities through Hong Kong and the Persian Gulf, which totalled £73 million in the first half of 1957 alone.

In response, UK exchange control permission for purchases of foreign currency securities from residents of the overseas sterling area was withdrawn at the begin-ning of July.[49] This effectively closed the route by which UK residents had acquired dollar securities through the Hong Kong market. Up to this point there had been no restrictions on capital flows from the UK to other sterling area countries and the change of policy in 1957 represented a major departure from the general movement toward freer trade and payments to which the British government was committed.

The introduction of new controls in the UK does not appear to have affected the volume of business on the dollar market. Weekly cash sales in the free market stayed high at US$3.5–4 million per week through to the end of the third quarter of 1958 despite a marked decline in activity in the Hong Kong gold market. The effect on exchange rates, however, was more significant, at least in the short term. The immediate effect was a slight rise in the Hong Kong sterling cross rate from $2.64 to $2.665, a rise in the London dollar security premium from 6.25 to 10.5 per cent, and a rise in security sterling from $2.63 to $2.71.[50] From this time, the Hong Kong free rate and the security sterling rate strengthened steadily, as is shown in Figure 4.3. The Hong Kong free rate discount was driven down to 2 per cent by February 1958 and stayed at this level for the rest of the year. However, this may have resulted from increased confidence in sterling after September 1957, and falling turnover in the gold market, rather than from specific action by the UK authorities against the Hong Kong Gap.

After the switching of dollar securities was banned in July 1957, switching of sterling securities continued. From September until December 1957, sales of sterling securities through the free markets amounted to £21.3 million, of which £19.7 million was through Hong Kong alone. For a year after the July controls on transactions involving dollar securities, the Treasury continued to lobby for restrictions to be imposed on sterling securities as well.[51] The purchase of sterling securities at a discount from non-residents through Hong Kong increased the supply of 'cheap sterling' that could be used to settle invisible debts to the sterling area. This cost the central reserves potential dollars that would have been sold at the official rate in London to purchase the sterling to settle these debts. In the end, however, it was decided that any further controls would be costly, difficult to make effective, and would seriously disrupt transactions among sterling area residents.[52] The Governor of Hong Kong warned that blocking the transfer of switch sterling would 'have grave repercussions locally apart from its effect on confidence in sterling'. He reported that according to local records £33.5 million of switch sterling had been remitted in the first half of 1957 and £29 million in the second half of the year.[53]

Ministers and officials in the Treasury continued to find the sterling leak through Hong Kong to be a nuisance, prompting several more investigations. After the advent of sterling current account convertibility in December 1958, leaks of short-term capital generally became a more important target for exchange control. At the same time, the volume of switch sterling transactions through Hong Kong accelerated because of the colony's increasing trade deficit with China. China's earnings of HK dollars were converted almost entirely to sterling, which was the preferred currency for China's foreign exchange reserves given the political conflict with the USA. This generated a large and growing demand for sterling in Hong Kong which was satisfied either by purchases of security sterling in New York, or of 'resident' sterling from the Persian Gulf, which could be bought at a slightly better rate than through London. Once in Hong Kong hands, this sterling could be used for any kind of international transaction. China's trade surplus with Hong Kong increased sharply from HK$300 million in 1954 to HK$900 million in 1959. It was then relatively stable at around HK$1 billion until 1963, but by 1965 Hong Kong's deficit with China had reached HK$2 billion.

Figure 4.5 shows the increasing volume of such transactions (the figures for 1964 are monthly averages). Table 4.5 shows the annual totals.

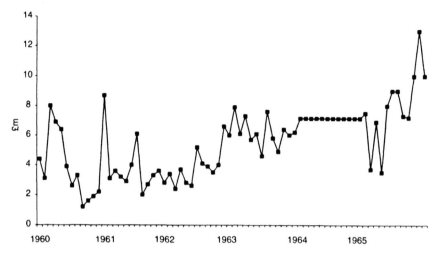

Figure 4.5 Sales of security sterling to Hong Kong 1960–5.

Table 4.5 Purchases of sterling by Hong Kong (£m)

	1960	1961	1962	1963	1964	1965
Security	44.3	43.8	48.2	74.6	85.7	95.1
Gulf	28.4	27	47.6	30.4	19.3	37.4
Total	72.7	70.8	95.8	105	105	132.5

Source: PRO T295/27.

After several further investigations, in February 1962 the Bank of England and the Treasury agreed (reluctantly in the case of the latter) that any controls imposed in Hong Kong or Kuwait would be ineffective. To stop the gap, stringent exchange control would have to be imposed in London on their relations with the UK. Ejecting them from the sterling area in this way threatened to reduce Britain's political influence in these territories. Since Hong Kong was a strategic colony and the Gulf was an important oil producer, any diminution in British influence could be dangerous. In addition, these territories had considerable sterling balances that might be diversified if they were outside the sterling area. On the other hand, the gap acted 'as a useful safety valve which enables non-resident sales of securities to take place without unduly depressing the security sterling rate'.[54] Thus, the leak provided a demand for security sterling, keeping this rate closer to the official rate than would otherwise be the case. If Hong Kong were prevented from buying security sterling, the discount in New York would fall, undermining confidence in the official rate. If the rate fell too far, the Bank of England would have to step in to support it. In this way, the Hong Kong Gap was performing an important task in

British sterling policy. The leak also reduced the pool of security sterling available for potential investors, encouraging new investment to take place across the official exchanges, and earning foreign exchange for the reserves.

By mid-1963, however, sales of security sterling through the gaps began to accelerate as Hong Kong's trade deficit with China expanded. In London, alarm bells began to ring in November, by which time sales of sterling securities through the gaps had reached £70 million for the first 10 months of 1963 compared with £36 million in the same period a year earlier. Attention turned again to stopping the gap by prohibiting the sale of sterling securities to Hong Kong residents.

At the end of the year, a substantial review of the situation convinced officials reluctantly once again to accept the status quo. Controls in the territories would be ineffective, and ejecting them from the sterling area was not politically or economically feasible. The Bank of England, however, argued for the elimination of security sterling so that Hong Kong would be forced to buy their sterling through the official exchange, thus earning dollars for the UK reserves.[55] Abolishing security sterling could be accomplished by allowing non-residents to sell their sterling securities for convertible sterling. The Treasury, however, saw no great advantage in unifying sterling while the security sterling rate was in line with the official rate. Leaving the Hong Kong Gap open would keep the rates in line without having to take the potentially irrevocable step of removing another exchange control.[56] There were also presentational difficulties involved in removing an exchange control (however ineffective) while confidence in sterling was weak.

There the matter rested until the beginning of 1965 when James Callaghan, Chancellor of the Exchequer, began a general review of ways to tighten exchange controls. In mid-January, he told the Prime Minister of his intention to collect a package of measures to tighten up the supply of sterling to the switch market.[57] After some delay, in August 1965 the Chancellor asked for an urgent brief on the Hong Kong and Kuwait Gaps and was advised again that no change was desirable or possible. Again, the key argument was that the security sterling rate was kept close to the official rate because of the demand for security sterling through Hong Kong.[58] The Bank of England and the Treasury kept their briefs up to date throughout the next four months in case they were asked about this issue again.

As pressure on the balance of payments persisted, the Chancellor remained concerned about the Hong Kong Gap.[59] The possibility of closing the Hong Kong and Kuwait Gaps was also discussed by Sir Dennis Rickett's Investment Group, which investigated ways in which to stem the outflow of capital from the UK at the end of 1965. Again, the Treasury and the Bank of England agreed to take no action, although a Bank of England representative was instructed to go to Hong Kong to assess the possibility of tightening the operation of exchange control in the colony.[60] This time, however, officials came out more strongly in favour of eliminating the restrictions on security sterling. If this pool of 'cheap' sterling were eliminated, Hong Kong would have to buy its sterling elsewhere. The rate through the Gulf would rise due to this increased demand, and Hong Kong would eventually be forced to buy sterling through the official exchange, thus earning dollars for the UK exchange reserves. This would help to offset the loss to the reserves that would occur due to the repatriation of non-residents' holdings of sterling securities once the proceeds were no longer blocked.[61]

In March 1966, Thomas Balogh argued strongly to the Chancellor that the Treasury/Bank of England position was flawed and that controls on the leaks through Hong Kong and Kuwait could and should be made effective, prompting yet another review of the situation.[62] The Treasury came back to the offensive on the unification of sterling in April 1966 with a fresh analysis of the problem, advising that 'the present policy is plainly unsatisfactory in itself. The only argument for continuing it is if the alternatives are shown to be worse.'[63] Eliminating security sterling was the preferred solution, not only for the reasons given above, but also because the Bank of England believed that allowing investments in sterling securities to be freely repatriated would make them more attractive to overseas investors, and might even generate an inflow of capital. Ejecting Hong Kong and Kuwait from the sterling area would have doubtful benefits because 'gaps' would merely arise elsewhere in the sterling area such as the Virgin Islands. Such a move would only be effective if the number of members of the sterling area were drastically reduced, a policy that A.K. Rawlinson of the Treasury was ready to advocate as a medium-term goal.[64] The Treasury, therefore, advocated abolishing security sterling as an interim measure. In the event, this policy was delayed a further year, partly due to the recurring danger of appearing to be further relaxing exchange controls at a time when sterling was weak. The Chancellor raised the issue again at a meeting to discuss the Hong Kong Gap in February 1967, and security sterling was finally abolished in April of that year.

This discussion of the ongoing deliberations through the 1950s and 1960s shows how uncomfortable officials and Ministers in London were about the free market in Hong Kong. The conflict between the laissez-faire attitude in Hong Kong and the interventionist governments in London was particularly stark over this issue. This account also shows that the impact of Hong Kong's financial markets was keenly felt in London and New York. Nevertheless, the Hong Kong authorities argued their case successfully in the late 1940s to retain the free market. In the 1950s and 1960s, they received support from the Bank of England, which was generally more sympathetic to deregulation. By this time, political as well as pragmatic obstacles prevented the UK authorities from bringing Hong Kong into line with the rest of the sterling area, and Hong Kong was used as an excuse to relax remaining restrictions on switch sterling.

Switch sterling activities of the Hongkong Bank

The switch sterling activities of the Hongkong Bank provide an example of the nature of this business. Table 4.6 shows the value of selected sterling transactions by the Hong Kong branch of the Hongkong Bank. Transfers of sterling from Singapore and Malaysia covered the bank's sales of HK dollars in these territories. After the imposition of controls on British residents' access to non-sterling securities in July 1957, the Hongkong Bank's purchases fell slightly but recovered by 1960, and by 1965 switch sterling purchases were close to four times the level of a decade before.

Table 4.6 Sterling transactions of the Hongkong Bank (£m)

	1954	1955	1956	1957	1958	1959	1960	1961	1962	1963	1964	1965	1966
Switch sterling purchases	24.5	25.8	25.5	36.0	35.5	31.5	40.4	37.8	47.9	45.4	76.9	92.6	56.9
Purchase of £ from Bank of Indonesia		6.8	23.1	12.3	8.7	4.7	12.7	7.8	0.0	2.1	3.2	2.0	
Transfers of £ from Singapore/Malaysia		18.1	19.2	22.0	20.3	20.0	13.2	17.2	14.4	22.4	36.7	33.1	31.4
Sales of £ to Bank of China		34.9	36.5	47.0	46.6	30.1	42.5	32.0	42.0	59.5	115.3	132.6	111.5

Source: Returns of Hong Kong Office, GHO201, HSBC.

The switch sterling was sold to other banks, and in particular to the Bank of China due to China's growing trade surplus with Hong Kong. By June 1965, the bank noted that 'It is becoming increasingly difficult to match our sales to Bank of China and if at any time offers of switch sterling become inoperable the immediate effect is a reduction in our overbought position (and in liquidity).'[65]

Offers of sterling came from the London office of the bank and also from the Middle East through Kuwait and the British Bank of the Middle East. The exchange controls introduced in July 1957 were expected to reduce the supply of switch sterling, and purchases in July only amounted to £818,627. They quickly recovered, however, and in the second half of 1957, purchases totalled £17 million. The Hong Kong branch noted in its returns for December 1957 that 'The new Bank of England regulations of July did not, therefore, affect this source of sterling and although purchases fell off slightly during the second half of the year, the year's total far exceeded the totals of previous years.'[66] The decline in the first half of 1958 compared with the same period a year earlier was attributed not to exchange controls, but to

> competition from some authorised Banks who were dealing directly in the Open Market. This has now been largely overcome by cutting out 'changeovers' and cutting our margin of profit on switch deals with the result that June purchases at £3.5 m were the highest since January 1957 with the exception of December in which we also purchased about the same amount.[67]

The Hongkong Bank bought the Mercantile Bank in 1959, and near the end of 1961, the Hongkong Bank began to purchase switch sterling through its new acquisition. The Mercantile was allowed to use all the free US dollars earned from the Hongkong Bank Group's commercial business to purchase switch sterling at brokers' rates. Mercantile were given first option on any US dollars available from the Group's Outward Bills departments and were offered first sight of the Hongkong Bank's offers of switch sterling from London. By 1962, however, Mercantile had sufficient offers of switch sterling from their own customers and the Hongkong Bank dealt almost exclusively through their brokers, Commercial Investment Co. Ltd and A.V. White and Co. In March 1963, the Hongkong Bank stopped offering Mercantile their free US dollar proceeds and offered them to the free market through Commercial Investment Co. Ltd instead.

In the second half of 1960, the Hongkong Bank began selling US dollar forward in London for up to six months. These transactions earned the London premium on US dollars, and allowed the New York office to invest the US dollars on the Eurodollar market in the meantime at favourable rates. In 1962 these forward sales of US dollars amounted to US$7.4 million, and in 1963 to US$3.6 million. Direct enquiries by Hong Kong residents about the Eurodollar market were not reported by the Hongkong Bank until the second half of 1966. At this time, Eurodollar deposit rates in London were up to 1.5 per cent better than the bank's customers could get on their deposits in San Francisco. In addition, the interest was tax-free, and these deposits provided a hedge against sterling devaluation. In 1966, the Hong Kong office of the Hongkong Bank placed about US$3.2 million of Eurodollar deposits in London on behalf of their customers.

Illegal transactions

In the late 1940s, the Hong Kong market became a primary route by which residents of Europe and North America could buy sterling 'cheaply' to settle their invisible debts to UK residents. If foreigners could manage to convert their currency into HK dollars (whether directly or through false invoicing of exports to Hong Kong), these HK dollars could then be converted to sterling or US dollars on the free market. The motivation was for sterling area residents to get access to scarce US dollars which their local exchange controls would not allow them, or for other foreigners to buy sterling cheaply to settle their debts to the UK or sterling area. For example, in August 1949 the Bank of England reported that they were aware of a sample transaction of £15,000 in legal fees due in London by a resident of Canada and paid for in sterling bought in Hong Kong.[68] At the time, such transactions were illegal under sterling area exchange control and so the volume of such transactions was difficult to determine. The Bank of England and the Treasury were convinced, however, that Hong Kong was a centre for such 'cheap sterling' deals, and this was the major motivation for the imposition of the No. 1 and No. 2 account system in 1950.

However, the new account system was not watertight, and there were periodic reports of illegal transactions through the market. In 1953 for example, the Tokyo branch of the Hongkong Bank advised the British embassy in Tokyo to cash sterling area cheques in Hong Kong and use the proceeds to buy US dollars on the free market to fund travel allowances.[69] Nevertheless, the volume of such transactions was considered to be relatively small. In 1965 an 'outside observer' put the total at about £100 million p.a., but the Bank of England estimated on the basis of their investigations that the amount was probably about one third this level (£30–40 million). The largest part of this amount was the sterling savings of Indian and Pakistani residents in the UK who used the market to remit their money to their home country. So-called 'real' exports of UK-owned capital through the free market were estimated to be about £10–20 million p.a.[70] By the end of 1965, the Bank of England and the Treasury were agreed that

> In recent years, the multiplication of authorised banks in Hong Kong has made the control there less reliable. Probably some transactions which are contrary to the rules do take place through these banks. This leak is though not large in respect of genuine UK residents. It is used by Indian and Pakistani residents of the UK; the dollars bought in Hong Kong are thought to be used to buy gold in Macao to be smuggled into India and Pakistan.[71]

A visit to Hong Kong by M.F. Culhane of the Bank of England in May 1966, however, revealed that the volume of illegal transactions through the free market was likely to be larger than the British had reckoned. This prompted the Bank of

England to initiate a campaign to increase prosecutions against transgressors.[72] It appeared to Culhane that there was a large volume of transactions which involved sterling credited to No. 2 accounts in Hong Kong from the UK, which was then converted to HK dollars and then to US dollars on the free market. The UK resident thus acquired US dollars illegally because the Hong Kong Exchange Control did not know that the sterling was from the UK. In Culhane's view this was possible because

> Hong Kong Control has in recent years become more and more casual in allowing the use of sterling from No 2 Accounts...without any enquiry about its origin or any alternative attempt to ensure that UK regulations were not being breached. In addition it seems more than likely that some of the Hong Kong Authorised Banks are slack.[73]

The problem was partly due to the growth in the number of authorised banks beyond the limited number envisioned when the controls were introduced in May 1950. Most of the leakage, however, was through non-authorised banks. Culhane performed a detailed survey of the exact practice of exchange control in Hong Kong, and found that permissions to authorised and non-authorised banks for transfer from No. 2 to No. 1 account were granted very easily with little investigation or requirement to identify that the transaction was related to legitimate trade. The practice of confirming that such transfers did not contravene UK control appeared 'to have fallen into disuse about 1962' according to Culhane's review of the paperwork in Hong Kong.[74] Culhane despaired of tightening the control up from the Hong Kong end, describing 'The atmosphere [in HK] is one of pride in complete free enterprise, which very much includes the avoidance or evasion of other centres' regulation, by smuggling, bribery, or less culpable (from the western viewpoint) means.'[75] He noted that 'local opinion is unanimous that the free market is an essential to Hong Kong's position as *the* Far Eastern financial centre' and that 'Cowperthwaite himself, perhaps a little casually, said he would rather leave the sterling area than abolish the free market'. Culhane concluded that 'to do any real good we have got to frighten off the UK remitters of funds' through prosecution, but that in addition the Hong Kong authorities should be reminded of their obligations.[76] By the beginning of July, the Bank of England reported that they had approached eight banks in London regarding transfers to Hong Kong.[77]

A planned visit of Sir David Trench, Governor of Hong Kong, to London in July 1966 offered an opportunity for the matter to be taken up at the highest level. Suggestions included revising Hong Kong's banking law, reducing the number of authorised banks, and increasing the staff of the Exchange Control. It was also necessary for the Exchange Controller to get support from the government 'which he at present did not get'.[78] The Governor of the Bank of England believed that 'there were some grounds for thinking that the Colonial Government did not take its responsibilities seriously enough'.[79] This was perhaps confirmed by Trench's response to the problem of illegal transactions. He 'seemed sympathetic' but not knowledgeable and believed the British concern over the leak to be exaggerated.[80] Soon after, however, he appeared to change his mind about the size of the illegal leak through Hong Kong. A.K. Rawlinson of the Treasury described his conversion:

> I learned the other day that he is now completely converted to our view, not by anything which you or I said at the official meeting, but by his own experience the following day when he went to Ascot. In the Paddock he was introduced to a lady. "This is Sir David Trench, the Governor of Hong Kong." Said the lady: "Ah, Hong Kong. How interesting. That is where I get my dollars."[81]

In September, Cowperthwaite was approached both in Hong Kong and while in London. His response was that something should be done if possible, and he agreed to yet another visit by a Bank of England official to advise on tightening up the control over illegal transactions. He stipulated, however, that it must be clear to the public in Hong Kong that closing the free market was not on the agenda.[82] At the meeting in London, Cowperthwaite assured the British officials of his willingness to cooperate but

> He did not think that Hong Kong banks could be expected to be familiar with the exchange control rules of the UK, or that they could investigate the provenance of instructions coming to them, possibly from another resident of Hong Kong who might be acting as an agent for a UK resident.[83]

Instead, he launched his own campaign to tidy up the exchange control legislation by replacing the Defence Finance Regulations.

The problem of illegal transactions dragged on and resulted in the appointment of an independent Exchange Controller, updating Hong Kong's exchange control notices, and further investigations in London.[84] At the end of 1966, Harris, the Hongkong Bank's nominee exchange controller, proposed the appointment of a permanent officer. He noted that other banks resented the current arrangement and were reluctant to reveal details of their transactions to a potential competitor, which made his position unworkable.[85] The Chancellor was reported to be unsatisfied that more could not be done, but successive studies failed to come up with any more radical proposals.[86]

This account of the British reaction to the free market has taken us a few years beyond the scope of this book. It is important to recognise, however, that the free market continued to be a thorn in the side of British exchange control, and continued to be an important conduit for international capital. Indeed, the advent of current account convertibility of sterling at the end of 1958 increased the importance of remaining capital controls imposed by the UK. From the beginning of the 1960s, as sterling came under increasing pressure to devalue, the Hong Kong market played an increasingly prominent role in the international system.

Conclusion

This chapter has detailed the structure and operations of the free exchange market in Hong Kong. It has shown that this market served local merchants and facilitated regional trade in Asia as well as trade between Asian markets and the United States and Europe. The foreign exchange services offered in Hong Kong also attracted entrepot business. Importantly for the emergence of Hong Kong as an international financial centre, this market attracted remittance business between third parties, and was also used as a centre to convert sterling to US dollars at a time when exchange controls elsewhere prohibited direct conversion. The result was the development of a sophisticated market in cash and securities. The market in Hong Kong had global importance as an important breach in the international monetary system, as well as regional importance as the hub of commercial traffic. The switch market was one of the most prominent global dimensions to Hong Kong's financial services since it reached far beyond the regional Asian economy to compete with other major financial centres in Europe, the UK and the USA. The account of British policy with respect to the market has highlighted the conflict between the interventionist philosophy in London and the firmly laissez-faire approach in Hong Kong. In the end, the latter prevailed, with lasting implications for the role of Hong Kong as an international financial centre.

5 The gold market, the stock exchange and insurance

This chapter reviews developments in three elements of the financial services offered in Hong Kong in the 1950s and 1960s: the gold market, the stock exchange and insurance. The operations of the gold market in the 1950s and 1960s were clandestine but the volume of transactions passing through the market was large, and it was developed into a major regional trading hub with global links. The history of the market exemplifies the conflict between the governments in Hong Kong and London. Unlike the case of the free dollar market, the gold market was officially closed after British pressure was applied, although this did not eliminate the trade. The Hong Kong Stock Exchange was more limited in scope in the early decades after the war. Its importance lay in attracting considerable overseas capital, and the impact of the share boom in 1960–1 on the banking system. Finally, Hong Kong was the regional centre for many international insurance providers that were attracted by the entrepot activities of the colony. In the 1960s, the market began to diversify into the provision of investment products for residents of Hong Kong.

The gold market

The Hong Kong gold market, although strictly speaking a commodity market, was closely linked to the financial markets since it attracted foreign capital, and there was a forward market in gold for speculators. Since the 1970s, the gold market has been acknowledged as a prominent part of the general services offered by Hong Kong as a regional financial centre. The ban on the import and export of gold was lifted in 1974, and by 1979 Hong Kong had developed the fourth largest gold market after London, New York and Zurich.[1] In the same year, the daily turnover in the market reached HK$1,400 million and US$4,720 million worth of gold was officially imported into Hong Kong.[2] Despite this rapid growth and its prominent position in Hong Kong's financial services, historians have not yet explored its postwar development.[3]

Size, structure and fluctuations in the market

The Hong Kong gold market dates back to before the First World War, when it primarily served the needs of the regional Chinese community who traditionally valued gold for hoarding both in bars and in ornaments. After a series of bankruptcies brought about by inadequate regulatory controls, a number of traders formed the Gold and Silver Exchange of Hongkong in 1932. The Exchange was registered with the Secretary of Chinese Affairs, although its activities were not subject to taxation.

Imports of gold into Hong Kong were banned in 1945 but a market in 0.99 fine gold already in the colony remained legal, and this predictably attracted smugglers.[4] In 1946, in order to lower the Hong Kong price, the Financial Secretary began to license limited imports for transhipment to Macao from whence it could be smuggled back to Hong Kong. At this time, the main sources of supply were Mexico and the UK, from where it was imported on behalf of customers in the USA, Britain and Europe, as well as for regional trade. In January 1947, for example, a load of HK$57 million worth of gold bars arrived from the UK by Lancastrian airliner, consigned partly to an American bank and partly to a British trading company.[5] Total gold imports in 1946 amounted to HK$20.2 million, of which HK$19.3 million was for transit to Macao.[6]

This post-war boom was soon to end, however, under pressure from beyond the colony. In 1947, the Chinese authorities outlawed trade in gold as part of their effort to shore up their monetary system, and in April 1947 the Hong Kong Financial Secretary announced that no further import permits would be issued. All outstanding permits were cancelled in order to support the Chinese policy.[7] Two months later, members of the IMF were asked to 'take effective action to prevent external transactions in gold at premium prices because such transactions tend to undermine exchange stability and to impair monetary reserves'.[8] The Bank of England and the Federal Reserve Bank of the USA immediately withdrew their permission to bullion dealers to operate in free markets such as Hong Kong.

In 1948, the British authorities began to examine measures which would bring Hong Kong exchange control into line with the IMF edict. The Governor of Hong Kong, Sir Alexander Grantham, strongly resisted pressure for the gold market to be closed. He complained to London that

> For almost a century trade in gold has been pre-eminent and traditionally in the hands of native banks of Hong Kong. Prohibition would inevitably arouse grave resentment and might have far-reaching consequences.[9]

Despite this plea, in November 1948 Grantham was instructed to put into effect a new system of exchange controls, which included eliminating the gold market.[10] After considerable procrastination by Grantham, the gold market was closed down by order of the Hong Kong authorities on 14 April 1949. The timing of the official announcement was ill-favoured by political events in China, so Grantham's procrastination was somewhat unfortunate. On 21 April the Communists crossed the Yangtse River and the takeover of China was assured. The Chinese currency, the Gold Yuan, collapsed and there was a flood of capital out of China and out of the Asian region generally. The US dollar exchange rate in Hong Kong soared, causing difficulties for importers and inflating the prices of consumer goods and the cost of living. Meanwhile, the gold market had been forced underground and the uncertainty caused gold prices to double, adding to the upward pressure on the dollar exchange rate.[11] This upward pressure was exacerbated by the suspicion that the closure of the gold market signalled an imminent sterling devaluation, generating a further speculative rush for US dollars.[12]

The reactions in Hong Kong and London to these dramatic events in the dollar and gold markets were completely contradictory. Grantham called for the re-opening of the gold market to ease pressure on the dollar, while the Bank of England chose to reconsider the possibility of closing the free dollar market altogether.[13] The difference between the British and Hong Kong positions can be explained partly by their different perceptions of the role of the gold market in the Hong Kong economy. Grantham insisted that gold was an important element in the domestic credit market due to its role as collateral. An abrupt end to the gold market would thus cause a contraction in credit in the colony. The Treasury, however, saw the market as essentially speculative and in violation of the IMF prohibition on premium gold markets.[14] In June 1949, F.J. Portsmore, a representative from the Bank of England, was sent to Hong Kong to review the situation.[15]

By this time, however, the financial situation had steadied. In large part this was attributed to local optimism about the future of trade with Communist China, and greater confidence in Britain's commitment to maintain political responsibility for the colony. The continued unofficial operation of the gold market and the resumed supply of smuggled gold lowered the gold price, and steadied demand in the dollar market. On the supply side of the US dollar market, a Chinese government organisation was reported to be selling substantial US dollars against HK dollars, and the start of the Dragon Festival meant that overseas remittances were seasonally high.[16] Portsmore reported that the flurry in the US dollar market in May was primarily due to political events and he therefore recommended that the official gold market should remain closed.[17]

The legislation merely made transactions in pure gold illegal, while leaving the market free to operate in 0.945 gold. The Ministry of Food representative in Southeast Asia described this amendment as a measure 'which to the onlooker might appear to disallow a glass of gin unless angostura had been added'.[18] Since importing 0.945 gold was still illegal, it was necessary to smelt 0.99 fine gold temporarily in nearby Macao, or smuggle it into Hong Kong to be smelted locally before reaching the market. In May 1953, P.L. Hogg of the Bank of England visited Hong Kong and reported that the refineries in Macao were very rudimentary and that about half of the gold continued to be smelted in Hong Kong.[19] Forty-four of the members of the Gold Exchange were allowed to issue their own gold bars but only one half of these members actually refined their own gold. The bar issuing members had to furnish a guarantee of HK$20,000 and the bars were subject to inspection by the Exchange, but the credibility of the various refiners varied. In 1950, for example, Wing Sing Loong Bank bars had a high reputation, while those of the Tak Cheong Bank generated suspicion of their exact fineness.[20] Refiners could earn extra profits by misrepresenting the fineness of their bars, and it was harder to detect fraud in 0.945 bars than in 0.99 fine gold.

In October 1953, restrictions on Hong Kong's gold trade were relaxed somewhat to allow imports into Hong Kong which were bonded for re-export – usually to

Macao. This marked a return to the situation of 1946/7. The gold was exported to Macao temporarily and then smuggled back to Hong Kong, cutting out the need to tranship gold in other ports such as Saigon. From this time, gold began to be flown directly into Hong Kong from Europe, Australia or South Africa on BOAC planes, stored temporarily in local bank vaults, and then re-exported to Macao by Catalina flying boat at a cost of HK$0.30 per ounce. In March 1954 the London bullion market was re-opened, and from this time most of the gold imported into Hong Kong came from Britain. Three companies in Hong Kong dominated the import market: Mount Trading Co. (which was a subsidiary of Samuel Montagu and Co. in London), Premex (the local agent of the Swiss firm, Bullion Exchange and Trading) and Commercial Investment Co. (part of the Wheelock Marden group).[21] Until the changes became effective in December 1953, official imports of gold into Hong Kong had averaged just over HK$400,000 per month. In December, the total recorded imports leaped to over HK$22 million, and averaged HK$25–40 million per month for the rest of the decade.

The Gold and Silver Exchange Association was limited to 197 members by 1951 and met each morning for three hours and a further two hours in the afternoon.[22] In 1953, P.L. Hogg reported that the market was 'housed in a modest building down one of the side streets [Mercer Street] in a principal shopping district' where 'a large crowd of Chinese gathers each morning'.[23] Members representing the native banks and other dealers bought their seats on the Exchange for a sum that varied with the amount of activity in the market. In mid-1951, a seat cost HK$27,000, although at the peak of business in 1949 the price was HK$77,000.[24] By 1954, as the market quietened, the price of membership fell to HK$8,000.[25] The dealers charged commission, which in 1951 amounted to one cent per tael in the cash or spot market and two cents per tael in the forward market. Each day in mid-1951, about 30,000 taels of gold were traded on the spot market and 100,000 taels in the forward market, generating daily earnings of HK$3,000–4,000 for the Exchange.[26] The Exchange paid out biannual dividends to its members and managed funds for the education, medical and sports interests of its members as well as owning property, including a pool, school and clinic.[27]

The volume of forward transactions was always considerably greater than cash sales. In the late 1940s, the forward market averaged about 400,000 taels per week, which was 10 times the volume of cash sales. Individuals could purchase gold bars and sell them forward through the Exchange on a daily basis, earning interest at a variable rate depending on supply and demand for cash bars at 11:30am each day. A charge of HK$75 per tael was levied on positions carried from one day to the next.[28] At its peak in early 1949, the interest ran at about 30 per cent p.a., falling to 12–18 per cent p.a. by the end of the year. This compared favourably with deposit accounts at banks, which earned only 1–2 per cent p.a.[29] The forward market became well established by 1948, and was initially dominated by Shanghai immigrants fleeing from the Civil War on the mainland.[30] It was reported that Shanghai financiers overbought gold futures in anticipation of a devaluation of the HK dollar and found themselves in financial difficulty vis-à-vis local and Cantonese speculators. Like the cash market, the forward market was supposed to take place within the Gold and

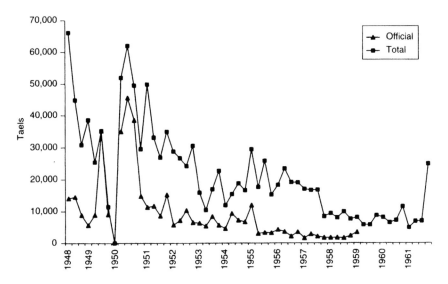

Figure 5.1 Weekly cash gold sales 1948–61 (last week of each quarter).

Silver Exchange, but in practice occurred directly. The *Far Eastern Economic Review* reported that during 1948 'a number of local gold bucketshops were well appointed supplying (like in good old Shanghai) the gamblers with all kind of refreshments (women were always prominent among the following of these gold brokers)'.[31]

Figure 5.1 shows the volume of cash sales on the market both inside and outside the Exchange during the last week in each quarter. The *Far Eastern Economic Review* stopped reporting regularly on the volume of trade in the gold market after 1961. In the immediate post-war period, regional instability generated a high turnover in the market. After the slump following the Korean War, the volume of trade enjoyed a brief rise due to increased demand in the Middle East after the Suez crisis of 1956. Imports of gold into Macao increased from 1.8 million ounces in 1955 to 2.25 million in 1956, but then returned to 1.9 million ounces in 1957.[32] In 1959 and 1960, gold markets were opened in Laos and Bangkok, and the Hong Kong market faced greater regional competition, although the Laos market was subsequently closed in October 1962.

An interesting feature of Figure 5.1 is that a substantial proportion of cash sales of gold took place informally in 'curbside' deals outside the Exchange, even though this was punishable by temporary suspension from the Association. The curbside deals allowed traders to evade the commission payable to the Exchange, and allowed smugglers to hide their identity. The proportion of such transactions increased when the price of gold rose slightly in 1951–3 and then again in 1956/7. In a meeting of the Gold and Silver Exchange on 10 May 1954, eight members of the Association were suspended from operations for three to four months for dealing in futures outside the Exchange.[33] One of these banks, Yue Tak Sing Kee Bank, failed after the suspension with an outstanding liability of over HK$0.5 million.[34]

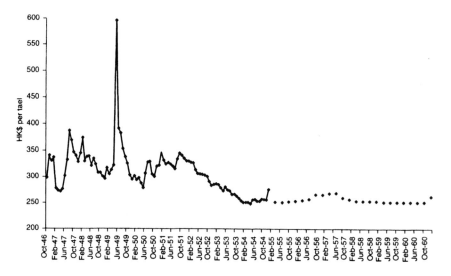

Figure 5.2 Gold prices 1946–60 (monthly 1946–54; quarterly 1955–60).

Figure 5.2 shows movements in the gold price from 1946 to 1960. The peaks and troughs reflect the impact of a variety of political and economic factors.

The outbreak of the Korean War in 1950 prompted a speculative boom. In July and August 1950 alone, 680,000 ounces of fine gold were imported into Macao. This gold was bought by speculators and native banks hoping to make a substantial profit, but they were ultimately disappointed as regional demand did not rise substantially.[35] Indeed, most native banks sustained considerable losses on their gold speculation as prices fell.[36] At the end of 1950, however, demand recovered after the freezing of Chinese US dollar assets encouraged Hong Kong and Chinese residents to switch assets into gold.[37] By the beginning of 1951, the Korean War turned against the Western allied interest, and gold hoarding resumed among the local and Chinese refugee population. In September 1951, the IMF relaxed its hunt against premium free gold markets and most gold-producing countries allowed newly mined gold to be sold to premium markets. This increased the supply and depressed the price. The Korean War armistice and large-scale selling of gold by the USSR in 1953 reinforced this trend and for the next decade the trend of prices was downward.

Table 5.1 shows the relative gold price in the Hong Kong market for 1946–53. After 1953 the Hong Kong price fluctuated narrowly around a cross rate of US$38 per ounce, which tended to be lower than other regional markets such as Tokyo and Bangkok. The higher prices in Hong Kong in the early 1950s were in part due to the hoarding encouraged by proximity to the Korean conflict. Also important, however, were the relative transactions costs of the Hong Kong market compared to other free gold markets. These costs included transportation, currency exchange risks, licences, and smuggling charges.

Table 5.1 Free market gold prices, closing price for December (US$ per oz.)

	London	Beirut	Tangier	Zurich	Bangkok	Bombay	Paris	Lisbon	Hong Kong
1946			63	47			62		51
1947			53	42			53		50
1948			57	43			49		49
1949			40	41			46		36
1950			40	40			41		45
1951	38.75	39	38.9	38.87	45.44	47.02	41.37	41.21	42
1952	37.55	37.5	37.45	37.47	40.87	43.67	39.03	40.18	38.67
1953	35.2	35.45	35.1	35.2	37.82	45.4	35.57	36.88	35.42

Sources: 1946–50, 'Lower Gold Prices and Demand', *Far Eastern Economic Review*, 25 September 1952, p. 411. 1951–3, *Daily Commodity Quotations*, Hong Kong, OK Printing Press.

The transactions costs in the market tended to be high firstly because of the illegality of the external trade, and secondly due to special circumstances in Macao, the intermediate source of gold for the market. Gold imports into Macao were subject to licences, which were controlled by a syndicate. Applicants for licences were required to deposit 1.2 million patacas on application; this sum to be returned after the application had been approved.[38] The official rate for the pataca was on par with the HK dollar, but the circulation of local currency was very small since the HK dollar was used as the primary currency in Macao. This made the deposit requirement hard to meet and effectively protected the monopoly of the gold syndicate, who had hoarded patacas at a par rate in anticipation of the requirement.[39] The cost of import licences varied with demand, ranging from HK$5 to HK$26 per ounce from 1945 to 1951.[40] Throughout 1951 the licence price fell in line with the gold price to HK$ 14 per ounce[41] and then to HK$7 in August 1953. This reflected both increased competition from the new free market in Bangkok, and falling world gold prices.[42] The cost of a licence subsequently increased to HK$9 and then HK$12 per ounce by the end of 1954.[43]

Table 5.2 shows estimates of the transactions cost of selling gold on the Hong Kong market based on contemporary press reports and information given to P.L. Hogg (of the Bank of England) by local dealers. In 1952, the total transactions cost of selling gold in Hong Kong amounted to the equivalent of US$3.23 per ounce on the official price of US$35 per ounce. For importers to make a profit, the premium on the gold price in Hong Kong had to be at least 9 per cent in 1952. In fact, the premium amounted to between 14.4 and 22.4 per cent in that year.

The costs for 1954 were only about US$2.00 per ounce both because direct imports into Hong Kong were allowed in October 1953, and because the Macao licence fee was lower. Illegal transport from Macao back to Hong Kong cost about HK$1–2 per ounce, and was handled by a number of Chinese firms reportedly connected with the native banks.[44] The *Far Eastern Economic Review* noted that at its peak this charge amounted to HK$5 per ounce.[45] Since the market price was consistently about US$38 per ounce for the rest of the decade, dealers made a profit of about US$1 or HK$6 per ounce.

Table 5.2 Cost of smuggling gold into Hong Kong (HK$ per oz. of gold)

	1952	1954
Saigon handling charge	0.25	—
Transport to Macao	1.40	0.30
Macao handling charge	0.25	0.25
Macao import license	14.00	7.00
Transport from Macao		1.50
Swap for 0.945 in Hong Kong	3.20	3.20
Total	19.10	11.75

Sources: 1952 estimates by P.L. Hogg, 11 May 1953, BE OV14/9; 1954 estimates from *Far Eastern Economic Review.*

Table 5.3 Hong Kong customs gold seizures (pounds)

1955/6	783
1956/7	391
1957/8	878
1958/9	35
1959/60	56
1960/1	244
1961/2	396
1962/3	242
1963/4	190
1964/5	421

Source: *Annual Departmental Reports, Director of Commerce and Industry*, Hong Kong.

The cost of smuggled exports from Hong Kong is not as easily calculated as for imports. In June 1954, the *Far Eastern Economic Review* estimated that the total premium for imports and exports was about HK$ 11 per tael or twice the estimate for imports alone in Table 5.2.[46] Smuggling exports to China was more expensive than exporting to Singapore or other regular destinations because of the greater risk of detection. Nevertheless, in June 1957 it was reported that 1,000 taels were being smuggled to Canton each week.[47] Fortunately for them, the prospects of being caught smuggling gold out of the colony appear to have been fairly slim. Table 5.3 shows annual seizures of gold in Hong Kong for 1955–65.

In February 1953, the reward for information related to gold smuggling was reduced from 40 per cent of the official value of the confiscated gold to a flat rate of HK$10 per tael.[48] The decision reportedly reflected the Hong Kong government's acquiescence to public pressure for a legal gold market, since it reduced the incentive to hinder the gold trade.[49] Confiscated gold accounted for less than 8 per cent of gold exports in any year. Official seizures were mainly on outward bound shipping; for example in 1956 111 pounds were found under the decking of a vessel bound for Indonesia,[50] and in 1957 133 pounds of gold were found concealed in a cargo of sweets bound for Singapore.[51] Hogg reported that most of the seizures were from outside the main smuggling rings.[52] In 1968, *The Economist* reported that professional gold couriers could usually charge a commission of 1 per cent of the value of their smuggled consignment but that the route between Macao and Hong Kong was so safe that junk owners only charged US$3.50 per pound or 24 cents per fine ounce. The article concluded that 'the authorities most closely concerned keep their eyes firmly glued to their official records, pick up the occasional smuggler when they can – and ignore the rest'.[53]

The restrictions on the market in Hong Kong had a profound impact on neighbouring Macao. Between 1947 and 1950, the Macao government earned 12.5 million patacas from the gold import duty on total imports of 6.25 million fine ounces. In the same period, the Macao gold syndicate earned an estimated 45–50 million patacas from their sale of licences, equivalent to about HK$60–100 million.[54] In 1951, 3.1 million ounces were imported to Macao generating a further HK$40 million for the syndicate, but only 1.6 million ounces of this gold was imported officially, so the Treasury revenue was 3.2 million patacas.[55] Once gold could be legally imported from Hong Kong after 1953, the volume of official imports into Macao increased and so did tax revenue. By 1967, the tax on gold imports accounted for 20 per cent of the government revenue of Macao.

Timothy Green asserts that Hong Kong continued to restrict the gold trade because it was such a vital source of government revenue for the Macao authorities.[56] When Britain considered opening the gold market in mid-1953, however, the cost to Macao was not the primary obstacle. A relaxation was rejected because recognition of the Hong Kong market would antagonise the Americans, who had a greater interest in maintaining the official exchange rate of the US dollar to gold.[57] Crick at the UK Trade and Supply Delegation in Washington argued that opening the market would officially allow convertibility for sterling at a fluctuating rate and might attract more sterling area capital to Hong Kong.[58]

After the London gold market opened in 1954, however, this situation changed and there is some support for the suggestion that stability in Macao was a factor in this breach of the Hong Kong government's otherwise stalwart anti-regulatory policy. A brief for a Bank of England visit to Hong Kong in 1959 reported that the Hong Kong government had been given the opportunity to re-open the local market to dealings by non-residents, but that they rejected this move on the basis that such a relaxation 'would have a catastrophic effect on the economic position of Macao'.[59] It must also be assumed that the difficulty of isolating non-residents would have made the regulations unenforceable.

Local business, however, objected strongly to the status quo. In 1957, it was reported that Hong Kong bullion dealers felt 'a burning sense of grievance' that most of the profit on the gold trade went to the Macao gold syndicate rather than to the Hong Kong government through local licensing.[60] In 1956 and again in 1960, the Hongkong Bank advocated the elimination of Macao in the gold trade. In 1960 Turner, then manager of the Hongkong Bank, wrote to Robert Black, Hong Kong Governor,

Suppose we cut out Macau altogether, allowed gold into Hong Kong and imposed a 10% duty on all gold coming in: that would bring us in £300,000 a month, or about $55 million a year, and I think the market could stand that 10% and possibly more, so $55m might well be a minimum. Granted there are snags and the UK might not like it, but at the moment we are subsidising Lobo, Ho Yin and Macau at a time when we badly need the subsidy ourselves.[61]

Turner's suggestion was not taken up and the gold market continued to operate in its clandestine way, generating high profits for the Macao government and for the Hong Kong bankers and merchants who were involved.

Hong Kong and the East Asian gold trade

Hong Kong was by far the most important gold market serving Asia. It was the crucial link between gold producers in South Africa, Australia and Canada, the premium gold markets in Europe, and Asian gold purchasers. The appendix shows the direction of gold smuggled in and out of Hong Kong. The financial institutions, insurance and communications services available in Hong Kong made the colony a much more attractive gold centre than neighbouring Macao with its rudimentary banking system and shallow harbour. Hong Kong also benefited from the restrictions that operated in other supply and distribution centres in the region.

The Philippines was the only significant gold producer in the region but their market was relatively undeveloped. In 1941 the average monthly production was 105,400 ounces, but this had fallen to 26,000 ounces at the end of 1949,[62] rising to 32,800 ounces by 1951.[63] After 1945, Philippine gold producers were required to sell 25 per cent of their newly mined gold to the government at the official cross rate of US$35 per ounce. This price was less than the prevailing Hong Kong free market price and not enough to ensure profitability of the mining process. Exports of gold to countries where it could be sold for more than the official price were prohibited. The remaining three quarters of the gold production was then ostensibly open to a 'free' market but was in practice bought by a Chinese cartel at uncompetitive prices. Of this amount, about a quarter was re-sold for industrial use and the rest disappeared to overseas markets including Hong Kong. In the early 1950s, therefore, approximately 15,000 ounces of gold were smuggled out of the Philippines each month, with the profits going to the traders rather than to the mining companies.

In September 1952, a gold bullion exchange for locally produced gold was suggested for Manila. The mining industry believed that establishing a market operating at higher competitive prices would sustain the industry and keep the gold in the Philippines.[64] The gold could then be used to import non-essentials from the USA. Despite pressure from the mining industry, a free exchange was not introduced and the Philippine government continued to stockpile local gold output through to the 1980s.

Bangkok and Singapore were the main distribution centres for gold throughout Southeast Asia, although restrictions on internal trade meant that gold markets did not flourish there. The Thai authorities prohibited the import of gold but allowed it to be held in bond for re-export. Until the end of 1952, Bangkok featured prominently as both an importer and exporter of Hong Kong gold. Gold was flown from Europe or South America to Bangkok and stored temporarily in a specially

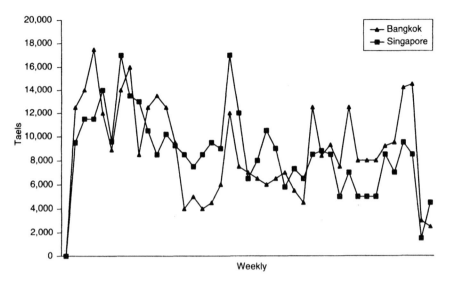

Figure 5.3 Smuggled gold exports from Hong Kong in 1952.

constructed vault at Don Muang Airport. The gold was then transferred to Catalina flying boats (often operated by the state-owned Siamese P.O.A.S.[65]) and flown to Porto Exterior at Macao. From there the gold was smuggled to Hong Kong and sold to exporters who smuggled it back to Thailand by ship into the port of Koh-Sihchang.[66] Thai gold importers used HK dollars generated by selling the US dollar proceeds of rubber exports on the Hong Kong free market. In 1952, it was estimated that this trade generated about US$2 million per month from Bangkok, accounting for about 30 per cent of the telegraphic transfer dollar sales on the free dollar market in Hong Kong.[67] Through 1951–2, smuggled exports from Hong Kong to Bangkok averaged over 7,300 taels per week.[68] Figure 5.3 shows weekly exports to Bangkok and Singapore in 1952, which accounted for almost all of the smuggled exports from Hong Kong in this year.

In October 1952, the Thai government proposed to establish an official gold syndicate to handle the import and distribution of gold. At this time illegal imports were estimated to be running at about 50,000 ounces per month[69] but the opening of the market was delayed, apparently due to the resistance of those who benefited from smuggling.[70] On 1 November 1952, a Financial Syndicate of nine Bangkok banks and one trading firm was established with an initial import quota of 40,000 ounces of gold which could be imported directly rather than smuggled through the Hong Kong market. In theory, any Thai citizen could apply for a licence, but in practice licences were only granted to the Thai Financial Syndicate controlled by Phao Sriyanondh, then Chief of Police.[71] The Thai Financial Syndicate in turn sold the gold to the Gold Dealers Syndicate of 25 local goldsmiths who actually negotiated the imports.[72] No official gold exports were allowed, although it was believed that a *considerable proportion of* newly imported gold was re-exported to Indochina.[73] The import quotas were supposed to fulfil domestic demand, but it was also believed that a 'considerable additional quantity' was smuggled in.[74] This is reflected in the periodic exports of gold from Hong Kong in the later 1950s shown in the appendix.

Open recognition of the unofficial gold trade operating throughout the region promised some rewards for governments from revenue on import licences, but there would be losses for those who had profited from the black market. In the case of Thailand, there was widespread corruption among Thai officials who offered 'protection' to gold smugglers in return for bribes.[75] Legalising the trade would eliminate these rewards. As noted above, however, the Thai gold market was a monopoly controlled by the Chief of Police, which suggests that similar interest groups continued to profit from the gold trade after liberalisation. The result of the opening of the Bangkok market was a re-routing of some of the Southeast Asian gold away from Hong Kong. This was reflected in the fall in the Hong Kong gold price seen in Figure 5.2. The Bangkok price of gold fell from US$45 per ounce (or 10 per cent above the Hong Kong market price) to US$41.25 once the market became legal.[76]

Between the opening of a legal market in Bangkok and the relaxation on imports into Hong Kong at the end of 1953, Saigon was the major transhipment port for the Hong Kong market. The gold arrived in Saigon chiefly from Paris, originally from South Africa, Australia, Canada, Mexico and the USA.[77] From Saigon, the gold was flown by Catalina flying boat to Macao where it was broken down into small bars and smuggled into Hong Kong.[78] A Catalina flying boat could carry up to 40,000 ounces per trip and it made the journey four or five times per month, accounting for up to 200,000 ounces per month.[79] Once Hong Kong allowed transhipments of gold consigned on a bill of lading to another destination, there was no need for transhipment in other Southeast Asian centres, and this trade ended abruptly.

After 1952, Singapore became the major market for Hong Kong gold exports. The role of Singapore in the market was revealed by Hogg's investigations in May 1953. He reported that Singapore gold imports were used

> partly to meet the up-country demand in Malaya and partly for redistribution round the whole of Southeast Asia.[80]

Singapore was consistently the largest importer of Hong Kong gold, averaging over 5,000 taels per week from 1953 to 1958. Indonesia was briefly the next largest market after 1955, absorbing 3,400 taels per week on average from 1955 to 1957. Other, less important destinations included direct exports to Korea, Burma, Japan and India. The gold was mostly supplied from South Africa, but also from Australia, Canada, Mexico, the USA and the Philippines. It arrived in the Far East mainly through Paris but also via Zurich, Brussels and London.[81]

In the 1960s, Hong Kong encountered more regional competition. In 1959, Laos legalised the entry of gold, and this was followed by greater relaxation of the market in Thailand in 1960. From 1960 to 1965, the Far East markets altogether sold about 60–70 tons of gold worth about US$1.1 million.[82] From 1960 to 1965, the Middle East (Dubai, Beirut, Bahrain and Kuwait) became a more important first destination for gold exports from London, increasing from less than 10 per cent to almost one third of total gold exports between 1960 and 1964. The share going to the Far East declined over the same period from 10 to 6 per cent.[83] Hong Kong maintained its position as the premier regional gold market because of the sophisticated financial and insurance services available in the colony as well as the transport infrastructure – in particular Kai Tak Airport. As will be seen in Chapter 6, Hong Kong also benefited from relative political stability compared to other countries in East and Southeast Asia.

Conclusion

The gold market was an important feature of commercial and speculative activity in Hong Kong. In London, the market was not condoned because this would have left Hong Kong as an even more exposed aberration in the international monetary system. After the gold market in London was opened in 1954, European companies quickly established themselves in Hong Kong to import gold directly. A proportion of the profit of the illicit gold trade was thus going to the UK and other European firms, which may explain the delay in relaxing the trade restrictions after the London market was re-opened. Also, the gold trade through Macao was a vital source of government revenue for the Macao authorities. The gold market is an example when the interventionist government in London prevailed over the laissez-faire intentions of the Hong Kong state. Because the market was condoned by the Hong Kong authorities, the actual impact was to enrich those who controlled the smuggling, at the expense of part of the competitive edge of the market for buyers. That the market continued to attract customers despite these difficulties suggests that the transactions costs were outweighed by the efficiency of the market in terms of associated services, communications, and concentration of expertise.

The stock exchange

Share trading began in Hong Kong after the first Companies Ordinance of 1865, and was brought into an organised stock exchange in the mid-1880s. By the start of the Second World War, there were two exchanges: the Hong Kong Stock Exchange and the Hong Kong Shareholders Association. Some trading took place during the war, and resumed unofficially soon after the Japanese surrender.[84] However, demand was low, the number of brokers had been drastically reduced, and prices fluctuated widely on the black market, destroying investor confidence. To restore the market, it was decided to merge the two exchanges into the Hong Kong Stock Exchange (1947) Ltd, which re-opened for business in February 1947.[85] Twenty-two dealers, predominantly Hong Kong Chinese, made up the initial membership of the new Exchange, although there was provision for 60 members.[86] By April the number had reached 54 brokers, with four applications pending. Brokers were required to be of British nationality or able to prove that they had resided in Hong Kong for at least five years.

Brokerage commission was first set at 1 per cent of the gross value of the transaction, where it remained for most of the period – except for a brief spell at 0.5 per cent during an increase in activity in the market from mid-November 1947 until May 1948.[87] Profits were not subject to capital gains tax, but transactions were subject to an ad valorem Stamp Duty of 0.2 per cent, bringing the total cost of trading to 1.2 per cent throughout the 1950s. This compared favourably with fees in European stock markets. Business took place on large wooden trading boards where bid and offer prices were quoted on a 'first come first served' basis. The regulations were lax and brokers acted both for their clients and on their own accounts.

At the outset, trading was thin and a delegation of brokers asked the Hongkong Bank to promote margin trading. The Hongkong Bank initially refused, on the grounds that this would merely encourage destabilising speculation.[88] Despite the lack of initial support for margin trading, banks in Hong Kong were closely involved in the market. In 1954, the Bank of East Asia established a nominee company which specialised in the management of stock portfolios for its customers.[89] It was noted in Chapter 3 that most banks offered loans based on shares as collateral (the Chartered Bank, for example). It will be seen below that the stock market boom of 1960–1 squeezed the liquidity of banks and helped to precipitate the banking crisis of that year. Finally, the Bank of East Asia and the Hongkong Bank had very active issues on the Exchange.

The activities of the Hong Kong Stock Exchange have generally been discounted as insignificant until the 1970s, when turnover increased substantially.[90] Figure 5.4 shows the amount of new capital raised on the stock market from 1954 to 1969. From 1959 to 1968 capital raised through the Stock Exchange amounted to less than 1 per cent of GDP, compared with 5.4 per cent in the period 1969–72. Table 5.4 shows that the manufacturing industry was not well represented among public companies until the 1970s. Until the 1970s, there were only 50–70 companies listed on the Exchange, of which less than half were subject to active trading. They were dominated by large, primarily service sector enterprises. Of the capital raised between 1958 and 1966, 43 per cent was raised by public utilities and a further 15 per cent by hotel, property and commercial enterprises. From 1954–65, just over HK$760 million of new capital was raised on the Stock Exchange. This compared with HK$4.9 billion in 1966–72.[91] The Stock Exchange was not, therefore, an important source of capital formation for Hong Kong's industrialisation.

A total of six industrial companies including two textile firms and one steel mill were active in the market in the 1950s. Nanyang Cotton Mills was the first cotton spinner to go public in 1954. The five rubber companies in Table 5.4 were all incorporated in Malaysia or Indonesia. Ten other companies were Shanghai concerns that did not trade after 1949. Between 1957 and 1965, 19 new companies were listed and one insurance company was removed from the list after it was taken over by a British firm. Of the new entrants, two bus companies went public in order to comply with the requirements for a government franchise, and several others (Taikoo Docks, Jardine Matheson and Local Property and Printing) needed to set a value on their shares for estate purposes.[92] This suggests that the primary motivation for listing was not always to raise extra capital. By the mid-1960s, there was active trading in only 25 companies, with periodic trading in a further 10 shares.

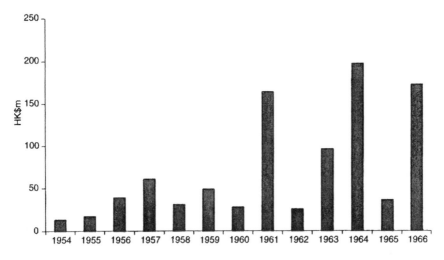

Figure 5.4 New capital raised on the Hong Kong Stock Exchange.

Table 5.4 Hong Kong Stock Exchange; number of quoted companies by industry groups

Industry group	April 1947	1957	1967	1972
Banking and finance	4	2	2	9
Insurance	4	3	2	4
Investment	0	3	4	9
Shipping	5	4	5	17
Other commercial	0	1	4	16
Docks and wharves	4	4	6	8
Hotels and property	6	5	8	76
Utilities	9	9	12	11
Textiles	2	2	4	17
Other industrial	4	4	5	13
Stores	9	5	8	10
Miscellaneous	10	4	4	15
Rubber	0	5	5	5
Total	57	51	69	210

Data include all quoted companies, domestic and foreign.

Source: Wong (1975) p. 90 and *Far Eastern Economic Review* various issues.

The Hong Kong market was small in relation to other Asian stock markets. From 1960 to 1965, new issues amounted to 1.23 per cent of GDP in Hong Kong, compared with 3.3 per cent in Malaysia and 2.5 per cent in Thailand.[93] Table 5.5 shows some comparative figures for other regional stock exchanges. The Hong Kong market was by no means as large as that of Malaysia and Singapore or Manila, but nor was it the smallest market among the developing countries in Asia.

Table 5.5 Asian stock markets 1967

	Date of establishment	Number of members (1967)	Quoted companies
Taiwan	1962	23	46
Korea	1956	40	50
Malaysia and Singapore	1960	91	256
Bangkok	1962	50	26
Manila	1927	180	135
Djakarta	1952	46	120
Hong Kong	1947	60	71

Taiwan: figures for 1971.
Manila: figures for 1970.
Malaysia: quoted companies for 1970.

Source: U. Tun Wai and H.H. Patrick, 'Stock and Bond Issues and Capital Markets in Less Developed Countries', *IMF Staff Papers*, 20, 1973, pp. 253–317.

The closest rival to Hong Kong was the Malayan Stock Exchange, which opened for public trading in 1960.[94] Direct telephone links between the trading rooms in Kuala Lumpur and Singapore were introduced in 1962.[95] By 1964, a total of 269 firms were listed, although this included 150 foreign firms, mainly tin and rubber companies. Foreign companies encouraged local shareholdings in Malaysia for political reasons, given the nationalistic nature of the governments. Still, this leaves 119 local companies, which was almost double the number of firms in the Hong Kong exchange. Both the Thai and the Malaysian stock markets were swelled by the large amount of government securities, which were mainly bought by central banks. The Hong Kong government, in contrast, offered only one public issue, the 1948 loan that raised HK$50 million. The government periodically considered issuing securities but their conservative spending policy reduced the need for public debt. It will be seen in Chapter 6 that the Financial Secretary showed some desire to issue treasury bills in the early 1960s but this was mainly to provide a liquid asset for the banking system.

The narrowness of the Hong Kong market in this period can be attributed partly to the predominance of small family firms that depended primarily on internal funds or 'friendly' loans.[96] Also, the banking system was well developed and competitive, especially after the expansion of bank services from 1959. Raising capital on the stock market, in contrast, required substantial dividend pay-outs to sustain share prices at a level which would attract further investment.[97] This made it an unattractive alternative to bank loans. Furthermore, there were repeated reports that, unlike the other financial markets in Hong Kong, the Stock Exchange did suffer from the political uncertainty that erupted in Asia periodically. On the other hand, shares were also a target for flight capital from overseas Chinese investors.

A further factor restricting activity on the Stock Exchange was the fact that high unit prices for many shares tended to exclude all but the wealthy from participating in the stock market.[98] In the 1940s, many investors were Chinese owners or managers of local banks, and brokers visited them daily to encourage business and deliver certificates.[99] In the 1950s, a few individuals such as George Marden (of Wheelock Marden and Co. Ltd) and Noel Croucher (a prosperous broker) had a large influence on the market.[100] Shares traded well above their par value, and were usually transferable only in collective 'boards' of minimum numbers.[101] For example, Hongkong Bank shares with a par value of HK$125 traded at over HK$1,450 in March 1961. At this point the shares were split, to provide five cheaper shares for each existing one, in order to increase the popularity of the stock. By the end of the year, however, the price of these split shares had increased from HK$209 to HK$450.[102] One interesting innovation was the establishment of a unit trust in August 1960 by Singapore interests. This company sold one million units of HK$1 each, allowing a broader range of local Hong Kong investors to participate in the stock market.[103] In contrast, the Jardine Matheson share issue in 1961, that led to the peak of the stock market boom of that year, was offered at HK$16 per share, with a minimum purchase of 300 shares. Even so, it was 56 times oversubscribed and the Hongkong Bank noted that 'Here in London considerable interest had been shown.'[104]

Figure 5.5 shows the monthly turnover on the Hong Kong Stock Exchange from 1949 to 1966. After a brief flurry of activity in 1946–8 due to capital flight from China, the market was less active through the political uncertainty surrounding the establishment of the Communist regime in China. Total turnover for the year 1948 was HK$159 million compared with HK$88.2 million in 1949. There was a mild increase in activity during the Korean War boom, followed by some growth through to the mid-1950s. This can be attributed to the inflow of capital from trouble spots in Southeast Asia, and remittances from Singapore and Malaysia at a time when the property market was dull and international trade was constrained by the UN embargo.[105] In August 1955, local British banks increased their interest rates in order to contain speculation on the stock market, which depressed activity. At the same time, the property market became a more attractive target for speculation, which

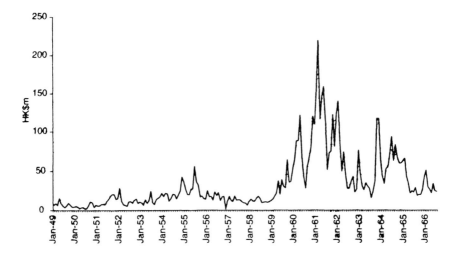

Figure 5.5 Hong Kong Stock Exchange monthly turnover 1949–60.

attracted funds out of shares. Due to the relatively small number of new issues, the narrow range of investors in the 1950s, and the small number of public companies, the value of transactions on the market was fairly low until the boom of 1959–61.

The first post-war stock market 'boom' began in October 1959, partly due to inflows of capital from overseas. Investors were attracted to the shares of companies with large landholdings once property values had soared in the wake of local and overseas speculation.[106] At the same time, the revival of international trade benefited the share value of banks and shipping companies.[107] The Hongkong Bank raised its overdraft rates for stockbrokers and borrowers against shares by 1 per cent in an effort to try to stem the speculation[108] but the turnover on the market recovered by February 1960. The monthly value of stock turnover reached its highest level in March 1961 at HK$219 million. Share prices on average doubled between 1959 and mid-1961, bringing dividend yields to levels similar to those of the US and Britain.[109] By June 1961, the cost of a seat on the Stock Exchange had quadrupled to HK$200,000.[110]

The boom was fuelled by the flotation of several new companies. Among the traditional Hong Kong companies, the Taikoo Dockyard and Engineering Company (HK) was listed in 1959, followed by Jardine Matheson in June 1961. Two bus companies, Kowloon Motor Bus (1961) and China Motor Bus (1962), were required to offer 25 per cent of their equity to the public as a condition of their franchise. Speculators hoped to reap quick returns from these well-established companies, and the demand for these new issues was extraordinarily high. The Kowloon Motor Bus issue was 5.5 times oversubscribed, China Motor Bus by 36 times, and Jardine Matheson by 56 times.[111]

As the market rose, the potential for high returns on the stock market drew deposits from local banks, catching out those without adequate reserves. Applications for the new issues had to be accompanied by signed cheques for the required amount, all of which were cleared through the banks although only a fraction would result in a final purchase since the issues were so oversubscribed. The result was a considerable drain on the liquidity of local banks. In correspondence with the Malayan manager of the Hongkong Bank during the Malayan stock market boom in 1962, Oliphant noted that

> We learnt our lesson here when Kowloon Motor Bus shares were issued and completely disorganised the market. We bought sterling from or gave temporary overdrafts to banks which were short and the interbank lending rate was held at 6.5%. The banks and Stock Exchange discussed the problem and subsequent issues have been handled on the ballot principle. Only cheques successful in the ballot are cleared, the remainder being returned direct to drawer.[112]

In June 1961, the boom was halted by the failure of a local bank and subsequent credit restrictions imposed to halt speculation. In his 1961 statement to shareholders, the Chairman of the Hongkong Bank noted that speculation during the year had 'put a severe strain on the resources of some of the smaller banks, one of which [Liu Chiong Hing] we had to assist to a very considerable extent'.[113] The market was dealt a further blow when an official enquiry into the provision of electricity in

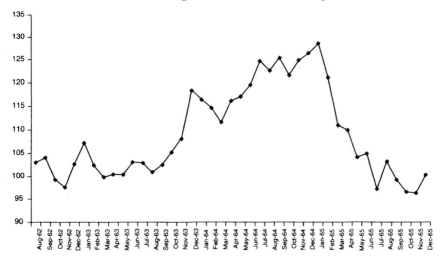

Figure 5.6 Far Eastern Economic Review share index (3 August 1962 = 100).

the colony recommended a merger of the two electric power companies. This delivered a 'paralysing blow to confidence' to the market and knocked hundreds of millions of dollars off the value of utility shares within one week.[114] By August, market turnover had fallen to one quarter of the March value. Continued uncertainty about whether the government would adopt the enquiry's proposals, and periodic international political disturbances (including the Cuban missile crisis) depressed the market from mid-1962 until 1964. Once the utilities policy was resolved, the market recovered, but it was then struck by the banking crisis of 1965.

The *Far Eastern Economic Review* constructed an index of share prices based on the market value of shares of 20 prominent listed companies in August 1962.[115] Figure 5.6 shows the movements in this index from 1962 to 1965. This shows the stagnation in prices during 1963 until the market recovered from the uncertainty described above. The banking crisis of April/May 1965 resulted in a fall in prices to below the levels reached three years earlier.

As the account of the movements in the stock market detailed in the previous section suggests, the Hong Kong Stock Exchange was often affected by substantial inflows of overseas capital that found at least a temporary home in Hong Kong shares. Francis Zimmern, one of the original members of the post-war Exchange, recalled that 'the 1950s was when Hongkong became a real international market, a lot due to the people who came from China'.[116] Shanghai brokers joined the exchange in the post-war period, thus facilitating the flow of capital from the mainland in the late 1940s. In the 1950s, remittances from elsewhere in Southeast Asia were frequently cited as affecting the market.[117] In 1960, the Chairman of the Hongkong Bank reflected that

There has been a phenomenal rise in local share and land values and it is doubtful whether the peak has yet been reached. Much of the demand seems to have come from overseas funds seeking investment and although this has not had the same effect on bank deposits, these have risen by over 30%. So much of the post-war development in HK has been due to an influx of capital from abroad that one would not wish to discourage the flow but I think there is little doubt that the present volume is unhealthy.[118]

Indeed, the preponderance of foreign capital in the stock market inhibited the efforts of the Hong Kong banks to curb speculation. In November 1959, interest rates were raised on advances related to share purchases but the Hongkong Bank noted that 'This had only a limited effect as new money from abroad continued to seek investment'.[119]

In summary, the turnover in the Hong Kong Stock Exchange was small compared to developed and developing countries. For 1959–64, the amount of new capital raised as a proportion of GDP amounted to about half that of the UK, USA and European stock markets. The market was vulnerable to a variety of influences including fluctuations in property values, local and international interest rates, and flows of capital in and out of the colony.

Hong Kong investment in foreign stock markets

Foreign stockbrokers channelling funds overseas had long operated in Hong Kong. At the end of 1946, the American firm of Swan, Culbertson and Fritz relocated from Shanghai to Hong Kong, re-naming themselves Sing Foong Co. Ltd, owned by three American stockbrokers and one Swiss stockbroker.[120] From the mid-1950s, brokers for foreign stock markets began to establish offices in Hong Kong in greater numbers, as they sought to take advantage of accumulated liquid funds in the colony. The funds raised by these companies were primarily destined for Wall Street, but there were also representatives from Japan, Australia, Canada, Switzerland and the UK, who offered services to clients from elsewhere in Southeast and East Asia as well as Hong Kong. Specialised brokers in Hong Kong represented firms who were members of the Tokyo or New York Stock Exchanges and dealt directly with customers in Hong Kong via direct lines to their principals. By 1965, for example, Merrill Lynch had their Southeast Asian regional office located in Hong Kong to promote investment in Wall Street, and Nomura Securities' affiliate Hong Kong International Securities Co. Ltd promoted investment in Tokyo. Trading on the London or Australian exchanges took place through members of the Hong Kong Stock Exchange who had agents abroad. In tacit recognition that these brokers performed offshore transactions, these firms were not subject to stamp duty. The export of capital in this way was made possible by the existence of the free exchange market, which allowed settlements for Hong Kong and overseas residents alike.

By 1964, there were five investment companies listed on the Hong Kong Stock Exchange engaged in the purchase of shares in Hong Kong and overseas for their investors.[121] In addition, Hong Kong residents could invest in a variety of mutual funds offered by American and European firms. In February 1964, Jardine Matheson introduced Capital Growth Plans Ltd, which was designed to capture the Hong Kong market through lower monthly subscriptions than the foreign mutual funds. Monthly payments into the Hongkong Bank were invested by the company in units of International Growth Funds located in Lichtenstein, with principal investments in Europe and America. The board of IGF included two residents of Hong Kong.[122]

There are no firm statistics on the value of such investments, but David Williams estimated that investment from and through Hong Kong in new issues of foreign currency securities in European financial centres amounted to US$65 million in the 10 years from 1957 to 1966 (slightly more than the total for France, and one third the level of the UK).[123] This estimate was based on press reports and bankers' opinions and included purchases of European and Japanese US dollar bonds and US corporate debentures. A different source estimated that by October 1966 HK$57 million (US$10 million) was leaving Hong Kong for Wall Street each month.[124] Williams noted in 1967 that 'Hong Kong banks are traditionally large-scale dealers in US securities' and that 'Hong Kong plays a role in the Far East similar to that of Switzerland in Western Europe, though on a smaller scale, as a channel for acquiring effectively tax-free investments'.[125]

Conclusion

The Hong Kong Stock Exchange was small relative to other regional markets, and the turnover was low relative to the 1970s. However, the boom in 1959–61 raised the profile of the Hong Kong market both domestically and internationally. Nevertheless, there is no doubt that it was not an important source of investment capital for industry, but it did attract considerable funds from overseas. It seems that Hong Kong's role as a clearing house for Asian investment in overseas stock markets was perhaps more important than the activity of the domestic Stock Exchange.

Insurance market

Almost nothing has been written about the insurance sector in Hong Kong, although it was undoubtedly an important service for traders and investors in the colony. The commerical activities of the port of Hong Kong attracted insurance companies from the mid-nineteenth century. Hong Kong then benefited from the removal of Shanghai as a commercial centre from the late 1930s.[126] By 1946, three smaller independent British companies that had operated in Shanghai had re-registered in Hong Kong, and the rest of the foreign companies quickly left Shanghai after 1949.[127] In 1947, 64 separate insurance companies operated in Hong Kong, of which 27 had direct representatives and the other 37 operated through local agents.[128] They included American, British, Australian, Canadian, Indian, Swiss and Norwegian companies. Four large Hong Kong firms were public companies, including Canton Insurance, Union Insurance Society of Canton, China Underwriters, and the Hong Kong Fire Insurance Co. Canton Insurance and Union Insurance were the largest publicly quoted Hong Kong companies. Union Insurance was the local giant with assets totalling £14.4 million in 1953, compared with Canton Insurance at £2.5 million. Both were established in Canton in the mid-1830s. In 1953, Canton Insurance bought a 100 per cent interest in Hong Kong Fire Insurance Co. and changed its name to Lombard Insurance in order to emphasise the international nature of its activities. Both Lombard and Union Insurance operated their global business from head offices in Hong Kong, with offices and subsidiaries in the UK, North America, Australia, New Zealand, and elsewhere in Southeast Asia. In October 1960, Guardian Assurance of London announced its bid to take over Union Insurance, and this was completed by the end of the year.

In addition to these public companies, there was a wide variety of foreign and private insurance companies with offices or agencies in Hong Kong. In 1951, for example, Jardine Matheson advertised its services as General Manager of Hong Kong Fire, General Agent for Canton Insurance and Agent for a further 10 major international assurance and insurance companies, most of them British.[129] Through the 1950s, there was a steady influx of foreign companies from Europe, America, India and Southeast Asia. By 1960, firms from 14 countries operated in Hong Kong.[130]

In 1960, the Hong Kong Fire Insurance Association had about 120 members and the Accident Insurance Association had about 90 members. Many firms, of course, offered both services, and in total there were about 150 insurance firms operating in Hong Kong either directly or through agencies.[131] No statistics for insurance activity are available, but in 1960 the *Far Eastern Economic Review* estimated that the established firms had probably tripled their business in the 10 years since 1950, and that total activity had perhaps increased five- or six-fold due to an influx of new firms into the Hong Kong market.[132] Fire and Accident business certainly grew for the listed Hong Kong companies. Premium income on fire insurance collected by Union Insurance grew from £2.7 million in 1952 to £3.6 million in 1959, while premiums on accident and general cover increased from £1.5 million to £5.5 million in the same period.[133]

A wide range of marine insurance was available at rates linked to underwriting costs in London. In 1959, there were 109 company members of the Hong Kong Marine Insurance Association, of which 48 were British and 17 American, as well as representatives of 12 other countries. In addition, there were local representatives of Lloyd's brokers in Hong Kong. Coverage was available for shipbuilding as well as hulls and cargo in transit. In 1960, the Hong Kong General Chamber of Commerce noted that the insurance of locally manufactured exports was an increasing share of marine insurance, although this posed some problems because of the low quality of some local packing, and the relatively undeveloped target ports, both factors that tended to increase the potential for claims.[134]

The marine insurance sector suffered from increased competition and falling cargo rates in the period 1951–60. Hong Kong insurers carried the extra burden of claims due to the embargo and other calamities in the early 1950s. Lombard Insurance suffered particularly in this decade, and had a disastrous year in 1951, when the claims ratio reached 105 per cent. The Marine department of the firm made consistent losses until 1959, generating discontent among shareholders. They felt misled by the company's directors about the seriousness of the 1951 results, which were hidden until losses of HK$905,000 were finally revealed in 1954.[135] In the following years, the firm was the only active listed company on the Hong Kong Stock Exchange which failed to maintain its pre-war dividend. Nevertheless, the board rejected calls to close the Marine department on the grounds that it was closely integrated with the Fire and Accident business, and that a profit could be shown on this account in the future. Their decision was vindicated when a profit began to appear in 1959. Union Insurance also struggled through the 1950s, but managed to sustain its net profits at about half a million pounds per year. In the mid-1950s their claim ratio on marine insurance was 75–77 per cent, close to twice the ratio for other types of cover.

Life insurance business increased sharply in the 1950s and was relatively more profitable than the traditional types of cover. Companies offering life cover were often distinct from other types of insurers, and they had no separate insurance association. Many offered endowment policies of 20–25 years as a personal investment product in addition to traditional life cover. The returns offered by foreign firms usually averaged 3.5–5.5 per cent while the local firms claimed returns of 6–8 per cent. In 1964, it was estimated that insurance companies received approximately HK$100 million p.a. in premiums for life insurance from 5 per cent of the population. Local insurance firms invested 70–80 per cent of their funds locally and sold mainly to wealthy Hong Kong Chinese residents.[136] The value of new business increased about 10 per cent per year in the decade after 1948 and then accelerated thereafter.[137] The record for individual firms was even more dramatic. American International Assurance (a China company before the war) reported the value of ordinary life assurance in force at £14 million in 1954, rising to £27 million in 1957. Premium income increased by almost 20 per cent p.a. in this period. In 1956, Wing On Life reported a 70 per cent increase in the amount of life business and in first year premiums received compared to 1955. The following year the company opened branches in Singapore and Malaya. By 1965, the life insurance business was dominated by 11 firms, of which only two were incorporated in Hong Kong.[138] Canadian, American firms, and an Indian firm (Life Insurance Corporation of India) dominated the market.

This sketch of the trend of insurance services available in Hong Kong confirms that the colony was the major regional base for many foreign insurance companies, as well as the source of domestic firms that operated globally. The Marine sector languished in the 1950s, but this was offset by the growth of accident and life insurance. The services available in Hong Kong no doubt facilitated the merchant activities of the colony, as well as providing investment opportunities for Hong Kong's increasingly wealthy population.

Conclusion

This chapter has examined three services offered by Hong Kong in the post-war period. Like the banking and exchange markets, they were founded in Hong Kong's pre-war position as a commercial entrepot. Banks and insurance companies dominated the stock market, and the major boom of this period was associated with the flotation of part of one of Hong Kong's traditional merchant 'Hongs'. The gold market, too, grew out of the traditional role of Hong Kong as a regional entrepot, but it gained a global importance in the post-war period because of restrictions on the gold trade imposed by the IMF. Hong Kong's insurance companies also date from the emergence of Hong Kong as a commercial entrepot. They subsequently realigned their activities to cover domestic exports, and increasingly to offer personal insurance for local residents. Lombard and Union Insurance also extended their operations abroad in this period. The influx of companies into Hong Kong, however, shows that the colony was still a regional centre for insurance despite the decline of the entrepot trade in the 1950s.

The Stock Exchange and the gold market have also offered insights into the role of regulation in Hong Kong. In the case of the gold market, supervision was devised and enforced not by the state, but by the Gold and Silver Exchange. The volume of transactions outside the exchange suggests, however, that these rules did not impinge greatly on the freedom of the market. The controls on external trade in gold were not rigorously enforced, but they did have the effect of raising transactions costs. The circuitous route of gold traffic enriched the Macao Treasury and those involved in smuggling. Like the free exchange market, the gold market prompted conflict between the British and colonial authorities. Unlike the case of the free exchange market, however, the British position prevailed and the market was curtailed. This was because the Governor of Hong Kong could not convince the British authorities that the gold market was as integral a part of the economy of Hong Kong as the free exchange market. The controls actually introduced, however, aimed not to eliminate the market altogether, but merely to draw Hong Kong nominally into line with British policy. The resilience in the local demand for gold, and for the speculative opportunities offered in the forward market ensured that it continued to operate. In the end, the underground market was tolerated, and indeed involved British companies. The difference in the British attitude perhaps lay in the benefits that the exchange market offered to UK residents, while the gold market largely served regional Asian markets.

The light hand of the Hong Kong authorities extended to the other services discussed in this chapter. The Hong Kong Stock Exchange was self-regulated, and benefited from lower transactions costs than existed in European or American markets. This left it vulnerable to the speculative fervour of 1960–1, which was followed by an even greater boom and crash in the early 1970s. The Hongkong Bank periodically tried to reign in the market by constraining domestic credit, but they were frustrated by the ability of the market to attract foreign capital. It was not until the speculative crisis of the early 1980s that greater prudential supervision was introduced. The insurance sector was also largely left to its own devices, organised into professional associations. In addition, Hong Kong company law required fire and marine insurance companies to deposit HK$100,000 with the government or on fixed deposit with a bank. Life assurance companies were required to put up HK$200,000 as security. An exception was made for companies that complied with the UK Assurance Companies Act in the UK. This prevented the kind of fraud that affected the Malayan market, where in 1961 over 50 bogus insurance companies swindled savings from the public, prompting greater state regulation. In summary, all three services provide examples of markets growing out of the pre-war economy of Hong Kong, favoured by the laissez-faire approach of the Hong Kong government, and related directly or indirectly to the free exchange market.

Appendix

Table A Smuggled gold exports from Hong Kong 1950–9 (last week of each quarter)

	Total	Singapore	Bangkok	Indonesia	Vietnam	India	Japan/Korea	Rangoon	Taiwan	Penang
1950	4,000	1,000	2,000		1,000					
	6,000	1,500	4,500							
	6,700	1,200	3,000			2,500				
	8,200	4,000	4,200							
1951	31,500	9,200	13,800			8,500				
	6,100	3,600	2,500							
	18,600	9,600	9,000							
	29,500	17,500	12,000							
1952	18,750	9,250	9,500							
	12,800	7,300	5,500							
	18,500	8,000	7,500		1,000		2,000			
	19,400	3,200		9,500			4,200		2,500	
1953	4,500	3,500				1,000				
	3,500	3,500								6,000
	13,500	4,000			3,500					
	11,500	6,000				2,000		3,500		
1954	11,000	5,500			800	3,000	700	1,000		
	7,500	4,000			1,500			2,000		
	7,500	3,500				1,000		2,000		
	7,800	4,000		1,000	2,000		1,300			
1955	8,500	5,500	2,000		1,000					
	9,000	3,500		4,500				1,000		
	18,000	6,000	3,500	6,500				2,000		
	9,500	4,500		3,000	1,000	1,000				
1956	19,500	9,000	3,500	4,000			1,500			1,500
	14,500	8,000		5,000			500			1,000
	12,500	5,500		5,000		1,000	1,000			
	9,500	4,500		3,500		1,000	500			
1957	8,500	6,000					1,000	1,500		
	8,000	4,500		2,000				1,500		
	10,500	6,500		3,000				1,000		
	8,000	5,000		2,000						
1958	11,000	6,500		3,000				1,500		
	6,500	5,000						1,500		
	10,500	7,500	2,000					1,000		
	8,000	3,500	2,000		2,500					
1959	5,500	3,500		1,000		1,000				

Source: *Far Eastern Economic Review.*

6   Hong Kong as an international financial centre

Previous chapters have traced the history of various financial and commercial services offered in Hong Kong. The present chapter seeks to place these activities in a global context by establishing Hong Kong's position as an international financial centre in the post-war period. This includes some quantification of international banking activity and an exploration of the sources of competitive advantage for Hong Kong. A final section links the international financial services sector with the finance of domestic industry.

The growth and competitiveness of international financial centres (IFCs) has attracted considerable interest from economists and historians.[1] These centres usually engage in capital export and/or import, they intermediate between foreign and domestic customers, and/or act as an entrepot for foreign customers.[2] Financial centres historically have tended to grow out of the commercial activity of the host country. The City of London, for example, evolved into an IFC as a result of Britain's domination of international trade in the nineteenth century. New York also benefited as the geographical focus of American commercial activity, but gained greater prominence after 1945 when the USA emerged as the major world creditor. In the case of London, Michie has argued that the commercial business lasted longer as an important element of the city's financial activity than it is usually portrayed.[3] In 1965, the identifiable net overseas earnings of commodity traders, export houses and the Baltic Exchange (which organised shipping) amounted to almost 25 per cent of the city's total net overseas earnings, and it is only from the 1960s that London's position as a port for physical trade began steeply to decline.[4] However, as a result of two World Wars, the great depression, government regulation, and the rise of MNCs, the international trade business gave way to specialisation in providing short-term credit and long-term investment facilities.

In judging Hong Kong's entitlement to the label IFC, we must consider Hong Kong in its historical context. This includes the strong commercial heritage of banking and financial services, which continued to dominate the activity in the colony throughout the 1950s and 1960s, and positioned Hong Kong as the regional centre for the exchange of information and expertise on Asian and Western market opportunities. We must also bear in mind that the period under review preceded the explosion of international financial activity that began in the 1970s. Certainly, the 1960s saw considerable innovation with the emergence of the Eurodollar and

Eurobond markets and certificates of deposit, but these instruments were relatively undeveloped and were focused on the major centres of London, New York and Continental Europe until the 1970s. It will not be argued that Hong Kong was an innovative IFC during this period; indeed the Financial Secretary of Hong Kong was content to allow Singapore to create the Asia dollar market in 1969. Hong Kong offered a narrow range of services, focused on commercial finance and banking, but this in part reflected the relatively unsophisticated nature of financial services at the time.

Hong Kong clearly fits into the model of an IFC emerging from an international commercial entrepot. The gradual agglomeration of services, expertise and infrastructure that generated the development of London and New York can also be seen in Hong Kong's transition from primarily commercial activity to a greater mix of commercial and financial activity. The collection of banking, merchant/marketing and insurance expertise that had serviced the entrepot of Hong Kong in the nineteenth and early twentieth centuries combined with the regulatory environment to make Hong Kong a major target for new entrants in the decades that followed. As Meyer notes, the continuity in Hong Kong's century-long history as 'the great Asian regional financial centre' allowed it to transcend competitors such as Tokyo or Singapore after the opening of China at the end of the 1970s.[5] In the first two decades after the Second World War, the colony began this transition from an exclusively commercial to an increasingly financial focus. With the stagnation of the re-export trade in the 1950s, many banks shifted toward new activities such as financing domestic industry, collecting capital from abroad, and channelling the increasing wealth in Hong Kong overseas. The dramatic rise in deposits and the influx of foreign banks into Hong Kong in the early 1960s shows that the colony was developing into a collection centre in these years. The flurry of activity in the first stock market and property booms in the early 1960s also attracted investors and speculators, establishing Hong Kong as a centre where fortunes unrelated to international trade could be won (and lost). The increasing sophistication of foreign security transactions and the growth of the exchange markets in these years further contributed to the emergence of Hong Kong as an IFC. The diversification of financial activity in the 1950s and 1960s set Hong Kong on its path to becoming a major IFC in the 1980s.

Some economists tend to define an IFC so narrowly as to exclude all but New York and London in the twentieth century. These centres can accurately be described as 'World Financial Centres' since their activities are literally global and they serve as a clearing centre for other financial centres. At the other end of the spectrum are Regional Financial Centres that service only the locale in which they operate, providing a more limited range of services to residents in neighbouring economies, but not intermediating between the region and the rest of the world. In the 1960s, Hong Kong obviously fell between these two classifications since it was a regional focus for international finance but also operated on a global stage, linking Asia with the UK, USA and Europe. In Dufey and Giddy's typology, Hong Kong was an Entrepot Financial Centre rather than an Offshore Banking Centre since it did not distinguish between foreign and domestic actors.[6]

Certain of Hong Kong's institutions, such as the stock market, and the remittance business had a clearly regional rather than global scope, although remittances came from North America as well as Asia, and there is evidence of British investment in the stock market. The gold market was part of the global trade in premium gold, channelling it from the suppliers in South Africa and Australia (through London after 1954) to end users in India/Pakistan and Southeast Asia, financed through bank accounts in the USA. After 1952, the gold price closely followed the world price, showing the integration of Hong Kong with the global gold market. The foreign exchange market and the banking sector serviced the regional needs of traders, remitters to family, and flight capital. However, both these institutions had a much wider geographical reach, moving Hong Kong from a strictly regional base to a centre with global significance. As in many aspects of Hong Kong's history, it is difficult to fit the colony's complex position with a convenient label.

It might be argued that Hong Kong should be more accurately described as an international banking centre than an international financial centre since the domestic securities and money market were relatively undeveloped. It was not until 1971 that the first merchant bank opened in Hong Kong, partly to circumvent the moratorium on new banking licences and partly due to the increased business associated with the stock market boom of the early 1970s. The lack of specific merchant banks in the 1960s does not imply, however, that these services were unavailable in Hong Kong. Banks in Hong Kong performed a wide range of financial services including foreign exchange, international brokerage and portfolio management, underwriting, discounting commercial bills, and providing business advice. Furthermore, as described in previous chapters, the banks were supplemented by a broad range of separate insurance houses, foreign exchange brokers, and gold merchants. The merchant houses, like Jardine Matheson and Wheelock Marden and Co., were agents for a large selection of international financial and insurance companies. This agency system allowed regional customers to have easy access to a wide range of financial service providers.

In summary, previous chapters have shown that Hong Kong had most of the attributes that are used to define an IFC. It hosted markets for various forms of capital, foreign exchange and insurance. In addition to these usual categories of financial activity, the gold market was active both in current and future transactions. Most of the financial sector's activities were related to commercial activity, but these markets also offered services not directly related to Hong Kong's visible trade. There is no doubt that Hong Kong was not a leading IFC in the first few decades after the war. It will be shown below that its global importance reached much greater heights in the 1980s. Nevertheless, previous chapters have argued that Hong Kong played more than merely a regional role in international finance in these years because of its unique position in the international monetary system. This in turn meant that in some respects Hong Kong was a more prominent IFC in the 1950s and 1960s, a period of relatively tight exchange controls, than it was in the 1970s when capital controls were gradually relaxed.

Reed has calculated the relative importance of different categories of international financial transactions to rank financial centres from 1900 to 1980.[7] This exercise reveals some interesting insights into the historical development of Hong Kong. Based on the number of private banks, the number of international banks head-quartered in the centre, and the number of foreign banks with offices in the centre, Hong Kong is identified as one of a group of second rank IFCs (behind London and New York) in the period from 1900 to 1930. This reflected the dominant role of Hong Kong in the finance of China's international trade in this period. After 1945, Hong Kong dropped out of the second rank of identified centres. By 1960, however, the position of Hong Kong was restored and it ranked alongside Paris, Tokyo, Hamburg and San Francisco (again, behind London and New York). At this time, the determining factors for the ranking were the range of countries with links to the centre. In Hong Kong's case, this was almost completely due to the international offices of the Hongkong Bank. Reed further refined his analysis for the period 1955–80 by adding variables that captured the amount of foreign financial assets and liabilities, and the spread of representative offices of banks as well as branches. Hong Kong again fell into a secondary group of centres ranked below London, New York and Paris in 1955–75, but dropped down into the third rank of IFCs by 1975, confirming the suggestion that Hong Kong was relatively more important in the 1960s than in the 1970s.

Reed's work was an attempt to move beyond rankings based merely on the number of international banks located in a centre, by including the range and international scope of these links as well as the size of assets and liabilities. The weakness of his analysis is that it excludes the correspondent relations of banks, which were a more prevalent link between financial centres but will not be captured by measuring international financial assets and liabilities. Another difficulty is the identification of international compared to domestic assets. In the case of Hong Kong, the liberal regulatory environment biases the colony's ranking since it was impossible to distinguish many foreign assets and liabilities in the Hong Kong banking system.

Bearing in mind these limitations, the most common way in which IFCs are judged is by the international activities of banks, measured by the number of branches of domestic banks located in other IFCs and the number of local branches of foreign banks. Chapter 3 showed that a few locally incorporated banks engaged in international branching activity – this is especially true for the Hongkong Bank. Most Hong Kong banks did not branch abroad because many were quite small in terms of capital. Their growth was constrained in part by the great value placed on maintaining family control. As noted above, the size and global reach of the Hongkong Bank in the 1950s and 1960s does much to push Hong Kong up the 'ranking' of IFCs, where the geographical reach of locally incorporated banks is an important factor. Table 6.1 shows the overseas branches of banks incorporated in Hong Kong in 1961, plus those of the Mercantile Bank since it was owned by the Hongkong Bank at this time (although incorporated in London).

From this it is clear that Asia was the main focus of branching and that the Hongkong Bank was overwhelmingly dominant. By 1965 the Hongkong Bank was on its way to becoming one of the world's largest banks, helped by the acquisition of the British Bank of the Middle East and the Mercantile Bank at the end of the 1950s. The Hongkong Bank also had a fully owned subsidiary in California and a

Table 6.1 Overseas banking offices of Hong Kong banks in 1961

	HSBC	Mercantile Bank	Bank of East Asia	Bank of Canton	Chiyu Bank	Total
Borneo/						
Sarawak	11					11
Burma	1	1				2
Cambodia	1					1
Ceylon	1	5				6
China	1		1		1	3
France	1					1
Germany	1					1
India	8	8				16
Indonesia	1					1
Japan	4	3				7
Malaya	21	13				34
Mauritius		1				1
Pakistan		3				3
Philippines	2					2
Singapore	3	2	1	1		7
Thailand	2	2		1		5
UK	1	2				3
USA	3					3
Vietnam	1		1			1
Total	63	40	3	2	1	109

separate hire purchase institution (Wayfoong Finance) in Hong Kong. Other Hong Kong banks exploited correspondent relationships with foreign banks to serve their customers' needs more cheaply than branches. It might be argued that the global presence of a single bank is too thin a basis on which to categorise Hong Kong as an IFC. Certainly, only the Hongkong Bank had direct links to New York, London and Paris through offices in these leading financial centres. But the importance of the Hongkong Bank, and the influence that it had on other institutions in Hong Kong, should not be discounted. The bank's international reputation facilitated the transactions of other banks in Hong Kong as well as attracting global business to the colony. Its vast resources also allowed it to operate as a lender of last resort along with the Chartered Bank, giving the financial system greater stability.

Another possible objection is that the Hongkong Bank is sometimes characterised as a British bank because it was part of the Exchange Banks' Association and was established and run by British expatriates, suggesting that its Hong Kong provenance was merely nominal.[8] The management of the bank, however, was firmly located in Hong Kong. The London Office was the home of an advisory committee, and liaised with British governments and the Bank of England, but policy decisions were made in Hong Kong based on local conditions and information.[9]

A second defining feature of an IFC is that it attracts the offices of foreign banks. Chapter 3 detailed the influx of foreign banks into Hong Kong after the war. By 1965, there were 29 such banks from 16 countries, including banks from all the major financial centres such as London, New York, Paris, Brussels, Amsterdam and Tokyo. These banks were attracted by the freedom from exchange control, relative political stability, and the volume of business available as the economies of East Asia grew. They served customers in their home country wanting to trade or invest in Hong Kong, on short term and long term, as well as channelling funds from Hong Kong residents to their home markets. The foreign banks also acted as correspondents for numerous other banks around the world.

Table 6.2 shows the number of foreign banks with branch offices in a variety of international financial centres. The figures for 1955–70 include all banks, while the data in the last two columns for 1970 and 1980 are taken from Choi *et al.*, and include only the world's top 300 banks. A comparison of the 1970 column with that of 1970A shows that Hong Kong ranked highly in earlier period partly due to the inclusion of smaller regional banks, although small banks are also well represented in the other centres. By the mid-1960s, Hong Kong surpassed Paris to rise from fourth to third place in terms of number of foreign bank offices. Table 6.2 also shows the number of full branches of foreign banks (in parentheses), and on this measure Hong Kong ranked second in the world in the 1960s. Branches were an expensive way of capturing business compared to agencies or correspondent relationships, so this commitment suggests that a significant volume of business was available in Hong Kong. This pattern may also reflect the difficulties of monitoring financial activity in Asia from the head office. It is notable in this regard that the large foreign banks tended to branch more densely in Asia than in Europe. Also, Hong Kong's open regulatory environment allowed foreign banks to open branches, while in other centres, such as New York, foreigners were restricted to agencies or representative offices that were not allowed to engage in a full range of banking activities.

Table 6.2 Number of offices of foreign banks (number of branches in parentheses)

	1955	1960	1965	1970	1970A	1980A
London	69 (54)	80 (59)	97 (72)	148 (118)	58	72
New York	40 (10)	61 (16)	67 (22)	96 (29)	54	80
Paris	24 (16)	32 (18)	41 (17)	52 (18)	35	52
Hong Kong	19 (19)	27 (26)	43 (36)	43 (27)	24	58
Tokyo	12 (11)	16 (15)	25 (15)	51 (17)	45	76
Singapore	15 (15)	17 (16)	15 (15)	28 (21)	13	54
Frankfurt/ Hamburg	17 (9)	23 (9)	34 (13)	55 (24)	39	59
Beirut	12 (12)	17 (13)	29 (13)	42 (17)		
Brussels	9 (8)	13 (10)	14 (9)	22 (12)	20	29
Amsterdam	6 (6)	4 (3)	8 (6)	10 (7)	23	21
Zurich	7 (4)	9 (3)	17 (6)	22 (9)	13	24

Sources: 1955–70 includes all banks, from Bankers Almanac and Yearbook; 1970A and 1980A include only the world's largest 300 banks, from S.-R. Choi, A.E. Tschoegl and C.-M. Yu, 'Banks and the World's Major Financial Centers, 1970–1980', *Weltwirtschaftliches Archiv*, CXXII, 1986, pp. 48–64.

By 1970 Hong Kong's relative position had declined from 1965, overtaken by Tokyo, Frankfurt/Hamburg and Paris, as well as the dual centres of Los Angeles/San Francisco and Milan/Rome, which are not shown in the table. Choi *et al.* rank Hong Kong as eighth in the world in 1970, rising to fifth by 1980. This was partly due to the relaxation of regulations that allowed more foreign banks to enter centres such as New York. Economic integration in Europe and the explosion of the Euromarkets enhanced the attractions of Paris and Frankfurt/Hamburg. The phenomenal growth of Japan, the dramatic increase in the size of its banks, and eventually deregulation of Japanese financial markets were responsible for Tokyo's rising prominence. While it would be wrong to suggest that Hong Kong was a more 'important' IFC than, say, New York or Zurich in 1965, this impressionistic analysis does confirm more quantitative data to follow. The general pattern is that Hong Kong's relative position as an IFC was probably greater before 1965 than it was in the following decade.

To give an indication of the extent of links between financial centres in 1965, and to correct somewhat for the bias toward small banks in Table 6.2, Table 6.3 shows the location of banks that had branch offices in at least four of the IFCs listed. The rapid multinational expansion of US banks in the early 1960s is reflected in the fact that five out of the 11 banks were American.[10] As noted above, the substantial overlap of branches of banks in Tokyo, Singapore and Hong Kong shows that multinational banks tended to locate branches more intensively in Asia, but not as readily in Europe, other than in London. Although Hong Kong hosted a number of relatively small banks from China and Southeast Asia, Table 6.3 shows that most of the major international banks were also represented in the colony.

The absolute value of international financial transactions in Hong Kong is impossible to calculate with any accuracy because the lack of foreign exchange control prohibited the collection of relevant statistics. Some quantitative assessments, however, can be made. It was reported in Chapter 3 that about half of the bank deposits belonged to overseas residents, mainly in the rest of Southeast Asia. This estimate yields a volume of about HK$3.5 billion (US$614 million) of overseas deposits by individuals rather than banks in 1965. Hong Kong banks' liabilities to foreign banks (rather than individuals) reported in this year amounted to a further US$146 million, giving a total value of overseas bank liabilities of some US$760 million.[11] This shows that inter-bank asset and liability figures do not give a reliable picture of the international operations of Hong Kong banks since non-bank deposits were much larger than those of other banks.

A comparative analysis is possible for deposit banks' foreign assets based on data collected by the IMF. Table 6.4 shows the foreign assets of deposit banks in various international financial centres from 1961 to 1990. This is an incomplete quantification of international financial services since it is restricted to a single stock measure of international banking, but it does give an indication of the course of Hong Kong's relative position.[12]

The table shows that from 1962 to 1966 the nominal value of Hong Kong banks' foreign assets increased by 133 per cent while total foreign assets held in the world's banks only doubled. During the 1970s, Hong Kong benefited from the dramatic

Table 6.3 Leading bank branches: location 1965

	London	New York	Paris	Hong Kong	Tokyo	Singapore	Frankfurt/ Hamburg	Beirut	Brussels	Amsterdam	Zurich
American Express	X	X	X	X	X		X		X	X	X
Bank of America	X	X		X	X	X				X	
Chase Manhattan	X	X	X	X	X	X	X	X			
Citibank	X	X	X	X	X	X	X	X	X	X	
Continental Illinois	X	X			X						X
HSBC	X	X	X	X	X	X	X				
Chartered Bank	X	X		X	X	X	X				
Bank of India	X			X	X	X					
Algemene Bank		X		X		X		X			
Sanwa	X	X		X	X						
Bank of Tokyo	X	X	X	X	X	X	X				

Source: *Bankers' Almanac and Yearbook*, 1965/6.

Table 6.4 Deposit bank foreign assets (US$b)

	1961	1962	1963	1964	1965	1966	1967	1968	1969	1970	1975	1980	1985	1990
UK	3.6	4.5	5.4	6.7	7.7	10.3	12.2	19.0	31.0	37.4	124.7	352.4	590.1	1069.0
USA	6.3	6.7	8.0	10.2	10.6	10.7	11.0	10.6	11.6	12.8	57.3	195.4	446.8	654.3
Japan	1.1	1.4	1.6	2.2	2.6	2.7	3.1	3.8	5.2	6.6	13.0	45.2	194.6	950.5
France				1.5	1.9	2.7	3.2	5.1	7.4	10.1	41.2	144.1	184.4	458.7
Switzerland	1.9	2.2	2.7	3.3	3.7	4.1	5.2	7.7	10.1	14.1	47.9	139.9	205.5	444.1
Luxemburg	0.2	0.2	0.3	0.3	0.4	0.5	0.7	1.1	1.9	3.7	30.2	104.8	131.5	355.1
Bahamas						0.0	0.0	0.1	5.1	7.2	55.1	125.5	143.1	164.0
Lebanon				0.5	0.6	0.5	0.4	0.5	0.5	0.6	2.1	3.7	2.5	2.8
Bahrein						0.0	0.0	0.1	0.1	0.6	2.1	31.4	50.7	59.3
Singapore							0.2	0.2	0.3	0.5	10.6	44.6	120.5	346.7
Hong Kong	0.3	0.3	0.4	0.3	0.5	0.7	0.6	0.9	1.0	1.2	9.0	38.0	101.2	463.8
Total	21.5	25.8	30.7	39.6	44.8	51.9	59.5	79.6	118.5	149.0	555.9	1,712.8	2,979.0	6,783.6

Source: IMF, International Financial Statistics.

Table 6.5 Deposit banks' foreign assets; share of all reporting countries

	1961	1962	1963	1964	1965	1966	1967	1968	1969	1970	1975	1980	1985	1990
United Kingdom	16.7	17.4	17.5	16.8	17.1	19.9	20.5	23.9	26.2	25.1	22.4	20.6	19.8	15.8
United States	29.5	26.1	25.9	25.7	23.6	20.6	18.4	13.3	9.8	8.6	10.3	11.4	15.0	9.6
Japan	5.0	5.3	5.1	5.5	5.7	5.1	5.2	4.8	4.4	4.4	2.3	2.6	6.5	14.0
France						5.2	5.3	6.4	6.2	6.8	7.4	8.4	6.2	6.8
Switzerland	8.7	8.4	8.9	8.3	8.3	7.9	8.8	9.6	8.5	9.5	8.6	8.2	6.9	6.5
Luxembourg	0.7	0.9	0.9	0.7	0.9	1.0	1.2	1.4	1.6	2.5	5.4	6.1	4.4	5.2
Bahamas						0.1	0.1	0.1	4.3	4.8	9.9	7.3	4.8	2.4
Lebanon				1.2	1.3	1.0	0.7	0.6	0.4	0.4	0.4	0.2	0.1	0.0
Bahrein						0.1	0.1	0.1	0.0	0.4	0.4	1.8	1.7	0.9
Singapore							0.3	0.3	0.3	0.4	1.9	2.6	4.0	5.1
Hong Kong	1.2	1.2	1.2	0.8	1.1	1.3	1.0	1.1	0.8	0.8	1.6	2.2	3.4	6.8
Total	100.0	100.0	100.0	100.0	100.0	100.0	100.0	100.0	100.0	100.0	100.0	100.0	100.0	100.0

Source: IMF, International Financial Statistics.

worldwide increase in international banking and captured a greater share of activity. Hong Kong banks' foreign assets rose more than 30-fold between 1970 and 1980 while total foreign assets increased by a factor of 19. The rise in the global value of foreign assets was accompanied by greater geographical diversification of international banking. Table 6.5 shows that in 1961, the UK and USA accounted for 46 per cent of the total but this fell to 41 per cent by 1965 and then to 34 per cent by 1970. This decline was mainly due to the retreat of the USA. The decline in US share was mainly taken up by European centres and by the new offshore tax havens in the Bahamas and Cayman Islands.

In the 1960s, Hong Kong's share of total international bank assets fluctuated. The share dropped in 1967 in response to the political instability in the colony associated with the Cultural Revolution in China, and then did not recover the 1966 level until the 1970s. In terms of global ranking, Hong Kong was thirteenth in the 1960s, rising only two places by 1980. The big surge in foreign assets came in the late 1980s; in 1985 the colony ranked eleventh, but by 1990 it was in fourth place behind the UK, USA and Japan. It must be remembered, however, that Hong Kong is being compared with entire countries, often including more than one financial centre.

There is no doubt that Hong Kong was a small centre by these measures in the 1960s, but this was a decade when London and New York dominated international financial activity. A more meaningful comparison might be made with comparable regional financial centres. Figure 6.1 compares the position of Hong Kong with that of Singapore and Lebanon. This shows quite clearly that Hong Kong's foreign assets were much greater than those of Singapore in the 1960s, and slightly less than Lebanon (mainly centred in Beirut and Tripoli). In the 1970s Singapore's activity

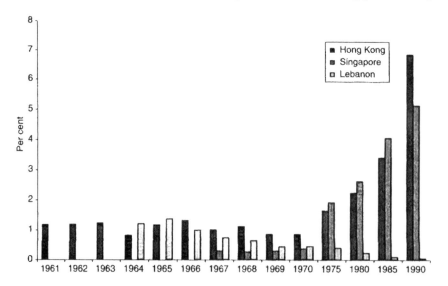

Figure 6.1 Deposit banks' foreign assets as a share of world banks' foreign assets.

increased sharply as a result of the Asia dollar market, although Hong Kong regained the lead by 1990. Figure 6.1 supports the evidence in Table 6.5, suggesting that Hong Kong's international banking activities declined relatively after 1965 and only recovered after the opening of China to the rest of the world in the 1980s. Although there is no quantitative data for the period before 1961, the subsequent figures tend to support the general argument that Hong Kong's importance as an international financial centre was greater for the period 1955–65 than for the following decade.

Writing in the mid-1970s, Johnson defined Hong Kong as a regional rather than an international financial centre. In his analysis, the main distinction lay in the size of the domestic economy; 'the major international financial centre developed from a strong base as a national financial centre in a large and powerful country with the natural market support of citizens of that country'.[13] Regional financial centres, by contrast, attracted foreign financial institutions mainly due to locational and legal advantages rather than on the basis of their national financial power. The distinction is not, however, as clear-cut as Johnson assumes. London was the premier IFC in the post-war period but this had little to do with the strength of the British economy (which was in relative decline from the end of the nineteenth century). London also benefited from locational advantages since Britain and Europe were the main target for the MNCs that attracted American banks to the city. Conversely, Hong Kong (like London and New York but unlike Panama) had a well-developed financial and communications infrastructure based on international trade, which became the foundation for the emergence of international financial activity.

Jao agrees with Johnson that Hong Kong was a regional financial centre, adding that 'Hong Kong's transformation from a sub-regional into a regional financial centre did not begin until about 1969' due to the double setback of the banking crisis of 1965 and the witholding tax on foreign currency deposits.[14] However, Jao does not address the period before 1969 beyond observing that 'most foreign banks then [before 1969] were content to confine their activities to financing Hong Kong's external trade and domestic economic activities'.[15] Certainly the volume and range of international financial services offered by institutions in Hong Kong increased in the 1970s as the colony participated in the globalisation that took hold of financial markets in this decade. It would have been strange indeed if Hong Kong did not experience a dramatic rise in the number of foreign banks, and a proliferation of services due to financial innovation in this decade. These were global phenomena of which Hong Kong was a major participant. On a relative basis, however, Hong Kong's position was well established before 1965, although with a smaller absolute number of banking offices and offering a narrower range of services as befitted the character of the international financial system of the time. Hong Kong's institutions were not innovators in the early 1960s, but they did provide traditional financial services to a wide range of customers in Asia. Moreover, the security switches and cheap sterling transactions offered by the free market elevated Hong Kong's role beyond the merely regional.

Jones suggests that both Hong Kong and Singapore moved from being 'sub-regional' centres in 1945–65 (focused on bilateral trade of the host with other countries) to 'regional' centres in the period 1965–75 (supplying financial services to an entire region).[16] The basis for Jones' categorisation is not clear since he does not address the quantitative evidence on international banking activity before 1965. Certainly on the basis of the evidence presented here, there is no case for grouping Singapore and Hong Kong together until the 1970s. It is true that much of Hong Kong's international financial activity in the first two decades after the war was ultimately related in some way to the colony's trade. For example, Chapter 4 showed that the security transactions that attracted so many European and American customers to the free market were indirectly related to Hong Kong's trade deficit with China. The importance of Hong Kong as a trade entrepot and increasingly as a manufacturing exporter was clearly at the heart of Hong Kong's international financial services. But the services of the banks were also used by customers in Asia and beyond for transactions unrelated to Hong Kong's visible trade. These included the financing of third party trade, and the international investment activities in the colony described in previous chapters. The importance of Hong Kong's markets to the functioning of the international monetary system, and in particular for the UK balance of payments as described in Chapters 2 and 4, lifts Hong Kong from a 'sub-regional' centre to one with much wider implications.

Jones puts greater emphasis on Beirut than Hong Kong, asserting that 'in the two decades after the Second World War, the most significant event was the advent of Beirut as a regional financial centre'.[17] The analysis presented here shows that the international bank presence in Beirut was much smaller than in Hong Kong, and that the recorded volume of foreign assets and liabilities was only slightly higher. The similarities between Hong Kong and Beirut are rarely mentioned, but they shared features that help to define the necessary characteristics for a regional IFC in this period. Both were small, open economies where the local currency had a reputation for stability. Banking practice in both territories was very liberal, which accompanied a laissez-faire attitude to economic policy as a whole. In 1956, Lebanon introduced a law enforcing banking secrecy, which increased Beirut's attractions for some customers. No such legislation existed in Hong Kong, but the identity of account holders was often difficult to ascertain and until 1965 there was no requirement to publish or report detailed balance sheets. In both centres there was no discrimination between local and foreign banks. Both were havens for regional flight capital, as well as the target for substantial remittances from overseas residents.

The main difference identified by Jones is the large percentage of total bank deposits that were denominated in foreign currency in Beirut (about 35 per cent in 1964).[18] Equivalent figures for Hong Kong as a whole are not available, but in 1965 foreign currency deposits (almost all US dollars) amounted to 8 per cent of deposits at the Hang Seng Bank, and 12 per cent at the Chartered Bank.[19] As Jones himself notes elsewhere, the large proportion of dollar deposits in Beirut was mainly due to factors unrelated to international commerce including the large American presence in Lebanon due to the American University, and the UN Relief and Works Agency which dealt with Palestinian refugees.[20] Hong Kong had a much more entrenched English-speaking international financial infrastructure developed over a century of entrepot trade with China. The communications infrastructure was also more developed in Hong Kong. But the most important difference between the two centres was that while Beirut operated a free exchange market it was outside the sterling area, and so did not enjoy the substantial benefits that Hong Kong did from this connection. It has been argued in Chapter 4 that Hong Kong was a unique gateway between tight exchange controls in the sterling area and the relative convertibility of the dollar area. This position, straddling the sterling and dollar worlds, was a vital factor in Hong Kong's prominence.

Today, Hong Kong faces a variety of competitors in the provision of financial services in East Asia. These include Tokyo, Singapore and, possibly, Shanghai in the future. In the 1950s and 1960s, in contrast, the local competition was left much further behind. The next two sections will review the institutional and political basis for Hong Kong's competitive position in the provision of international financial services.

Competitive advantage of Hong Kong

The determinants of the competitive advantage of an IFC include geographical position (and time-zone), regulatory environment and tax system, legal, economic and technological environment, and political stability.[21] Again, these various factors cannot be divorced from their historical context. Time-zone, for example, has become most important in the last 50 years once technological improvements in communication allowed 24-hour global trading. Political stability and regulatory freedom will be more important in periods when there is widespread political instability and tight regulatory control elsewhere. It will be seen that both of these aspects were important sources of competitive advantage for Hong Kong in the period under review. Given these features, a skilled labour force and a highly developed communications infrastructure will enhance the attractions of the centre. These last two features will usually be the product of historical development from a primarily commercial toward a more mixed commercial and financial centre, although some states such as the Bahamas and Cayman Islands have deliberately created offshore banking centres from scratch.

Hong Kong had several advantages over potential competitors for the provision of international financial services in the post-war period. Most obviously, Hong Kong had a century of tradition as a major trading entrepot because of its harbour facilities and its geopolitical location off the coast of China. In the post-war period, these physical advantages of Hong Kong were enhanced by the construction of the Kai Tak Airport and the improvement of telegraph links to major financial centres in Europe and America. Hong Kong's post-war financial development built on the sophisticated banking and financial services sector which had been developed to service Hong Kong's trading activities in the century before the war. This left an agglomeration of banks and financial talent in the post-war period that was unrivalled in East Asia. Importantly, the widespread use of English in the colony, and the domination of this language in the banking and financial community was an added advantage, shared in Asia only by Singapore. Like London, Hong Kong benefited from the 'remnants of history' left by a strong trading tradition, but combined with this were features specific to the post-war period.

A major advantage Hong Kong had over its neighbours was relative political stability. This might seem to be overstated since it was noted in Chapter 3 that the possibility of instability in the future encouraged some banks to view their presence in Hong Kong rather gingerly, at least until 1960. Although the future of Hong Kong was uncertain in the long term, the immediate commitment of the UK and the USA to the continued Western control of Hong Kong was assured after the spread of the cold war to East Asia. The threat that China would invade Hong Kong in this period was not a serious one, and the prospect that Hong Kong would return to China in 30–40 years was well outweighed by the benefits the colony offered in the present. This was reinforced by the economic and political turmoil that plagued most other territories in East Asia during this period.[22]

The major disruption, of course, was the Korean War of 1950–2, which generated considerable flight capital to Hong Kong. Indochina and Indonesia gained independence after the Second World War, but the ensuing regimes were inherently unstable and hostile to the international community. The Communist takeover of North Vietnam in 1954 further destabilised the region. In Indonesia, Sukarno nationalised Dutch, British and American property, expelled Dutch nationals, and aligned the country with the USSR in the 1960s. Chinese businesses and bankers, who dominated the financial sector in many Southeast Asian economies, found themselves increasingly under threat from nationalist regimes seeking to restore economic power to indigenous populations. Corruption was another factor that raised transactions costs in many countries, especially in the Philippines and Thailand. These threats encouraged wealthy Chinese to collect assets in the relatively secure haven of Hong Kong where the economic dominance of the Chinese population was never threatened.[23]

A brief survey of banking developments elsewhere in Asia serves to show the hostility of other centres toward international finance. In South Vietnam, the government established a central bank in 1954 and began actively to promote local banks to replace the existing Chinese banks. Foreign banks were allowed to continue to operate, but foreigners were prohibited from engaging in certain types of trade.[24] The nationalist regime in Malaysia was also a threat to foreign banks, which found their activities gently squeezed in favour of local banks.[25] After the Central Bank of Malaya was established in 1959, foreign banks were restricted to opening branches only in large urban areas and they were 'encouraged' to invest more of their funds locally.[26] The Chinese populations in Malaya and Singapore were unsettled by the 'malayanisation' of the economic and political system, which also generated capital flows to Hong Kong. In Thailand, from 1955 the entry of foreign banks was generally limited to one per country, and from 1962 they were banned from opening branches. Foreign banks in Thailand were subject to reserve requirements of 10 per cent, half of which needed to be maintained in deposits with the Bank of Thailand and half in notes and coin.[27]

The story in each of these countries is the promotion of indigenous interests over international interests (sometimes through nationalisation), and curbs on the activities of the immigrant Chinese population.[28] Usually these policies were enforced by the establishment of a strongly interventionist central bank, and generally on the principle that international finance was incompatible with domestic economic development. Together, these trends increased the attractiveness of Hong Kong as a centre for regional activities and as a haven for capital as well as capitalists. The role of flight capital will be discussed in greater detail later in this chapter.

The third main source of Hong Kong's competitive advantage was its regulatory environment. The colonial administration was particularly loathe to intervene in the financial activities of its residents. The phrase 'laissez-faire' is not an accurate description of Hong Kong government policy as a whole given the considerable public housing, education, and health programmes initiated in this period. In terms of the financial system, however, the government (with few exceptions) was vehemently non-interventionist. In Chapter 3 it was shown that the banks themselves pressed for greater regulation, but the Financial Secretary resisted on doctrinaire grounds. In 1970, Cowperthwaite explained the unwillingness even to collect basic balance of payments or GDP statistics since

> We have no practical use for them and are not prepared to go to the expense and trouble (not least on the part of businessmen and bankers who have more important things to do) of collecting them.[29]

Trade statistics were collected because they were of interest to business in planning their future policy, and such data were necessary in the negotiations against the exclusion of Hong Kong products in Europe and the USA.

Among the few exceptions to this non-interventionism were the 15 per cent withholding tax on interest, and the restriction on new bank licences imposed after the second banking crisis of 1965 and maintained until 1978. The tax on interest was low relative to other countries, and only became really significant in 1968 after Singapore abolished its 40 per cent tax on interest earned by non-residents. Unlike Singapore, the proceeds of financial transactions on behalf of third parties through Hong Kong were not subject to tax since they were not considered earned in Hong Kong. This remained a considerable advantage.

The restriction on bank licences after 1965 had an important impact on the structure of banking. Unable to open new branches, representative offices of foreign banks were increasingly attracted to Hong Kong, mainly to collect foreign currency deposits and to provide links to other financial markets. By 1970, there were representative offices of 22 foreign banks from seven countries operating in Hong Kong. The restrictions on new banking licences also prompted the expansion of deposit-taking companies and other non-banking financial institutions from the early 1970s.[30] Another result of the moratorium on bank licences was the merger/takeover of medium-sized Hong Kong banks by foreign banks. Chapter 3 showed that this process began in 1962 when Dai-Ichi Kangyo Bank took a 33 per cent interest in Chekiang First Bank. Over the next 10 years, American, British, Canadian and Japanese banks acquired equity in another nine Hong Kong banks.

In contrast to its competitors, the regulatory environment in Hong Kong in the period before 1965 was remarkably liberal. The attractions this offered to foreign banks and overseas customers both in Asia and in the rest of the world have been discussed in Chapters 3–5. The freedom to repatriate earnings and investments, the unwillingness and inability to discriminate between Hong Kong and foreign customers, and the open field for competition all contributed considerably to the attractions of Hong Kong relative to other financial centres. In the case of exchange transactions, it was shown in Chapter 4 that Hong Kong had many advantages even over London for particular types of business. The liberal regulatory environment for commerce was combined with a stable political and legal order, which the Hong Kong manager of the Indian United Commercial Bank described as 'unrivalled in the Far East'.[31]

One potential weakness of the non-interventionist policy was the failure to provide liquid government paper or discount services for the banking system. There was no secondary market in government bills in Hong Kong, and the financial system remained dominated by banks. The government ran a persistent revenue surplus despite maintaining a low rate of tax (partly due to lucrative land sales) and so had no need to issue significant debt. There were two government bonds outstanding in the 1960s but neither was actively traded.[32]

The Financial Secretary considered issuing Treasury Bills in mid-1960 in response to a temporary cash shortage and a predicted fiscal deficit, but ultimately this proved unnecessary. The main disadvantage of local borrowing was the high interest rates that would have to be offered to exceed domestic commercial rates. In March 1961, Cowperthwaite announced in his budget speech an intention to start issuing Treasury Bills, but the subsequent surplus eliminated the fiscal need for the cash.[33] A year later Cowperthwaite was again tempted to proceed with an issue in order to provide liquid local assets and rediscount facilities for the banking system, but as he put it to Tomkins, there was

> No point in borrowing at say 6% to earn say 4% on deposit with the Hong Kong and Shanghai Banking Corporation, however convenient a Treasury Bill issue may be as a liquid asset for the other banks.[34]

The government did not need access to short-term capital because it had adequate reserves on deposit with the Hongkong Bank and the Chartered Bank. The state's borrowing requirements tended to be for the medium term to fund land reclamation and other public works, but again this was a costly way to raise funds. Instead of issuing debt, in 1962 the government applied to reduce the currency reserve backing from 128 to 110 per cent, so releasing £9.5 million for development purposes.[35] In the same year an official lottery was proposed to raise funds for welfare and social spending.[36]

This leads to the fourth factor that strengthened Hong Kong's position vis-à-vis potential competitors. As noted above, Hong Kong straddled the sterling area and the non-sterling area which meant that banks had intimate connections with the City of London, as well as operating on a large scale in US dollars. This was the primary source of Hong Kong's global rather than regional advantage in international finance. Hong Kong became a centre for investors wishing to exchange sterling and dollar securities, or to convert currencies outside the national exchange controls that prevailed during this period. Hong Kong had long been an important regional exchange centre due to the entrepot business of the port. After the Second World War, however, these free markets became of global importance in the context of strict exchange controls operating in most countries. After the advent of official current account convertibility of sterling and most European currencies in December 1958, the attractions of Hong Kong increased because most countries continued their restrictions on capital account transactions.

In summary, Hong Kong had all three of the classic attributes of an IFC: political stability, infrastructure and regulatory freedom. In addition to these defining attributes, Hong Kong benefited from its commercial past, which left a legacy of financial expertise and institutions. These advantages were heightened by political instability and poor communications in the Asian region, and by tight regulation over the world as a whole. It might be argued therefore that the first two factors were responsible for establishing Hong Kong as a regional financial centre, and the last gave Hong Kong its global importance.

Hong Kong vs Singapore 1945–65

Singapore bears the closest comparison to Hong Kong; indeed, one study asserts that 'for an observer in the late 1940s, Hong Kong and Singapore looked almost identical'.[37] Both were city-states, populated overwhelmingly by Chinese, which flourished under colonial administration in the pre-war period, and found their main activity as trading and financial entrepots. Singapore was the hub of Malayan tin and rubber exports, as well as providing services to merchants elsewhere in Southeast Asia, particularly Indonesia. As in Hong Kong, this entrepot business fostered local banks and attracted international banks to the colony.

In 1945, Hong Kong and Singapore hosted a similar number of foreign banks (nine in Hong Kong compared with 10 in Singapore). By 1965, however, only a further nine had opened offices in Singapore (including the Bank of Canton and the Bank of East Asia who arrived from Hong Kong in the early 1950s)[38] compared with 20 who had arrived in Hong Kong (excluding the China state banks). By 1965, there were 11 banks with head offices in Singapore, bringing the total number of banks in Singapore to 30. The dominant local Singapore bank was the Overseas Chinese Banking Corporation (OCBC) which, along with several other Singapore banks, had branches in Hong Kong.[39] This compares with 86 locally licensed banks in Hong Kong.

From these bald statistics, the contrast between the banking systems in Singapore and Hong Kong is stark. In 1961 Singapore had about 50 banking offices, and although by 1963 this had risen to 90, it still compared poorly to 231 offices in Hong Kong.[40] All of Singapore's banks kept accounts in London, and sterling accounted for 85 per cent of the foreign exchange turnover in 1963,[41] whereas in Hong Kong the US dollar exchange was more significant. In common with Hong Kong, there was a dramatic increase in bank deposits with the total for Malaya and Singapore quadrupling between 1947 and 1965 from M$634 million to M$2,477 million.[42]

Despite its smaller absolute size, the financial services sector was slightly more important to the economy of Singapore than was the case in Hong Kong. In 1960, financial and business services accounted for about 10 per cent of Hong Kong's GDP compared with 11.3 per cent for Singapore.[43] However, rather than reflecting greater productivity in Singapore, the large presence of financial services in the colony's GDP was due to relatively slow economic diversification. By 1960, only 12 per cent of Singapore's GDP came from manufacturing compared to 25 per cent in Hong Kong in 1961.[44] Singapore's communications were also inferior to those of Hong Kong. In 1965, the volume of telegraph messages was 22 per cent greater in Hong Kong than in Singapore. Singapore only began sending Telex in 1963 and had only 6 per cent of the volume of Telex traffic in Hong Kong by 1965.[45]

Singapore differed markedly from Hong Kong in that it did not host a free market in foreign exchange, nor an open gold market. The relative freedom of markets in Hong Kong and also in Bangkok provoked some resentment in Singapore. In 1949, P.J. Keogh of the Bank of England toured Southeast Asia and reported that

> In Singapore, we heard about the trade problems of a great entrepot centre endeavouring to maintain a strict exchange control and at the same time compete with neighbouring centres where irregular Sterling–Dollar cross rates prevailed.[46]

Seven years later, at the Malayan Constitutional Conference in London, the Malayan delegation challenged the British government to explain why Hong Kong was allowed to operate a free market while Singapore was not.[47] They were given the standard rationalisation that Hong Kong needed a free market to trade with China (where a broken cross rate operated), but this argument had lost its persuasiveness given the Chinese trade embargo and the nationalisation of China's external commerce. More convincingly, the Malayans were reminded that Singapore's main US dollar-earning entrepot business was with Indonesia, who required the surrender of all US dollars at the official exchange rate.[48] Although Bangkok operated a free market, the Bank of England argued that as Thailand was only a small part of Singapore's entrepot trade this did not justify opening such a market in Singapore.

To some extent, these explanations smack of ex post rationalisation since Singapore might have captured more Southeast Asian entrepot business had a free market been allowed to operate. Privately the Bank of England pointed out that Malaya needed economic and financial stability in order to develop, and this would be hindered by a fluctuating exchange rate, which would also involve an exchange barrier with sterling. Furthermore, the Malayan currency was statutorily linked to sterling, while the Hong Kong currency link was based on an understanding between the Hong Kong Exchange Fund and the banks. Hong Kong was not obliged by law to back its currency with sterling or to redeem it in sterling.[49]

The Malayans reportedly were satisfied with the British explanation, but David Marshall, Chief Minister in Singapore, was not entirely convinced. Immediately after the meeting of the Finance Committee of the Conference, H.S. Lee, the Federation of Malaya's Minister of Transport, approached the Chartered Bank (of which he was a customer) for a fuller explanation that he could use to dissuade Marshall from advocating a free market for Singapore.[50] The issue was deemed important enough for Morford, manager of Chartered Bank, to be coached in his reply by the Bank of England. Morford asked for advice and was instructed to argue that a free market would discourage the confidence and stability necessary to attract overseas capital and domestic investment for development, especially given the political instability presented by self-government. He was told that

> It may be argued that Hong Kong's free market has attracted capital. But this is speculative capital probably invested in speculative ventures and ready at the least provocation to get into gold or dollars. Malaya needs to encourage the more permanent long term investor.[51]

With respect to Singapore as separate from Malaya, a free market posed some threat to the entrepot trade since

> A free market would involve, at best, some form of exchange control between Singapore and sterling which would hamper the financing of trade and, at worst (with an independent Singapore managing its own currency) accentuate or lead to breaking the fixed exchange rate between Singapore and sterling which is the basis of the stability and acceptability of Singapore's currency. Indonesians, Malayans and others who, in addition to using the entrepot, also hold substantial balances there would become nervous about fluctuating rates in Singapore and might develop their own direct channels (a thought never far from their minds).[52]

It was thus argued that instability in the exchanges would encourage traders to operate through London rather than Singapore. Also, fluctuating rates would complicate the status of Singapore and the Federation of Malaya with the IBRD and the IMF. Also, such a policy was not consistent with Singapore's expressed desire to stay in the sterling area. The entrepot business of Singapore did not require competitive exchange rates with other centres, and a fluctuating rate was an unnecessary risk in an unstable political environment. More fundamentally, the Hong Kong free market was a point of some controversy in the IMF and in British exchange control, but was tolerated mainly because it could not be eliminated. There was no enthusiasm in London deliberately to introduce such complications in another sterling area territory.

As described above, the political problems of Hong Kong's neighbours and potential competitors were a major source of the colony's competitive advantage. In the case of Singapore, the political uncertainty that accompanied the drawn-out independence process of the Federation of Malaya from the mid-1950s (culminating in independence in 1957) was accompanied by monetary uncertainty because a common currency circulated in Singapore and Malaya. From 1955, negotiations began to create a central bank in Malaya which was considered an essential symbol of political independence from Britain. The problem for Singapore was whether to join such a central bank and under what terms. The looming political independence of

Malaya, combined with increasing political hostility between Singapore and Kuala Lumpur, made business, banks and the government in Singapore nervous about the future of the free port on which the colony's prosperity depended.[53] The development plans of the Federation of Malaya promised to require protectionist trade and payments policies. Protection was inconsistent with the free port of Singapore and complicated the possible union of the two economies, although the gulf in economic ideology and goals between the two regimes was not fully recognised in Singapore. After Singapore's independence in 1959, Goh Keng Swee, Finance Minister of Singapore, announced his government's aspirations for a common market with Malaya, but was rebuffed by Tan Siew Sin of the Malayan government who retorted that 'one cannot have a free port and a common market at the same time. You must choose one or the other.'[54]

At the beginning of 1956, G.M. Watson (sent from the Bank of England to advise on the new central bank for Malaya) canvassed the views of banks in Singapore. At this time, there was no formal clearing system in Singapore and it was hoped by many that a central bank would rectify this situation.[55] All banks stressed that confidence in the currency was an overriding consideration, which ruled out a substantial reduction from the 100 per cent currency reserve cover. Most banks also supported the introduction of a banking ordinance so long as it did not unfairly discriminate between banks. The merchants approached by Watson stressed the need to maintain a currency union between Singapore and Malaya after Malayan independence in order to allow the smooth administration of their business.[56] A group of rubber brokers based in Singapore believed that the rubber market would stay in Singapore after the separation of Malaya due to the continued supply of Indonesian rubber, but they warned that 'any lessening in confidence or possibility of fluctuating exchange rates might tend to reverse this trend and decrease the importance of the Singapore market compared with London'.[57]

When banks and business were consulted again in August 1957, they were unanimously agreed that the free port of Singapore must not be sacrificed to Malayan control, and that a currency union with an exchange rate fixed by law to sterling was a minimum requirement for the continuation of Singapore's prosperity.[58] In the end, this is close to the eventual agreement: the Central Bank of Malaya began operations in January 1959, did not issue currency, and its powers did not extend to Singapore. Instead, a pan-Malaysian currency board continued to operate, signalling the commitment of Singapore to its Malayan hinterland. The focus of Singapore's economic interests continued to be northward, sealed by the union of Malaya and Singapore in Malaysia in 1962. During 1963, the possibility of high liquidity ratios being imposed on Singapore's banks to conform to the new practice in Malaysia was a major preoccupation of G.P. Stubbs, the Singapore manager of the Hongkong Bank, although ultimately these ratios were not enforced.[59] The racial and political conflict between the two former colonies further postponed Singapore's hopes of generating enough international confidence to become a more sophisticated international financial centre.

In summary, the mid-1950s to mid-1960s was a decade of political and economic turmoil as the future of Singapore's relationship with its hinterland was carved out. This financial uncertainty, the Singapore government's association with Communists, the Indonesian 'confrontation' which disrupted trade with Singapore from 1963[60] all made Singapore a less attractive haven for international finance than Hong Kong in these years. In contrast, although the eventual return of Hong Kong to China was inevitable, there was rarely an imminent threat of a collapse of the existing system until 1967. The 'long term' in Hong Kong only extended for about five years in investment terms, but most international financial activity is on considerably shorter basis than this, and so was little affected by the looming return of Hong Kong to China in 1997. Hong Kong held the advantage over regional competitors through lower tax rates and freedom from nationalist threats or exchange controls.

The international financial centre and industrialisation

A basic motivation for this book is that the post-war historiography of Hong Kong's economy has been dominated almost exclusively by the story of the post-1950 industrialisation. As a consequence, the international financial activities of the colony have been relatively neglected. In some respects, of course, these two aspects of the economy overlap in ways that have not yet been explored. This section examines the nature of the relationship between international finance and domestic manufacturing.

The links between financial development and industrial development or economic growth has been the subject of lively debate in the economics literature since the late 1960s, although the exact nature of that relationship has yet to be determined.[61] More recently, the 1997 financial crisis in Asia has led to criticism of financial systems in developing countries. In particular, the enthusiasm for financial liberalisation during the boom years of the 1980s may have outstripped the institutional development necessary to allow such liberalisation to be sustainable.[62] Hong Kong was an exceptional case in that its very liberal financial system had a long history and it maintained its currency peg throughout the crisis, although suffering a historically severe recession. This resilience had much to do with the depth and breadth of the financial market with greater emphasis on equity (reducing the exposure of the domestic banking system) and relatively transparent markets, which aided confidence. The maturity of Hong Kong's financial markets due to their long history was a fundamental factor in the survival of Hong Kong's financial system.[63]

The specific relationship between international financial activity and economic growth has not been as well researched as the potential of the financial system to mobilise domestic savings for domestic investment. An exception is Tuan and Ng, who suggest that there have been positive externalities from the international financial sector for Hong Kong's export industries since the 1980s.[64] The contribution of the financial sector to GDP should, therefore, extend beyond the traditional direct measures (such as employment and specific contribution to GDP) to include the indirect impact on growth. Some aspects of this have been discussed in Chapter 1. The direct impact on employment, tax revenue, and economic policy sovereignty were seen to have been relatively minor. The indirect impact on construction, property prices, and tourism are difficult to separate from the impact of industrialisation.

The impact of the IFC on the provision of capital to domestic industry is the subject of the present section.

Jao has asserted that the increased competition in the banking sector provided by the influx of foreign banks gave entrepreneurs greater access to credit on favourable terms, both in the 1960s and since.[65] Reed has also emphasised that IFCs in developing countries will give borrowers in these countries direct access to more efficient capital.[66] On the other hand, Tuan and Ng suggest that the IFC may have crowded out local manufacturers because they cannot compete with the returns on the short-term global investment of loanable funds.[67] Gorostiaga has argued that the establishment of an IFC in Panama perpetuated the country's neo-colonial status and ultimately sapped its domestic development by diverting scarce resources in terms of labour and capital.[68]

The first and most obvious link between international finance and the domestic economy in Hong Kong is that the cotton textile sector which pioneered the transformation into an exporting economy was initially financed from foreign capital which fled mainland China in the period 1945–50. The same attributes which made Hong Kong an attractive international financial centre, also contributed to its success as the host for the Shanghai industrialists who relocated in Hong Kong in this period. Thus, relative political stability, the communications infrastructure, and freedom from regulation were important sources of advantage for manufacturing as well as finance.

The IFC also attracted capital from elsewhere in Asia. Szczepanik estimated that the inflow of capital and invisible earnings amounted to 40 per cent of national income in the period 1947–55. Approximately two thirds of investment in industry was financed from abroad in these years.[69] Through the following decade (1954–63), a further HK$4.4 billion flowed into Hong Kong from overseas Chinese in China and elsewhere in Southeast Asia, about half of which came from Malaysia, Singapore and Indonesia.[70] Table 6.6 shows Japanese estimates of inflows of capital from overseas Chinese into Hong Kong. Wu estimated that most of this inflow remained in Hong Kong; two thirds invested in real estate, 18 per cent in industrial and commercial investments, and 15 per cent in portfolio investments

Table 6.6 Flow of Chinese-owned funds into Hong Kong (HK$m)

	Total	Annual average
1949	300–400	300–400
1950–2	600	200
1953–5	1,000	333
1955	600	600
1956–8	1,600	533
1959	300[a]	720
1964	1,000	1,000
1965	1,000	1,000

[a] June to October 1959 only.

Sources: 1949–64, Report by JETRO (1964) cited in Y.L. Wu and C.H. Wu, *Economic Development in Southeast Asia; The Chinese Dimension*, Stanford, Hoover Institution Press, 1980, p. 95. 1964/5 from Wu and Wu, *Economic Development in Southeast Asia*, p. 95.

such as the stock market.[71] Wu and Wu concluded that 'it is probably safe to say that Chinese funds have been a primary factor in making Singapore and Hong Kong the principal financial markets serving Southeast Asia'.[72]

The link between the domestic and international sphere was exaggerated by the fact that Hong Kong's manufacturing was highly import-dependent and most of the product was destined for export. The free market in Hong Kong facilitated the import of raw materials and allowed exporters to offer keenly competitive prices. Indeed, it was argued in Chapter 4 that if the free market were closed, Hong Kong exporters would have lost their competitiveness. In turn, the accumulation of wealth derived from manufacturing and trade attracted branches of overseas banks and brokers who sought to channel these savings into international markets. A further link is suggested by Jao's survey of the Hongkong Bank's lending to industry from 1950 to 1966 in which he found that one of the most important criteria for the approval or rejection of a loan request was

> the foreign exchange turnover generated by the client's business and his willing-ness to give a major, if not exclusive, share of this turnover to the Bank, since the spread between the buying and selling rates of foreign exchange is one of the most lucrative sources of bank profit in Hong Kong.[73]

In this sense, the high trade content of Hong Kong's manufacturing made it a more attractive prospect for the commercial banking establishment in Hong Kong.

During the period of industrialisation, large local manufacturers (especially in the Shanghai textile sector) worked closely with the traditional export houses such as Jardine Matheson to find markets in Europe and North America for their products, and to arrange trade finance. Cantonese manufacturers had weaker links to the Western financial establishment in Hong Kong, but maintained traditional ties to smaller banks and merchants. These smaller factories tended to produce lower quality goods destined for elsewhere in Asia, and manufacturers exploited their own regional business networks and built up their capital through re-invested profits and loans from local banks. In a 1978 survey of 415 small manufacturers, about half of the orders for small firms came from large and small import–export companies.[74] Meyer asserts that the synergy between 'expert local exporters, trade financiers and bankers with long experience in Asian and global markets' was vital in the support of Hong Kong's new industrialists.[75]

In contrast to Meyer, Choi has argued that the links between established financial institutions and local industry were close, but ultimately detrimental to the long-term development of industry. He argues that the financial establishment had no interest in industrial restructuring in the 1960s and was preoccupied instead by the commercial profits that came from labour-intensive manufacture for export.[76] He cites the failure of the government to respond to the demands of the Chinese Manufacturers' Association (a predominantly Cantonese organisation) for greater industrial protection through restrictions on free trade. The Hong Kong Federation of Industries (pre-dominantly Shanghai industrialists) had closer links to the government and Western finance, which enhanced their access to capital and other resources. As a result, they identified with the interests of the financial elite and so accepted the status quo, behaving as the 'lap dog' of government.[77] Choi's case depends on there being a substantial domestic market that could have supported import-substitution industrialisation. Given the relatively small domestic market, however, and the shortage of domestic resources, Hong Kong's industry would always be dependent on international trade. The finance of imported supplies and exported finished goods were vital short-term sources of credit for domestic industry. In this context, the distinction between financing trade and financing production is a false one.

The debate about the link between the international financial sector and domestic industry clearly revolves around the provision of bank lending for domestic industry. On the supply side, it is important to determine whether the IFC attracted a net inflow of capital, which was invested in domestic industry. On the demand side, the question is whether the presence of the IFC crowded out industrial investment by diverting loanable funds to other sectors, or if the foreign nature of many financial institutions created an expensive information gap between industry and banks. As in most developing and developed countries, there were persistent reports of a sizeable fringe of unsatisfied borrowers who felt that their financial needs were not met by the banking system. In January 1959, the Governor appointed a committee to investigate whether there was a need for an industrial bank in Hong Kong, and if the government should be responsible for establishing it. Included in the committee were representatives of the Bank of East Asia, Hang Seng Bank, the Chartered Bank and the Hongkong Bank. The terms of reference for the enquiry were quite detailed (requiring advice on the governance of such a bank, and the interest rates that it should charge), which suggests that the government was taking the matter seriously.[78]

After a year's deliberations, however, the committee found the case for an industrial bank 'not proven'.[79] The Chinese Manufacturers' Association was convinced that there was a need for such a bank, but they were unable to supply specific examples of worthwhile projects that had been refused finance. The Director of Commerce and Industry, and the Hong Kong General Chamber of Commerce both asserted that they were not aware of a considerable unsatisfied fringe of borrowers.[80] Indeed, the Director of Commerce and Industry remarked that with regard to industrial finance 'casual observations by industrialists themselves are often conflicting and usually reflect immaturity of outlook or obvious self-interest'.[81] He suggested that the small entrepreneur was not interested in planning for the long term, focusing instead on short-term profits in potentially short-lived industries. In the Director's view, this made such enterprises essentially speculative and not deserving of longer-term support from banks.[82] In contrast, although the Chamber of Commerce agreed that there was no need for greater provision of short-term capital, it did recommend the establishment of a 'development finance corporation' to support the diversification of Hong Kong's manufacturing. It also believed that if the British government would offer guarantees for longer-term loans to secure them against political risk, the banking system would be able to provide sufficient capital to industry.[83]

The conclusion of the Industrial Bank Committee that no new institutions were required was confirmed by an investigation by the London-based Economist

Intelligence Unit (EIU) solicited by the Federation of Hong Kong Industries and published in March 1962. The point of this study was to assess the prospects for diversifying Hong Kong's industrial base, which included industry's access to capital. The report confirmed that in almost all cases initial finance came from personal savings, and that even once a firm was mature 'the degree of self-financing is abnormally high'.[84] Like the Industrial Bank Committee, the EIU found that funds available from banks were adequate, noting that perhaps 75 per cent of industrial loans came from the Hongkong Bank and the Chartered Bank, although this reflected large loans to large business. Small and medium-sized business relied on private lending at high rates, and on short-term trade credits from merchant companies. The only positive recommendations were that the government should collect and publish statistics on banking and industrial profits, and that greater use should be made of the stock market.

Lending by banks was inhibited by the industrial structure of Hong Kong manufacturing which was (and is) based on small units, usually considered unattractive targets for loans.[85] The patchy evidence available suggests that the small firm structure of manufacturing in Hong Kong continued to inhibit borrowing from banks. A survey of small and medium-sized manufacturers in Hong Kong in 1987 found that 71 per cent found their initial investment capital from their own savings. Only 0.7 per cent borrowed exclusively from banks for this initial investment, although a further 27 per cent borrowed from a combination of banks, family and friends.[86] A similar survey of over 400 established small businesses in 1978 found that, after the initial startup, only 17 per cent identified lack of finance as a major problem. In this decade, the labour shortage was much more important for industry.[87] However, in 1996, 60 per cent of a sample of small and medium-sized enterprises described the inability to borrow from banks as a major concern.[88]

The EIU report also suggested that part of the 'Macmillan Gap' in Hong Kong might be blamed on the excessively international outlook of the banking system where profits were higher and achieved at shorter term compared with domestic industrial finance.[89] Certainly the foreign banks operating in Hong Kong were not geared toward lending to the domestic market, although they were sometimes keen competitors for deposits. As in Hong Kong, some have suggested that banks in the City of London were too committed to overseas finance to provide the necessary funds for British industry.[90] In the UK this prompted a government enquiry in 1931, the Macmillan Committee, which identified market failure in the provision of loans to small companies. Unlike the Hong Kong case, the British government responded by encouraging specialised institutions to deal with this apparent market failure, but they were not successful in finding viable and profitable projects whose needs had not been met by the conventional banking system. The failure of these efforts in Britain confirms the fears of the Industrial Bank Committee in Hong Kong, that banks captured most viable projects and that the remaining fringe were too risky to be commercially viable. Banks are profit-led institutions whose main concern is the security of depositors and not the development of the economy as a whole.

Between 1972 and 1976, the government operated a 'Loans for Small Industry Scheme' to help small entrepreneurs purchase machinery and equipment in order to improve productivity. Essentially, the government agreed to underwrite loans from HK$50,000 to HK$250,000 at an interest rate of 9 per cent p.a. Applicants had to spend HK$1,000 for a feasibility study by the Hong Kong Productivity Centre (a government organisation). In the event, only 10 loans were made and the scheme was abandoned due to lack of demand. Most of the complaints about the programme from small business related to the non-refundable HK$1,000 fee, and to the restriction of the loan to the purchase of capital equipment. In 1978, industrialists expressed a greater desire for working capital than for longer-term investment for machinery.[91] It will be seen below that the banks readily provided such finance in the form of overdrafts, packing loans, and other trade finance.

Despite this indirect evidence that the banks serviced the needs of Hong Kong industry adequately, market failure in Hong Kong may have resulted from information asymmetry caused by the cultural gulf between industry and banks. If the Western banks of the IFC were distant from local industry, the Chinese banks in Hong Kong should have had an advantage in local lending through their closer personal contacts with the Chinese community. The Chinese Manufacturers' Association observed in 1959 that 'the commonly known sources of finance for medium and small factories are the Chinese banks, the native banks or private financiers at rates of interest ranging from 1.2% to 2% per month'.[92] The contrast between Western and Chinese banking was clear when the Hongkong Bank took over 51 per cent of the Hang Seng Bank in response to the banking crisis of 1965. At the end of 1964, the Hang Seng Bank showed a balance of almost HK$500 million in outstanding loans and advances, of which over HK$400 million were secured loans and overdrafts.[93] The loans were overwhelmingly to small and medium-sized enterprises, secured against property. The Chinese banking practice of lending long based on short-term deposits, and using a potentially overvalued asset such as property as security was shocking to the Hongkong Bank when they examined the Hang Seng's books as part of their takeover of the bank in 1965. In July, P.E. Hutson, Assistant Manager and Chief Accountant of Hongkong Bank advised that

> While it is obvious that we cannot change Hang Seng from being a Chinese Bank, run in the Chinese way, it is equally obvious that unless we can impress them with the vital necessity of changing the unacceptable banking practice of borrowing short and lending long, there will continue to be the ever prevalent risk that they will be unable to maintain the liquidity ratios required. We can but hope that if we guide them with patience all may yet be well and our investment secured; but we MUST be firm.[94]

By September 1965, Hutson reported that

> From working with them, one has the feeling that the older generation are paying mere lip service, but that the younger executive is willing to concede the necessity for change and the wisdom of conservatism in banking.[95]

The dangers of Chinese banking practice were evident in the failure of the Hang Seng Bank, whose liquidity ratio had fallen to 17 per cent in February 1965, prompting the crisis. Chapter 3 showed the frequency of failures of other Chinese banks with low liquidity ratios.

By the 1940s, Shanghai industrialists had lost their close links with British banks in China, so after arriving in Hong Kong they used informal and formal intermediaries to re-establish their credibility.[96] These arrangements included hiring individual businessmen as brokers, or firms such as China Engineers Ltd borrowing from the Hongkong Bank and re-lending at higher rates to cotton spinners. As will be noted below, the Hongkong Bank eventually took the initiative and hired its own Chinese intermediary in 1964 to try to capture more industrial business. The fact that loans were forthcoming through an intermediary supports the contention that it was the cultural gap and lack of personal contact that inhibited the large Western banks from lending to Chinese business, but there is considerable evidence that the Western banks were aggressive in trying to find viable targets for industrial loans. Conversely, large and small Chinese banks made a much smaller contribution to industrial lending.

By the mid-1960s, as industry expanded and the banking system grew more competitive, the opportunities that European-style banks lost because of the gap between the local entrepreneur and the banking establishment were becoming more obvious. The Hongkong Bank tried to reduce the transactions costs of negotiation and enforcement of lending agreements by appointing an 'industrial consultant' in the early 1960s. He promoted joint manufacturing ventures between Hong Kong and foreign investors, but this proved unsuccessful. They also tried to form a link with local entrepreneurs by employing H.J. Shen as Chinese manager for the Hong Kong office, and introducing a factory inspection group to reduce the transactions costs of local industrial loans.[97] H.J. Shen was Managing Director of East Sun Textiles Co. and a former central banker with the Bank of China who had acted as an intermediary for Shanghai industrialists since the 1950s. This appointment shows that aspects of the traditional Compradore system were still useful to the bank.[98]

Another strategy to expand industrial lending was to widen branch networks, which increased the direct contact between the bank and potential borrowers. The Mongkok branch of the Hongkong Bank was particularly active in lending to local industry, and hosted the bank's Industrial Banking Department.[99] In 1959, the Hang Seng also set up a special section devoted to the finance of industry. As noted in Chapter 3, the Chartered Bank also used its branches to increase its lending to local industry. Outstanding overdrafts of the Kowloon branch at the end of 1965 (shown in Figure 6.2) show a greater commitment to textiles and other industry than either the Hong Kong office of the bank or the banking sector as a whole, although total overdrafts of the Kowloon branch were less than 10 per cent of those held at head office.[100]

The Chartered Bank overdraft records also allow an analysis of lending by ownership of the company.[101] All but two of the companies with outstanding overdrafts at the Kowloon branch of the Chartered Bank in 1965 were Chinese-owned[102] (one was British and one Australian), while most of the overdrafts of individuals were held by British citizens. At the Hong Kong head office, there is the suggestion of bias against Chinese customers in some sectors. Of the outstanding overdrafts greater than HK$10,000 (US$1,750) in 1965, 79 per cent of trading company overdrafts

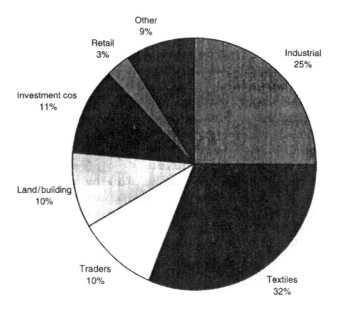

Figure 6.2 Chartered Bank Kowloon branch; overdrafts outstanding end 1965.

were Chinese but they accounted for only 41 per cent of the value of overdrafts to this sector, suggesting that Chinese customers tended to have smaller overdrafts. Similarly, 64 per cent of land/building companies were Chinese but they accounted for only 35 per cent of the value of overdrafts to this sector. The Chartered Bank's exposure to Chinese companies was particularly strong in the textile sector, where all but one company was Chinese-owned. Overall, 64 per cent of overdrawn accounts were by Chinese clients but they accounted for only 51 per cent of the total value of overdrafts over HK$10,000 at the Hong Kong office of the Chartered Bank. Of course, this may have more to do with the size of operations of the companies than with the nationality of their owners.

Despite efforts to attract more local industrial business, by the mid-1960s the old style of lending to established businesses and taking a close interest in their progress was still attractive to most banks. In May 1965, the Hongkong Bank manager suggested that

> deposits obtained by means of cheaply run collecting agencies should be used in substantial advances to concerns of outstanding importance. In this way foreign banks might exert influence (possible through Board representation) and preserve respect more effectively than by continuing to compete with indigenous banks in the financing of small businesses.[103]

Jao has argued that the Hongkong Bank was not a 'universal' bank in the German or French model because typically it did not have an equity stake in the businesses of its customers.[104] However, given the relatively small business community in

Hong Kong, bankers had a prominent role on the boards of most of the large companies in the colony and so were able to exert an influence. It will be remembered from the discussion of the 1965 Banking Ordinance in Chapter 3, that members of the non-executive Board of Directors of the Hongkong Bank were represented on the boards of over 100 other companies operating in the colony.[105] The major growth areas for links between the board of the Hongkong Bank and the local business community between 1950 and 1960 were in the fields of engineering, insurance, real estate and manufacturing. The tendency of bankers to sit on the boards of industry was also true of other banks in Hong Kong. Li Tse-fong, manager of the Bank of East Asia, for example, sat on the board of such British and American companies as China Provident Loan and Mortgage, China Underwriters, AS Watson's, North Point Wharves, and Green Island Cement as well as having close connections to the Chinese family firms Wo Fat Shing and Nam Wo Hong, which were prominent in shipping, rice and real estate.[106]

The nature of domestic lending by Hong Kong's banks is not identifiable until 1965 when the Banking Commissioner began to collect information on advances by sector. These figures understate industrial lending to the extent that some banks made personal loans to particular entrepreneurs, which would not be recorded as industrial loans. Advances related to the import of raw materials and export finance were also important to industry but were not part of 'industrial loans'. Figure 6.3 shows the breakdown of bank loans and advances in December 1965. Loans for international and wholesale trade accounted for 29 per cent of the total, which was greater than the direct share of manufacturing. A survey of banks by the Industrial

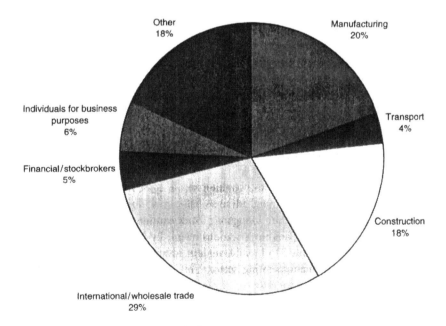

Figure 6.3 Analysis of bank loans and advances 1965.

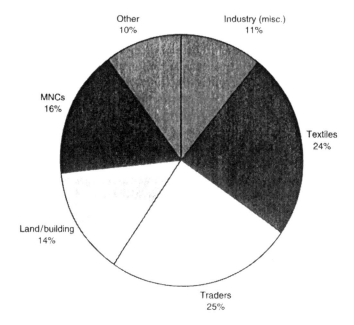

Figure 6.4 Chartered Bank Hong Kong office; share of total overdrafts 1965.

Bank Committee found that loans for industrial investment amounted to 18 per cent of total loans and advances in 1957 and 21 per cent in 1958, which is closely in line with the 1965 data despite the rapid growth of the banking sector in the intervening years.[107] These proportions were not far out of line with the contribution of manufacturing to GDP in these years.

Detailed evidence is available for the Chartered Bank in Hong Kong, and is presented in Figure 6.4, which shows that overdrafts to manufacturers were a considerably larger share of such loans by the Chartered Bank than for the banking sector as a whole in 1965.[108] The multinational corporations were mainly large oil companies operating in Hong Kong. The overall share of industry was even greater a decade earlier in 1955, absorbing 46 per cent of total overdrafts (of which 29 per cent was to textile firms alone).

The increased competition in the banking sector eroded the dominance of the Hongkong Bank, whose share of total advances fell from 45 to 34 per cent in the short period 1958–62.[109] However, the Hongkong Bank continued to dominate loans to domestic manufacturing, as Jao's investigations reveal. By June 1966, the Hongkong Bank was responsible for only 31 of total loans and advances, but accounted for 48 per cent of lending to the manufacturing sector. This was due to the bank's relatively smaller share of loans related to transport, the construction industry, and commerce.[110]

If the cultural gap between Western banks and Chinese entrepreneurs was responsible for the failure of many firms to get access to bank loans, then we would expect that Chinese banks would have a greater proportional share of total manufacturing loans, but this was evidently not the case. For most of this period the Bank of East Asia was the largest Chinese-controlled bank, but it was notoriously conservative in its lending practice, maintained very high liquidity ratios and tended to service only large and well-established Chinese clients. Sinn noted that 'up to the mid-1960s, due to its historical background, the Bank [of East Asia]'s clientele had been confined to a narrow social sector – well-established firms and individuals, both Chinese and foreign, with direct or indirect personal connections with the Bank'.[111] At the other extreme, the small banks were preoccupied with speculation on the stock market, the gold market, foreign exchange, and in real estate during these decades because these sectors offered more competitive returns on investment than lending to industry.[112] As noted in Chapter 3, borrowing from small banks was expensive because of the high returns on alternative investments and the poor security on offer for industrial borrowing. This supports the contention that the activities of the IFC crowded out domestic industrial borrowers, but this related mainly to the smaller banks, with smaller overall resources.

It is beyond the scope of this study to determine the contribution of the Hong Kong financial system to the industrial development of Hong Kong. It is generally recognised, however, that the relationship between finance and industry in Hong Kong has not been the same as elsewhere in Asia.[113] In Japan, South Korea and Taiwan, state-led development programmes have relied on finance channelled through the banking system to industry. In Hong Kong, the laissez-faire attitude of the state to the financial system and the heavy international focus of banking activities may have resulted in a greater reliance on internal funding of industry and informal channels of credit. But direct loans are not the only way that the financial system influences the pattern of industrialisation. As noted above, the range and sophistication of international commercial services available in Hong Kong, especially the free exchange market, substantially increased the competitiveness of Hong Kong's manufacturing. These attributes also attracted considerable overseas capital to Hong Kong, some of which ultimately found its way into domestic investment.

In the most comprehensive account of Hong Kong's post-war financial system, Jao concluded that

> The growth of the real sectors and the banking sector are continuously reinforcing each other. It is this powerful interacting mechanism that accounts for the remarkable growth of the Hong Kong economy during the post-war era.[114]

The Hong Kong government seems to agree that the financial system was central to the development of Hong Kong. In 1987, the Hong Kong Annual Report cited seven interlocking factors to account for the growth of the economy since 1945.[115] These were the free port and free trade, lack of exchange control, the long accumulation of commercial and financial experience, favourable location, and the hard work and entrepreneurial instincts of the population. Stammer suggested that the financial system of Hong Kong was growth-inducing rather than 'demand-following' since it provided stability and security for the inward flow of capital in the post-war period as well as directly providing loans for industrial expansion.[116] The fact that a well-developed banking network preceded domestic industrial development suggests that the financial system may have been 'supply-leading'.[117] In turn, as the manufacturing base expanded, the predominance of international trade in production (both imports and exports) sustained the international commercial activities of the banks in Hong Kong through the end of the 1960s and 1970s, until the opening of China marked a resurgence of international finance.

7 Epilogue and summary

This final chapter brings together some of the themes of earlier chapters and offers a brief sketch of subsequent events.

Epilogue

The story in this book ends when Hong Kong was on the brink of its second most serious post-war crisis. In 1966, China embarked on the disastrous Cultural Revolution. In May 1967, political riots and protests disrupted the reputation of Hong Kong as a capitalist paradise, and shocked the international community into remembering that the prospects for Hong Kong were intimately connected with those of China. The free dollar market rate soared, the stock market slumped, and capital fled the colony. Total bank deposits fell by about HK$1 billion between April and October 1967.

The banks, and especially the Hongkong Bank, drew heavily on their reserves abroad and were able to weather the crisis without a contraction in the money supply. For the Hongkong Bank, the cost of the 1967 disturbances were mainly the loss of income on assets in London that had been drawn down, the fall in the value of stock portfolios, and temporary costs for transport and ex gratia payments to employees.[1] The riots reinforced the need to keep large liquid reserves in New York and London in case of a crisis in Hong Kong.[2] In London, the crisis prompted the Treasury to prepare plans to insulate the UK from a potential financial crisis should it prove necessary to evacuate Hong Kong, a mission rather insensitively code-named 'Operation Junkheap'.[3]

Six months later, in November 1967, Hong Kong faced a further challenge with the devaluation of sterling against the US dollar. This episode marked a turning point for Hong Kong in the sterling area, and represented the culmination of the growing estrangement between London and Hong Kong over financial matters that had been brewing since the end of the Second World War. The HK dollar initially followed the pound, as was expected of a colonial sterling area currency. This quick decision avoided losses to the balance sheet of the Exchange Fund and major banks in Hong Kong, but it generated resentment amongst those who operated in US dollars. Five days later, the HK dollar was revalued by 10 per cent against the pound, so that the net devaluation against the US dollar was 5.7 per cent. Authorised banks were compensated for losses incurred as a result of the changes in parity. In May and June 1968, the Hong Kong government led the sterling area's retreat by negotiating form of exchange guarantee for its sterling reserves. Other countries subsequently sought similar arrangements, and a general solution (which included Hong Kong) was negotiated in September 1968. Under these Basle Agreements, the UK guaranteed the value of sterling reserves for sterling area countries for five years, and in return these countries agreed to maintain most of their reserves in sterling. The sterling area system was sustained in the short term, but its days were numbered.

Before the five years were up, the pound was floated in June 1972. The distinction between the free market and the official exchange market in Hong Kong was eliminated, exchange controls were relaxed, and the HK dollar was pegged to the US dollar. Once the US dollar supplanted sterling, Hong Kong ceased to be part of a colonial monetary system or part of the sterling area. Due to the ensuing instability of the US dollar, the HK dollar was allowed to float in November 1974.

In September 1983, political uncertainty prompted by Sino-British negotiations about the return of Hong Kong to China created Hong Kong's most severe currency crisis. The result was a return to a two-tiered exchange rate system, albeit a very different one from that which had prevailed in the first two decades after the war. The Exchange Fund set an official 'linked' rate for issuing banks' transactions through certificates of indebtedness, while all other transactions operated at rates set by supply and demand. The 'linked rate' system stabilised the exchange rate through bank arbitrage between the free and official rates.

Through the 1970s Hong Kong fought for its share of the globalisation of financial markets. In 1969, a new stock exchange was opened, called The Far East Exchange Ltd. It aimed to widen the number of brokers, to encourage more companies to issue capital, and to attract foreign capital into local issues. The stock market and property markets promptly boomed in 1971–3, but the bubble burst abruptly, prompting a stock market crash in 1973.[4] Nevertheless, the banking system expanded dramatically in this decade. About 200 deposit-taking companies were established to circumvent both the moratorium on bank licences, and the interest rate agreement among established banks. When the moratorium was lifted in 1978, there was a rush to take advantage. Fifty-four new banks had opened by 1982, and the total number of banking offices doubled from 759 to 1,474.[5] Similar to the period 1961–4, the banking system subsequently suffered from a series of crises caused by the expansion in the number of banks combined with the weak regulatory environment. As in the 1960s, a representative was sent from the Bank of England to advise on a new system of regulation, and in 1986 a much more comprehensive Banking Ordinance was introduced.

The new legislation finally sought to solve the problems that had plagued the Hong Kong banking system since the 1960s. It restricted the involvement of banks in the ownership of land and other commercial businesses, and further constrained lending to employees, directors, or firms in which a director of the bank (or their family) has a managing interest. The ordinance also increased the transparency of Hong Kong's banking, which proved invaluable in the wake of the 1997 Asian financial crisis. Hong Kong banks generally avoided the excesses of financial institutions elsewhere in Asia, although the shock waves of the crisis deeply affected the Hong Kong economy. Paradoxically, while many Asian countries were deregulating their financial systems in the 1980s and 1990s, Hong Kong was moving in the opposite direction, increasing the level of prudential supervision.

While these domestic and international problems occupied the government and banks in Hong Kong, Singapore effectively positioned itself as a major competitor. After the final break from Malaysia in 1965, Singapore embarked aggressively on a successful plan to industrialise and ultimately to rival Hong Kong as an international financial centre. Singapore pioneered the Asian dollar market in 1968, opened a non-resident gold market in 1969, and started the Asian Dollar Bond market in 1971.[6] One considerable advantage for Singapore was the 15 per cent witholding tax charged on interest earned in Hong Kong. In 1970, Cowperthwaite argued that the tax was low, that it did not apply to interest earned abroad by Hong Kong banks, and that Hong Kong had 'no ambitions to be a tax haven nor to attract the kind of money that flows into tax havens. We are not fond of gimmicks.'[7] Nevertheless, the tax gave Singapore the advantage in the establishment of the offshore Asian dollar market. In the same interview, Cowperthwaite asserted that this was not a blow to Hong Kong's role as an international financial centre since 'the use of a substantial proportion of the Asian dollar deposits in Singapore are in practice managed by the Hongkong offices of the banks concerned'.[8]

Although Singapore remained the collection point for Asian dollar deposits, Hong Kong developed its advantage in loan syndication and the Asian Bond market. In 1982, the witholding tax on foreign currency deposits was removed, and a year later the tax was removed from onshore HK dollar deposits. By 1986, Hong Kong had surpassed Singapore in terms of the size of the Asian dollar market and Asian dollar bond issues. In these activities, Hong Kong's continued dominance has been attributed to the greater volume and sophistication of financial institutions, the larger number of skilled lawyers and accountants, more sophisticated printing facilities, and lower corporate tax rates.[9]

The most profound event affecting the international financial activity of Hong Kong was Deng Xiaoping's Open Door Policy, launched in December 1978. This effectively marked the re-entry of China into the international capitalist economy, with the establishment of market-oriented enclaves along the south coast of China. The opportunities offered by the huge market and resources of China had captured the imagination of business people around the world since the first Western discovery of China. Finally, in 1979, it seemed that the full potential of this vast country could be exploited. This generated a considerable boom for investment in, and trade with, China, most of which went through Hong Kong's financial markets. In addition, land and labour costs in Hong Kong had reached the point where shifting production to the lower-cost mainland was irresistible. The result was a 20-year boom in investment and trade between Hong Kong and South China, which drew the territories ever closer together into an integrated region. This process culminated in the political shift of jurisdiction over Hong Kong from the UK to China in July 1997. Almost immediately, however, Hong Kong entered its worst recession since the 1950s as the East Asian financial crisis spread from Thailand.

Summary

The history of Hong Kong's financial institutions is tightly bound up with the development of the colony as a whole, yet this is an aspect of Hong Kong that has been relatively neglected in the enthusiasm to explain the colony's industrial 'miracle'. The financial sector in this period is most commonly characterised as a declining relic of the pre-war entrepot role of Hong Kong, that was famously ended with the embargo on trade with China imposed by the USA and then the UN in 1951. In fact, however, Hong Kong increased its global links in the 1950s and 1960s, linking markets in the USA, UK, Western Europe, the Middle East and South Asia, as well as traditional entrepot neighbours in East and Southeast Asia. The British government and the International Monetary Fund (IMF) certainly found Hong Kong's markets an important part of the international monetary system and a worrying breach in the controls on international investment in this period. The financial history of Hong Kong illuminates the inconsistency of the Bretton Woods system, and clarifies that it was not a monolithic system of exchange controls with fixed exchange rates. Free markets did exist and they mattered on a global scale.

In a narrower context, the financial history of Hong Kong is also important to the economic history of the colony because it illustrates the development of the famous 'laissez-faire' policy of the Hong Kong government. It is really only in the financial sector that Hong Kong's administration in the 1960s can be considered completely liberal, and the evidence presented here suggests that the benefits of this 'laissez-faire' attitude might be overstated. Weak regulation contributed to instability in the banking system, which was not ultimately self-correcting. On the other hand, freedom from exchange controls, and an effectively floating exchange rate profoundly shaped the pattern of Hong Kong's industrialisation, based as it was on imported raw materials and the production of cheap exported goods.

This book has explored the changing institutional and regulatory environment in Hong Kong in the first two decades after the war. In doing so, it has emphasised the importance of Hong Kong in British policy as well as the conflict between priorities in London and those in Hong Kong, between the interests of finance and the state, and between traditional and modern financial activity.

The traditional native banks persisted alongside the growing sophistication of the financial services sector. They benefited from government protection, both in terms of the defence of the gold trade, the free market, and their continued inclusion in the Banking Ordinance of 1964. The native banks arguably gained most from the lax regulatory environment in Hong Kong. These banks had always been outward oriented, financing trade in goods and gold and remittances, and this tied the traditional sector into the developing international financial centre. Their domination of the gold trade and the free dollar market made them indispensable to the foreign banks and other Hong Kong modern banks, and created links to banks in financial centres around the world. Nevertheless, in the 1950s and 1960s they faced increasing competition from the modern banking sector, and their unstable foundations shook the banking system as a whole in a series of crises that persisted through to the 1980s.

Hong Kong's most important long-term relationship has always been with China, but here there were also important frictions. Chapter 2 showed how Hong Kong/China relations in the period 1945–51 forged the pattern of this connection for the following 30 years. The free markets in Hong Kong were initially an irritant for the Nationalist and Communist regimes, and provoked political as well as economic conflict between Britain, Hong Kong and China. After the imposition of financial and trade embargoes by the end of 1951, however, the foreign exchange markets in Hong Kong became an indispensable resource for China. Hong Kong's free markets ensured anonymity and international access for the Communist regime, and the foreign exchange surplus that China earned from Hong Kong was vital to the country's economic prospects. Chapter 4 showed that China's trade surplus pushed Hong Kong into a long-running dispute with London over the 'gap' in the sterling area exchange control.

The discussion of the free market and the gold market exposed most clearly the conflict between the government in London and the government in Hong Kong. The colonial government fought hard, and usually successfully, to protect financial and commercial activity in the colony against repeated attacks from the metropole. In the case of the gold market, London won a nominal victory, although the market continued to operate in defiance of the restrictions. The position of Hong Kong as an aberration in sterling area exchange control was clearly uncomfortable for London both because of its effect on the British balance of payments, and on the reputation of the UK in institutions such as the IMF. Nevertheless, it was acknowledged that the free market on balance benefited Britain, first by generating foreign exchange, and later by supporting sterling in international exchanges.

Cain and Hopkins' much debated concept of Gentlemanly Capitalism has some relevance here. It is their contention that British imperial policy was driven by the commercial and financial interests of the City of London.[10] The example of the free exchange market contradicts the concept of 'gentlemanly capitalism' only insofar as successive Chancellors of the Exchequer and Treasury officials persistently fought *against* the interests of financiers in Britain and Hong Kong. In the end, however, it was these commercial and financial interests (supported by the colonial government in Hong Kong) that won the day. The reasons for this were both political (London did not want to be seen to be undermining a strategic outpost) and practical (it was difficult to make further exchange controls effective).

The account of the heated disagreements between Hong Kong and London over relations with China, the gold market, and the free market should put to rest the contention that the Hong Kong government sacrificed the interests of the colony to those of the metropole. In the 1940s, Hong Kong's governors fought hard against the subvention of the colony's interests to those of China in the financial and customs agreements discussed in Chapter 2. They also defended Hong Kong's interest against repeated attacks from London with respect to the gold market and the free exchange market. The latter conflict simmered for two decades until the collapse of sterling in 1967. By the end, the British government found it almost impossible even to engage the Hong Kong Governor or the Financial Secretary over the issue. *Far from sacrificing* Hong Kong's interests to the interests of the City of London, the government protected the free markets because they served the needs of local finance and industry, not financiers in London. In addition, Hong Kong's switch operations in the 1960s were important as a source of sterling for China, and so formed part of the crucial link between the two territories in these difficult years.

The complex relationship between local financial interests and London was also evident in the history of the banking system. The Bank of England was only reluctantly drawn into the debate over regulating the banking system. The contrast between Oliphant's and Tomkins' approaches to banking legislation revealed different attitudes to foreign vs Hong Kong banks, with the Hongkong Bank hoping to increase its competitive position by restraining the operations of foreign banks. Tomkins rejected such protection. Also, Oliphant was relatively insensitive to local Chinese banks, in his assertion on the exclusive use of English in company reports. On the other hand, Tomkins had to bow to the political environment in Hong Kong, by including the native banks in the new ordinance. More fundamentally, Tomkins sided with the Hong Kong government by rejecting the banking system's pleas for greater intervention in the monetary system.

This episode also revealed a new aspect of 'positive non-interventionism'. Unlike previous accounts that have stressed the collusion between financial interests and the state in Hong Kong,[11] the banks were shown to have instigated and maintained pressure for greater regulation. Several smaller banks went even further than statutory regulation, and would have supported the introduction of a central bank. However the state (in the person of Cowperthwaite) resisted this pressure, driving the banks to control interest rates themselves. In the end, the regulatory framework was too weak to protect against banking panics, and required frequent revision to tighten it up. Instead of providing prudent regulation, the state was forced to introduce a moratorium on the entry of new banks into the system after the crisis of 1965. The state successfully resisted the demands of the financial sector, rather than acquiescing to its interests.

The interests of industry and finance were sometimes in conflict. Chapter 6 showed the pressure from industry for more finance from local banks, but this reflected both the risky nature of venture capital and the problems of lending to small companies, which are common in developed as well as developing countries. On the other hand, the competitive alternative opportunities for banks in Hong Kong such as the gold market, stock market and real estate may have reduced the funds available for industrial lending. In contradiction to the colonial exploitation paradigm, there seems to be little evidence that the internationally oriented financial sector as a whole ignored local industry. The two largest international banks, Hongkong Bank and the Chartered Bank, used most of their funds locally and accounted for the bulk of industrial lending. They also went to considerable effort to find worthwhile projects while large Chinese-controlled banks, such as the Bank of East Asia, maintained high liquidity ratios and a cautious lending strategy. The Hang Seng Bank, which was more amenable to lending to small and medium-sized business, ended up insolvent in 1965. Indeed, it seems that it was the smaller Chinese banks that were most distracted by the speculative opportunities offered by the IFC, reducing the funds available for industrial lending and contributing to high interest rates.

On the other hand, the interests of finance often coincided with those of industry. The free exchange market was essential to international financial activity, but it also facilitated inward flows of capital for short-term investment since it allowed this money to be easily repatriated in a crisis. This inward flow was crucial, especially in the early phase of industrialisation in the 1950s. More clearly, the exchange system offered incentives to the export industry. Imports of inputs could be made at the official rate, while the proceeds of exports could be exchanged at the favourable free market rate. Finally, the banking system gave considerable financial support to traders, indirectly benefiting Hong Kong's industry.[12]

The institutions of Hong Kong's financial services sector were all closely intertwined. Without the free market, the gold market could not have functioned, and the stock market and banking system would not have attracted funds from overseas. Some parts of the banking system were heavily involved in the gold trade and the stock market, and all were engaged in foreign exchange business. Thus, there was considerable synergy among the various institutions. Nevertheless, by 1965 Hong Kong was certainly not a fully developed international financial centre in the sense that it became in the 1980s. Some of its markets, such as the stock market, were primarily regional. Others, however, such as the foreign exchange market, the banking system, and the gold market were global in scope and impact. In the period 1945–65, these markets matured, stretched the boundaries of international regulation, and established Hong Kong as the premier Asian financial centre. The legacy of these post-war decades is the range and degree of expertise available in Hong Kong today.

Furthermore, the debates in these first two decades after the war established the principle that there could be no distinction between onshore and offshore financial transactions. The Hong Kong government enforced this principle with respect to the gold market, the foreign exchange market, and the banking system in the 1950s. Freedom from exchange control was also defended successfully by the Hong Kong government, and became the foundation of Hong Kong's competitive advantage in the provision of financial services. Although outdone in some categories by Singapore in the 1970s, the breadth and sophistication of Hong Kong's financial services sector ensured its continued dominance in the decades that followed. The expansion of the 1960s placed Hong Kong in a good position to take advantage of the process of globalisation that accelerated in the 1980s.

In conclusion, the obstacles and conflicts that Hong Kong faced in the post-war period shaped the nature of the financial system for the next three decades. The conflicts and collusion between the Hong Kong government, the London government, local financial institutions, and mainland Chinese interests all expressed themselves in these first two decades after the war. The result was a financial centre that served the local and international community in ways that were not possible in other markets. The unique position of Hong Kong in the international monetary system ensured that its presence was felt by policy-makers in London and Washington, and that its institutions attracted customers worldwide. After a relative lull in the 1970s, Hong Kong re-emerged to claim its position as a major international financial centre. In the next century, although the jurisdiction of London has been removed; the future of Hong Kong will still depend on the relationship between the local government, mainland interests, and local financial institutions. As in the 1960s, the regulatory framework is the key to the prosperity of the territory.

Notes

1 Hong Kong in the international economy

1 In 1901, the official population of Hong Kong was 301,000.
2 The first two volumes of F.H.H. King's monumental history of the Hongkong Bank deal with the period before 1864–1919. More recently, see S.P.-Y. Chung, *Business Groups in Hong Kong and Political Change in South China, 1900–25*, London, Macmillan, 1998, and the first half of D.R. Meyer, *Hong Kong as a Global Metropolis*, Cambridge, Cambridge University Press, 2000.
3 Y.C. Jao, *Banking and Currency in Hong Kong; a study of Postwar Financial Development*, London, Macmillan, 1974. F.H.H. King, *The Hongkong Bank in the Period of Development and Nationalism, 1941–1984; From Regional Bank to Multinational Group*, Vol. IV of the History of the Hong Kong and Shanghai Banking Corporation, Cambridge, Cambridge University Press, 1991.
4 F.H.H. King, *The Monetary System of Hong Kong*, Hong Kong, 1953. E. Szczepanik, *The Economic Growth of Hong Kong*, Oxford, Oxford University Press, 1958. K.R. Chou, *The Hong Kong Economy; A Miracle of Growth*, Hong Kong, Academic Publications, 1966. J. Riedel, *The Industrialization of Hong Kong*, Tubingen, J.C.B. Mohr, 1974.
5 W. Shao, *China, Britain and Businessmen; Political and Commercial Relations, 1949–57*, London, Macmillan, 1991. D. Clayton, *Imperialism Revisited; Political and Economic Relations Between Britain and China, 1950–54*, London, Macmillan, 1997.
6 For some recent examples, see M. Enright, E.E. Scott and D. Dodwell, *The Hong Kong Advantage*, Oxford, Oxford University Press, 1997. S.W.K. Chiu, K.C. Ho and T.-L. Lui, *City-States in the Global Economy; Industrial Restructuring in Hong Kong and Singapore*, New York, Westview, 1997. Y.P. Ho, *Trade, Industrial Restructuring and Development in Hong Kong*, London, Macmillan, 1992. T.F.-L. Yu, *Entrepreneurship and Economic Development in Hong Kong*, London, Routledge, 1997.
7 See, for example, R. Buckley, *Hong Kong; The Road to 1997*, Cambridge, Cambridge University Press, 1997. S. Tsang, *Hong Kong; An Appointment with China*, London, I.B. Taurus, 1997. F. Patrikeeff, *Mouldering Pearl; Hong Kong at the Crossroads*, London, Coronet Books, 1989.
8 C.P. Kindleberger, *The Formation of Financial Centers; A Study in Comparative Economic History*, Princeton Studies in International Finance, 36, Princeton University, 1974.
9 Classic texts include G. Dufey and I.H. Giddy, *The International Money Market*, New Jersey, Prentice-Hall, 1978, and H.C. Reed, *The Pre-eminence of International Financial Centres*, New York, Praeger, 1981. See also the collected papers in R. Roberts, *International Financial Centres, Vols 1–4*, Hants, Edward Elgar, 1994. For a survey of the literature, see Y.C. Jao, *Hong Kong as an International Financial Centre; Evolution, Prospects and Policies*, Hong Kong, City University of Hong Kong, 1997, pp. 11–15.
10 This figure includes debt and equity. A. Tsui, 'Lessons from Hong Kong's Experience of the Crisis', in D.H. Brooks and M. Queisser (eds) *Financial Liberalisation in Asia; Analysis and Prospects*, Paris, OECD/Asian Development Bank, 1999, pp. 43–7, p. 43.

11 See, for example, Y.C. Jao, 'Hong Kong as a Regional Financial Centre; Evolution and Prospects', in C.-K. Leung *et al.* (eds) *Hong Kong; Dilemmas of Growth*, Canberra, Australian National University, 1980, pp. 67–73, and, most recently, *Hong Kong as an International Financial Centre*. See also G.W.L. Hui, 'Ranking Hong Kong as an International Financial Centre', *Hong Kong Economic Papers*, 22, 1992, pp. 35–51.

12 Jao, *Hong Kong as an International Financial Centre*, p. 31. This calculation includes representative offices, subsidiaries and agencies.

13 Y.C. Jao, 'Hong Kong's Role in Financing China's Modernization', in A.J. Youngson (ed.) *China and Hong Kong; The Economic Nexus*, Hong Kong, Oxford University Press, 1983, pp. 12–76. pp. 24–5.

14 See Jao, *Hong Kong as an International Financial Centre*, p. 53.

15 Net immigration into Hong Kong 1946–50 has been estimated at close to a million people compared to a population in 1945 of 600,000. E. Szczepanik, *The Economic Growth of Hong Kong*, p. 154.

16 In 1962 the Chinese authorities suddenly opened the border for emigrants, which resulted in a further increase of perhaps 10,000 people.

17 Chang's work in 1966 was made at the behest of the government and he appears to have relied on confidential tax files as well as other indicators in his analysis. L.C. Chau, 'Estimates of Hong Kong's Gross Domestic Product 1959–69', *Hong Kong Economic Papers*, 7, September 1972, pp. 11–33, p. 13.

18 Chau, 'Estimates', p. 20.

19 E.K.Y. Chen, 'The Economic Setting', in D. Lethbridge (ed.) *The Business Environment in Hong Kong*, Oxford, Oxford University Press, Hong Kong, 1980, p. 8. Jao, *Hong Kong as an International Financial Centre*, p. 75.

20 Jao, *Hong Kong as an International Financial Centre*, p. 73.

21 Chau, 'Estimates', pp. 11–32.

22 H.G. Johnson, 'Panama as a Regional Financial Center', *Economic Development and Cultural Change*, January 1976. I. McCarthy, 'Offshore Banking Centers; Benefits and Costs', *Finance and Development*, 16(4), December 1979, pp. 45–58. See also T. Huggins and C. Greene, 'The Economic Contribution of the Financial Sector in the Bahamas; A Ten Year Overview 1977–1987', *Central Bank of the Bahamas Quarterly Review*, 15(2), June 1988, pp. 31–40, included in R. Roberts (ed.) *Offshore Financial Centres*, Hants, Edward Elgar, 1994, pp. 411–20.

23 See, for example, A.H. Choi, 'State-Business Relations and Industrial Restructuring', in T.-W. Ngo (ed.) *Hong Kong's History; State and Society under Colonial Rule*, London, Routledge, 1999, pp. 141–61.

24 For a wider description of Hong Kong's pre-war industrial sector, see T.-W. Ngo, 'Industrial History and the Artifice of Laissez-Faire Colonialism', in T.-W. Ngo (ed.) *Hong Kong's History; State and Society under Colonial Rule*, London, Routledge, 1999, pp. 119–40.

25 *Hong Kong Textile Annual*, 1954.

26 S.-L. Wong, *Emigrant Entrepreneurs; Shanghai Industrialists in Hong Kong*, Hong Kong, Oxford University Press, 1988.

27 *Hong Kong Textile Annual*, 1954, p. 8.

28 Y.-P. Ho, *Trade, Industrial Restructuring and Development in Hong Kong*, London, Macmillan, 1992. E.Y.K. Chen, 'Foreign Trade and Economic Growth in Hong Kong; Experience and Prospects', in C. Bradford and W. Branson (eds) *Trade and Structural Change in Pacific Asia*, Chicago, University of Chicago Press, 1987, pp. 333–78. J. Reidel, *The Industrialisation of Hong Kong*, Tubingen, J.C.B. Mohr, 1974.

29 *Far Eastern Economic Review*, 14 July 1949, p. 52.

30 C.R. Schenk, *Britain and the Sterling Area; From Devaluation to Convertibility in the 1950s*, London, Routledge, 1994.

31 The Hongkong and Shanghai Bank will be referred to herewith as the Hongkong Bank. The Hongkong Bank issued 90 per cent of the Hong Kong currency. The Mercantile

Bank and the Chartered Bank issued the remainder. This differed from other colonies where the currency was issued by official currency boards.

32 In 1949, the backing for the note issue was 116 per cent. F.H.H. King, *The Hongkong Bank, Vol. IV*, p. 123.

33 A.H.Y. Chen, 'The Legal System', in J.Y.S. Cheng (ed.) *Hong Kong in Transition*, Hong Kong, Oxford University Press, 1986, pp. 88–119. C. Patten, *East and West; China, Power and the Future of Asia*, New York, Times Books, 1998. S. Tsang, *Hong Kong; An Appointment with China*, London, I.B. Taurus, 1997.

34 The free market rate for US dollar tended to fluctuate at a premium to the official rate. For a discussion of the free market in Hong Kong, see C.R. Schenk, 'Closing the Hong Kong Gap; The Hong Kong Free Dollar Market in the 1950s', *Economic History Review*, XLVII(2), 1994, pp. 335–53.

35 Szczepanik, *The Economic Growth of Hong Kong*, pp. 142–3.

36 *Estimates of Gross Domestic Product 1961–1994*, Hong Kong, Census and Statistics Department, 1995.

37 I.B.R.D. Mission, Report on Hong Kong, 1967 (unpublished). Cited in K.A. Wong, 'The Stock Market in HK; A Study of its Functions and Efficiency', unpublished Ph.D. Thesis, University of Liverpool, 1975. This amount is also cited by L. Wu and C.H. Wu, *Economic Development in Southeast Asia; The Chinese Dimension*, Stanford, Hoover Institution Press, 1980.

38 A. Shai, *The Fate of British and French Firms in China 1949–54; Imperialism Imprisoned*, London, Macmillan, 1997, p. 19. W. Shao, *China, Britain and Businessmen*, p. 32.

39 Shao, *China, Britain and Businessmen*, p. 32.

40 Fujian and Guangdong Trade Corporations had agents in Hong Kong. The China Resources Corporation was the agent for most Chinese state trade organisations. State corporations dealing in light industrial products, arts and crafts, food, native produce all had separate agents in Hong Kong.

41 The share of the Communist Bloc in China's total trade increased from 33 per cent in 1950 to 82 per cent by 1955. C.-H. Li, *Economic Development of Communist China; An Appraisal of the First Five Years of Industrialisation*, Berkley, University of California Press, 1959, p. 186.

42 Shao, *China, Britain and Businessmen*, p. 52.

43 This involved reducing the range of goods to those covered by the embargo on the Soviet Union. The USA continued strict controls on its exports to China.

44 Jao, 'Hong Kong's Role', p. 18.

45 Jao, 'Hong Kong's Role', pp. 123–4. See Choi, 'State-Business Relations' for other references to this claim.

46 China did try to encourage inward investment from Hong Kong and other overseas Chinese, but was not successful.

47 Mah's figures are in line with those of Jao, based on Japanese data. Jao, 'Hong Kong's Role', pp. 40–1.

48 Correspondence between P.G. Rynd (Beijing) and A.S. Adamson (HK), 29 July– 8 August 1950, SHG 741.7, HSBC.

49 Yoxall (Shanghai manager) to Wallace (in London), 8 October 1951. The Hongkong Bank resisted this edict on the grounds that the Bank of China could not enforce regulations governing banking practice abroad, and because this would leave the remitting bank with a liability if the remittance was not paid in China. SHG 760.5, HSBC.

50 Two surveys in the mid-1990s ranked Hong Kong as the freest economy in the world. B.T. Johnson and P.T. Sheehy, *1996 Index of Economic Freedom*, Washington, Heritage Foundation, 1996. J. Gwartney, R. Lawson and W. Block, *Economic Freedom of the World 1975–1995*, The Fraser Institute, 1996. Cited in Jao, *Hong Kong as an International Financial Centre*, p. 60. See also H. Smith, *John Stuart Mill's Other Island; A Study of the Economic Development of Hong Kong*, London, Institute of Economic Affairs, 1966. A. Rabushka, *Hong Kong; A Study in Economic Freedom*, Chicago, University of Chicago Press, 1979.

51 N.C. Owen, 'Economic Policy in Hong Kong', in K. Hopkins (ed.) *Hong Kong The Industrial Colony: A Political, Social and Economic Survey*, Hong Kong, Oxford University Press, 1971, pp. 141–206, p. 141.
52 Yu attributes this phrase to Sir P. Haddon-Cave while he was finance secretary in Hong Kong in 1978. T.F.-L. Yu, *Entrepreneurship and Economic Development in Hong Kong*, London, Routledge, 1997, p. 5.
53 Ngo, 'Industrial History'. See also Ngo, 'Colonialism in Hong Kong Revisited', in T.-W. Ngo (ed.) *Hong Kong's History; State and Society under Colonial Rule*, London, Routledge, 1999, pp. 1–12.
54 For various aspects of public housing, see D.J. Dwyer (ed.) *Asian Urbanization; A Hong Kong Casebook*, Hong Kong, Hong Kong University Press, 1971.
55 Y.W. Sung, 'Fiscal and Economic Policies in Hong Kong', in J.Y.S. Cheng (ed.) *Hong Kong in Transition*, Oxford, Oxford University Press, 1986, pp. 120–41, p. 124.
56 The US and UK figures are 29.5 per cent and 34.2 per cent respectively. W.F. Beazer, *The Commercial Future of Hong Kong*, New York, Praeger, 1978, p. 27. Haggard has further argued that the Hong Kong government's spending programmes reflect merely 'public goods that have always been accepted as necessary to the functioning of a market economy' and so are not inconsistent with laissez-faire. S. Haggard, *Pathways from the Periphery; The Politics of Growth in the Newly Industrializing Countries*, New York, Cornell University Press, 1990, p. 121.
57 For a review of Cowperthwaite's character, see F. Welsh, *A History of Hong Kong*, London, Harper Collins, 1997, pp. 461–3.

2 Hong Kong and China 1945–51

1 See, for example, L.C. Chau, *Hong Kong; A Unique Case of Development*, Washington, World Bank, 1993, and I. Islam and A. Chowdhury, *Asia-Pacific Economies; A Survey*, London, Routledge, 1997, p. 183.
2 The political relationship between Hong Kong, Britain and China in these years has attracted considerable attention. See, for example, S.Y.-S. Tsang, *Democracy Shelved; Great Britain, China, and Attempts at Constitutional Reform in Hong Kong, 1945–1952*, Oxford, Oxford University Press, 1988. Wm. R. Louis, 'Hong Kong; The Critical Phase, 1945–49', *American Historical Review*, 102(4), October 1997, pp. 1052–84. R. Buckley, *Hong Kong; The Road to 1997*, Cambridge, Cambridge University Press, 1997, Chapter 3.
3 For histories of China's international economic relations in this period, including some reference to Hong Kong, see D. Clayton, *Imperialism Revisited; Political and Economic Relations between Britain and China, 1950–1954*, London, Macmillan, 1997, and W. Shao, *China, Britain and Businessmen; Political and Commercial Relations 1949–57*, London, Macmillan, 1991.
4 Confidential letter to RIIA from Shanghai, 9 March 1947 (believed to be written by Cyril Rogers, adviser to the Central Bank of China), PRO FO371/63388.
5 For an account of Shanghai during the Civil War, see M.-C. Bergere, 'The Other China: Shanghai from 1919 to 1949', in C. Howe (ed.) *Shanghai: Revolution and Development in an Asian Metropolis*, Cambridge, Cambridge University Press, 1981, pp. 26–30. For a contemporary account of the dislocation during the post-war American occupation, see Ogden (Shanghai consulate) to Wallinger (Nanjing embassy), 12 July 1946, PRO FO371/53575.
6 Board of Trade, *Report of the United Kingdom Trade Mission to China, October to December 1946*, HMSO, 1948, p. 151. The final draft of the Mission, 21 August 1947, can be found in PRO FO371/63307.
7 Rubber merchants and investment houses dominated the activities of these firms. *Far Eastern Economic Review*, 30 October 1946, p. 8.
8 *Far Eastern Economic Review*, 13 November 1946, p. 10.

9 Colonial Office, *Colonial Annual Reports: Hong Kong 1947*, HMSO, 1948, p. 33.
10 Memorandum by the China Association left with Creech-Jones, 6 March 1947, PRO FO371/63387. In January 1947, the Hong Kong correspondent for *The Economist* observed that 'there is a growing tendency for goods ultimately destined for Shanghai and its hinterland to be discharged here [Hong Kong]'. *Far Eastern Economic Review*, 8 January 1947, p. 17.
11 Confidential letter to RIIA from Shanghai, 9 March 1947 (believed to be written by Cyril Rogers), PRO FO371/63388.
12 Telegram from Lance, UK embassy, Shanghai, to Thomas, Hong Kong, 24 September 1947, PRO FO371/63346.
13 Letter from T.V. Soong (Chinese Finance Minister) to Foreign Office, 13 January 1947, PRO FO371/63339.
14 Account of L.H. Lamb of a meeting with George Yeh (China's Vice Minister for Foreign Affairs), 25 August 1947, PRO FO371/63350.
15 For a more detailed account of the Hong Kong free market, see C.R. Schenk, 'Closing the Hong Kong Gap: The Hong Kong Free Dollar Market in the 1950s', *Economic History Review*, XLVII, 1994, pp. 335–53.
16 In February 1947, the *Far Eastern Economic Review* correspondent for the Shanghai Exchange Market remarked that 'Covering the exchange markets last week one felt almost like a war correspondent' because of the police action against market dealers. *Far Eastern Economic Review*, 19 February 1947, p. 97. In early 1948, Chiang Kai-Shek's son was sent to Shanghai to drive out the black market. His tactics of imprisonment and even execution were described as 'Hitlerite' by the British.
17 L.H. Lamb, British embassy, Nanjing, to G.V. Kitson, Foreign Office, London, 2 May 1947, PRO FO371/63350. These sentiments are also expressed by Lamb in a letter to Kitson dated 14 April 1947, PRO FO371/63349.
18 Letter from D.F. Allen, UK Shipping Representative in the Far East, to F.V. Cross, British embassy, Washington, 7 January 1948. Allen mentions 'the notorious ex-gangster Tu Yueh-sen' as a leader of the Shanghai shipowners. PRO FO371/69559.
19 Figures from the Chinese Inspectorate-General of Customs sent by J.C. Hutchison, Commercial Counsellor, British embassy, Shanghai, to Board of Trade, London, 25 May 1946, PRO FO371/53575.
20 Hsiao, Liang-lin, *China's Foreign Trade Statistics 1864–1949*, Harvard University Press, Harvard, 1974.
21 In February 1947, wages and prices were frozen and the Chinese abandoned the old exchange rate of CNC$3,320 per US dollar and adjusted to CNC$12,000, but this rate too was soon undervalued.
22 *Far Eastern Economic Review*, 11 December 1946, p. 9.
23 State monopolies on exports included tung oil, wolfram ore. *Far Eastern Economic Review*, 23 April 1947, p. 190.
24 Tyrell, British consulate, Canton, 27 September 1948, PRO FO371/69569.
25 K.-N. Chang, *The Inflationary Spiral: The Experience in China, 1939–50*, Cambridge, Massachusetts, Technology Press of Massachusetts Institute of Technology, 1958, p. 311.
26 'Recorded and Unrecorded Trade between China and Hong Kong', *Far Eastern Economic Review*, 16 April 1947, pp. 177–8. Also cited in Report by H.H. Thomas (British embassy, Shanghai) to N.E. Young (UK Treasury), 26 April 1947, PRO T236/682.
27 In March 1949, the Bank of England reported that estimates in the *Far Eastern Economic Review* 'are as accurate as those of most newspapers and probably more so than many'. Bank of England Memorandum, 28 March 1949, PRO T236/2034.
28 Chinese Maritime Customs seizures of smuggled goods amounted only to about 0.6 per cent of the value of imports and exports in 1946. Seizures in Shanghai and Lappa accounted for about half of the total. *Far Eastern Economic Review*, 2 April 1947, p. 166.
29 Chang, *Inflationary Spiral*, p. 340. These figures were calculated on a similar basis to the calculations of the *Far Eastern Economic Review* for 1946.

30 Chang, *Inflationary Spiral*, p. 338.

31 For a full account of these negotiations, see C.R. Schenk, 'Commercial Rivalry between Shanghai and Hong Kong during the Collapse of the Nationalist Regime in China, 1945–1949', *International History Review*, XX, (1) March 1998, pp. 68–88.

32 UK embassy, Nanjing, to Foreign Office, 10 February 1947, PRO T236/681.

33 Telegram from H.H. Thomas, Shanghai, to Foreign Office, 18 April 1947, PRO T236/682.

34 Telegram from Hong Kong to the Secretary of State for the Colonies, 24 May 1947, PRO T236/681.

35 Memorandum by Heasman (Bank of England), 12 December 1950, BE OV 104/89.

36 In case of a deficit in the US dollar pool, Young suggested that China should cover half of the deficit and the UK the other half. Telegram from Hong Kong to Secretary of State for the Colonies, 31 May 1947, PRO T236/682.

37 Loombes (Bank of England) to N.E. Young (Treasury), 4 June 1947, PRO T236/683. See also BE OV104/87.

38 Thomson memorandum, 21 July 1947, BE OV104/87.

39 Ibid.

40 Sidney Caine to N.E. Young, 29 July 1947, BE OV104/87.

41 F.F. Powell to N.E. Young, 5 August 1947, BE OV104/87.

42 Telegram from UK embassy, Shanghai, to Hong Kong, 18 June 1947, PRO T236/683. H.H. Thomas (Shanghai) to Follows (Hong Kong), 4 December 1947, BE OV104/87.

43 Grantham (Hong Kong) to Thomas (Shanghai), 4 December 1947, BE OV104/87.

44 H.H. Thomas to N.E. Young, 6 January 1948, BE OV104/87.

45 Treasury memorandum, 31 December 1948, PRO T236/1812.

46 Report by Portsmore, Bank of England representative on a visit to Hong Kong, 20 April 1948, PRO T236/2033. The total capital flight from China to Hong Kong from 1947 to 1949 has been estimated at about HK$500 million (US$100 million). Chang, *Inflationary Spiral*, p. 320.

47 Memorandum by H.H. Thomas, British embassy, Shanghai, 2 April 1948, PRO FO371/69566.

48 Extract from *North China Daily News*, 20 June 1948, PRO FO371/69575.

49 Telegram from UK embassy, Shanghai, to Hong Kong, 27 March 1948, PRO FO371/69565.

50 Telegram from UK embassy, Shanghai, to Foreign Office, 24 June 1948, PRO FO371/69567.

51 Telegram from UK embassy, Shanghai, to Hong Kong, 19 July 1948, PRO FO371/69567. In 1947, China's attempts to get Hong Kong to ban the movement of Chinese currency to Hong Kong by searches at the border on the Canton–Kowloon railway were rejected by the Hong Kong authorities.

52 Report by H.H. Thomas, UK Financial Counsellor, UK embassy, Shanghai, 2 April 1948, PRO FO371/69566.

53 Telegram from UK embassy, Shanghai, to Foreign Office, 28 October 1948, PRO FO371/69569. See also Report from Canton by G.F. Tyrrell, HM Consul General, 16 October 1948, PRO FO371/69619.

54 Report of the General Economic Situation in China for July 1948 by Lamb (Nanjing), 4 September 1948, PRO FO371/69618.

55 Ibid.

56 Chang, *Inflationary Spiral*, p. 385.

57 W.P. Montgomery, UK Trade Commissioner in Hong Kong, Telegram to Foreign Office, 9 March 1949, PRO FO371/75789.

58 Note by Portsmore, 28 March 1949, BE OV14/3. In January 1949, the Central Bank of China was reported to be using the free market in Hong Kong to purchase sterling to settle their debt to De la Rue for printing currency. Note by Keogh of a visit to Shanghai, 28 February 1949, BE OV66/2.

59 Grantham (Hong Kong) to Secretary of State for the Colonies, 28 August 1949, BE OV104/87.

60 For a more complete account of the impact of currency substitution on the economy of Hong Kong, see C.R. Schenk, 'Le Passe d'Une Region; Les relations monetaires entre Hong Kong et la Chine dans les annees quarante', *Economie Internationale*, 78(2), 1999, pp. 155–78. Also C.R. Schenk, 'Another Asian Financial Crisis: Monetary Links between Hong Kong and China 1945–50', *Modern Asian Studies*, 34(3), 2000, pp. 739–64.

61 Telegram from Hong Kong to the Secretary of State for the Colonies, 22 February 1947, PRO T236/681.

62 Based on March 1947 = 100, the RPI peaked at 112 in December 1949. *Hong Kong Government Gazette*, 1949–50.

63 Morse (Hong Kong) to J.L. Fisher (Bank of England), 17 May 1946, HSBC GHO154.

64 A.S. Adamson (Shanghai) to Morse (London), 5 September 1945, HSBC GHO154. Adamson was released from internment on 16 August 1945.

65 Adamson (Shanghai) to T.J.J. Fenwick (Hong Kong), 25 September 1945, HSBC GHO154.

66 Ibid.

67 C.M. Jamieson (Canton) to A.S. Adamson (Hong Kong), 23 July 1947, HSBC GHO179.

68 Adamson (Hong Kong) to Jamieson (Canton), 16 July 1947, HSBC GHO179. In July 1948, the Bank of England also observed that the note issue of the Hongkong Bank was expanding very rapidly to satisfy demand for the notes in China. Note by Portsmore (Bank of England), 20 July 1948, BE OV14/3.

69 Memo by Granger-Taylor, 31 December 1948, PRO T236/1812.

70 This calculation is based on a circulation of HK$300 million at the exchange rate current at the end of December 1947.

71 Quoted in the *South China Morning Post*, 26 May 1949, PRO T236/5111. The Communist newspaper *Renminribao* reported that 'particularly in the years 1948–1949 the Hongkong currency dominated the Kwangtung markets. It was the standard currency on which prices were based in cities and the countryside' and they estimated that about half of Hong Kong's note issue circulated in China, of which 88 per cent was in South China, mostly in Canton. Translation from *Renminribao* (People's Daily), 12 February 1950, HSBC GHO179.

72 Minute by P.D. Coates (Foreign Office), 27 January 1949, PRO FO371/75851. The British Commercial Secretary in Shanghai, I.C. Mackenzie, expressed the same opinion in November 1948. I.C. Mackenzie, First Secretary (Commercial) Shanghai to British embassy Nanjing, 15 November 1948, PRO T236/1812. About three million ounces of gold were shipped from China to Formosa as the KMT retreated. Chang, *Inflationary Spiral*, p. 321.

73 Report from *New China News Agency*, 14 February 1949, PRO FO371/75851.

74 Telegram from Stacey (Shanghai) to Morse (Hong Kong), 29 May 1949, HSBC SHGII 268.

75 Telegram from UK embassy, Shanghai, to Foreign Office, 3 July 1949, PRO FO371/75846.

76 The value of the PDU was based on the price of rice, cloth, fuel and edible oil and had a unit value of RMB302 on 14 June which rose to RMB522 by 2 July due to inflation in the price of rice. PRO FO371/75846.

77 W.P. Montgomery (Hong Kong) to Board of Trade (London), 5 December 1949, PRO FO371/75858.

78 Translation from *Renminribao*, 12 May 1950, HSBC GHO179.

79 Translation of *Kuang-chou*, Chinese People's Association for Foreign Cultural Relations, Canton, Kuang-chou Literary Press, 1959. US Government translation published by Joint Publication Research Service.

80 T. Ling and H. Lei, *The Circulation of Money in the People's Republic of China*, translated by Joint Publications Research Service, 1959, p. 8.

81 Breakspeare's Report, 1 April 1950, PRO FO371/83336.

82 Ibid.

83 Extract from *Xinwenribao*, 5 May 1950, PRO FO371/83359.

84 Report by Breakspeare (Hong Kong), 1 September 1950, PRO FO371/83337.
85 Translation from *Renminribao*, 12 February 1950, HSBC GHO 179.
86 Breakspeare's Economic Report of China – September 1950, PRO FO371/83337.
87 Yoxall (Shanghai) to Morse (Hong Kong), 10 January 1951, HSBC SHG 741.8.
88 Grantham (Hong Kong) to Secretary of State for the Colonies, 12 October 1950, BE OV104/46.
89 Ibid.
90 W.P. Montgomery to A.S. Gilbert (Board of Trade), 22 March 1949, PRO FO371/75853.
91 Report by W.P. Montgomery, 14 July 1949, PRO FO371/75857.
92 The impact of the blockade on Hong Kong was reinforced by the disruption of rail links between Kowloon and Canton.
93 The blockade was the cause of fruitless negotiations between the British and the Nationalist forces in Tamsui. R. Boardman, *Britain and the People's Republic of China 1949–72*, London, Macmillan, 1976, p. 80.
94 On 29 and 30 May 1950, two British ships owned by Jardine Matheson and Butterfield and Swire entered the port of Shanghai and regular trade links were resumed. B. Hooper, *China Stands Up; Ending the Western Presence 1948–50*, London, Allen and Unwin, 1986, p. 83.
95 Most of the blockade runners at this time were destined for the northern ports of Tianjin and Yingkou. Report by W.P. Montgomery, Hong Kong, 12 October 1949, PRO FO371/75858.
96 Ibid.
97 Report by W.P. Montgomery, Hong Kong, 17 October 1949, PRO FO371/75858.
98 In the first months of the blockade, it was estimated that Tianjin and Yingkou received more than 80 per cent of blockade running ships. Shao, *China, Britain and Businessmen*, p. 44.
99 Memorandum by the Chief of Naval Operations, 16 November 1949, Papers of the US Joint Chiefs of Staff.
100 Yoxall (Shanghai) to Morse (Hong Kong), Report on Chinese Trade in 1950, 10 January 1951, HSBC SHG741.8.
101 Monthly Economic Report of China for October 1949, 11 November 1949, PRO FO371/83336.
102 From Reports by W.P. Montgomery, 12 October and 2 November 1949, PRO FO371/75858.
103 Report by W.P. Montgomery, 17 October 1949, PRO FO371/75858.
104 'Economic Reports from Shanghai', *Far Eastern Economic Review*, 3 November 1949, p. 564.
105 Report by W.P. Montgomery, Hong Kong, 5 December 1949, PRO FO371/75858.
106 Monthly Economic Report for China for December 1949, 11 January 1950, PRO FO371/83336.
107 Ibid.
108 Boardman, *Britain and the People's Republic of China*, p. 14.
109 Report by W.P. Montgomery, 14 July 1949, PRO FO371/75857.
110 Report by W.P. Montgomery, Hong Kong, 5 December 1949, PRO FO371/75858.
111 Report by W.P. Montgomery, Hong Kong, 17 October 1949, PRO FO371/75858.
112 Report by W.P. Montgomery, 5 December 1949, PRO FO371/75858.
113 Report by W.P. Montgomery, Hong Kong, 5 December 1949, PRO FO371/75858.
114 'New Trade Routes', *Far Eastern Economic Review*, 3 November 1949, p. 569.
115 Ibid.
116 'Commercial Markets', *Far Eastern Economic Review*, 10 November 1949, p. 603.
117 Imports were valued cif, which included the charges associated with running the blockade. Exports were recorded fob and so would not be so affected by these charges.
118 Raikes (NY) to Adamson (Hong Kong), 26 December 1950, HSBC SHG756.3.

119 Telegram from Raikes (NY) to Adamson (Hong Kong), 28 December 1950, HSBC SHG756.3.
120 Telegram from Consul General, Shanghai, to Foreign Office, 13 June 1949, BE OV104/45. See also Telegram from Shanghai to Foreign Office, 6 July 1949, PRO FO371/75852.
121 Telegram from Foreign Office to Washington, 13 July 1949, BE OV104/45, PRO FO371/75852.
122 Telegram from Washington to Foreign Office, 13 July 1949, PRO FO371/75852.
123 Raikes (NY) to Dunkley (Tianjin), 26 July 1950, HSBC SHG756.3.
124 Raikes (NY) to Dunkley (Tianjin), 13 December 1950, HSBC SHG756.3.
125 Telegram from Shanghai to Foreign Office, 5 January 1950, PRO FO371/83357.
126 Telegram from Shanghai to Foreign Office, 23 March 1950, PRO FO371/83358. Shao reports that such transfers did not begin until July 1950. Shao, *China, Britain and Businessmen*, p. 61.
127 Yoxall (SH) to Adamson (HK) enclosing a report by Russell to his Hong Kong office, 16 February 1951, HSBC SHG741.8.
128 Yoxall (SH) to Adamson (HK), 27 February 1951, HSBC SHG741.8.
129 Announcement by the Bank of China, Shanghai, 29 March 1951. Appointed banks were members of the exchange. HSBC SHGII 958.
130 See, for example, Clayton, *Imperialism Revisited*, and Shao, *China, Britain and Businessmen*.
131 An exception is R. Buckley, *Hong Kong; The Road to 1997*, Cambridge, Cambridge University Press, 1997, pp. 42–7.
132 Buckley, *Hong Kong*, pp. 44–5.
133 Dean Acheson to Mr Souers enclosing a paper for President on 'US Policy Regarding Trade with China', 4 November 1949. Papers of the US Joint Chiefs of Staff.
134 Telegram from H.A. Groves, British embassy, Washington, to P.W.S.Y. Scarlett, Foreign Office, 12 February 1949 PRO FO371/75853.
135 Telegram from H.A. Groves, British embassy, Washington, to P.W.S.Y. Scarlett, Foreign Office, 15 March 1949, PRO FO371/75853.
136 Telegram from H.A. Groves, British embassy, Washington, to Scarlett, Foreign Office, 22 March 1949 PRO FO371/75853.
137 Ibid.
138 Memorandum from the State Department, 21 April 1949, PRO FO371/75853.
139 Telegram from Foreign Office to Washington, 28 May 1949, PRO FO371/75854.
140 Telegram from Foreign Office to Washington, 24 June 1949, PRO FO371/75854.
141 Telegram from Commonwealth Relations Office to Commonwealth, 5 July 1949, PRO FO371/75854.
142 Ibid.
143 Clayton suggests that including Japan in the embargo negotiations began after 1952, although it is clear that this was a part of the British case from the beginning of negotiations. Clayton, *Imperialism Revisited*, pp. 174–5.
144 British companies had already been asked. Telegram from Foreign Office to Washington, 29 July 1949, PRO FO371/75854.
145 Telegram from Grantham to Secretary of State for the Colonies, 28 June 1949, PRO FO371/75855. Grantham reiterated these points in a Telegram to the Secretary of State for the Colonies, 10 October 1949, PRO FO371/75857.
146 Telegram from Grantham to Secretary of State for the Colonies, 15 July 1949, PRO FO371/75855.
147 Telegram from Nanjing to Foreign Office, 4 July 1949, PRO FO371/75855.
148 USA Aide-Memoire, 3 August 1949, PRO FO371/75857.
149 Memo by Dening for Secretary of State, 11 August 1949. Minister of State agreed in a minute dated 12 August 1949, PRO FO371/75857.
150 UK Aide-Memoire to State Department, 12 September 1949, PRO FO371/75857.
151 Note from Graffety-Smith to Heasman, 8 December 1950, BE OV104/89.

152 Note by Heasman for H. Brittain (HMT), 12 December 1950, BE OV104/89.
153 The following departments were represented on the Working Party, but the Bank of England and the Treasury did most of the work: Colonial Office, Commonwealth Relations Office, Board of Trade, Admiralty, Treasury, Ministry of Supply, Ministry of Defence, Foreign Office. The report of the Working Party was not circulated to Ministers, but rather to Chiefs of Staff. Between the Working Party's only two meetings (on 1 February), the UN declared China an aggressor, paving the way for UN sanctions.
154 For a more detailed account of the British and American positions in 1951, see Clayton, *Imperialism Revisited*, pp. 92–3.
155 'Exports of Petroleum Products to China', *Far Eastern Economic Review*, 3 November 1949, p. 567.
156 This generated considerable hostility in the US Congress. Buckley, *Hong Kong*, pp. 43–4.
157 Report on Chinese Trade in 1950 by Yoxall (SH), sent to Morse (HK), 10 January 1951, HSBC SHG741.8.
158 J.F. Nicoll to J.B. Sidebotham, 23 April 1951, PRO FO371/92385.
159 J.B. Sidebotham to J.F. Nicoll, 6 June 1951, PRO FO371/92385.
160 Controls on Hong Kong's exports of rubber and pharmaceuticals had been agreed in March 1951.
161 This point is also made by E. Szczepanick, 'The Embargo Effect on China's Trade with Hong Kong', *Contemporary China*, II, 1956–7, pp. 85–93.
162 D.R. Meyer, *Hong Kong as a Global Metropolis*, Cambridge, Cambridge University Press, 2000, p. 188.
163 Buckley notes that smuggling continued but does not attempt to quantify it. Buckley, *Hong Kong*, pp. 43–4. See also Meyer, *Hong Kong*, p. 188.
164 Office of International Research, US State Department, 'The Current Situation in Macao', 3 October 1951.
165 Ibid.
166 Memo by Chief of Naval Operations for Secretary of Defence and Joint Chiefs of Staff, 7 September 1951, Papers of the JCS.
167 The official was subsequently dismissed by the Hong Kong government whose 'attitude appeared to be that if we wanted the figures we [the Bank of England] could come and get them'. Note of Second Meeting of Hong Kong Working Party, 26 April 1954, PRO T231/705.
168 *Far Eastern Economic Review*, 12 May 1955, p. 609.
169 Office of Information Research, US State Department, 'Economic Cost to Hong Kong of a Complete Severance of Trade with Communist China', 22 December 1952.
170 Ibid. Live pigs made up most of the meat imports and all live pigs came from China. In 1950, recorded imports were 275,000 head and slaughters were 535,000 head. The figures for 1951 were 300,000 and 600,000. Due to greater vigilance on junk traffic, the figures in the first 10 months of 1952 were 285,000 imports and 320,000 slaughters.
171 Office of International Research, US State Department, 'Chinese Communist Imports from Non-Communist Countries Rose in the Third Quarter of 1952', 22 December 1952. Pakistan's exports of cotton comprised the largest single source of imports for China in 1952.
172 S. Tsang, *Democracy Shelved: Great Britain, China, and Attempts at Constitutional Reform in Hong Kong 1945–52*, Hong Kong, Oxford University Press, 1988, pp. 171–2.

3 The banking system

1 This contrasts with Malaysia and Singapore where restrictions on deposit-taking by commercial banks encouraged the development of non-bank financial institutions.
2 J.W. Powell, in *China Weekly Review*, 30 November 1946, quoted in *Far Eastern Economic Review*, 11 December 1946, p. 8.

3 *Far Eastern Economic Review*, 19 November 1947, p. 596.

4 T.K. Ghose, *The Banking System of Hong Kong*, Singapore, Butterworths, 1987, p. 63.

5 The official definition was an institution which engaged 'in the receipt of money on current or deposit account or in payment and collection of cheques drawn by or paid in by a customer or in the making or receipt of remittances or in the purchase and sale of gold or silver coin or bullion'.

6 Kan Tong-po, Chairman of the Bank of East Asia, was the only Chinese to serve on the Committee until his death in 1964.

7 Speech by J.J. Cowperthwaite, 9 July 1963, *Hong Kong Legislative Council*, p. 211.

8 The Exchange Banks' Association was established in 1897. Chinese bankers made up the less formal Chinese bankers' association, which met regularly to exchange information. The Bank of East Asia was the most prominent member of this group.

9 See, for example, comments by H.J. Tomkins in a letter to R.H. Heasman of the Bank of England, 17 February 1962, BE OV14/21.

10 For an account of the historic links between native Chinese and foreign banks in Shanghai before 1937, see D.R. Meyer, *Hong Kong as a Global Metropolis*, Cambridge, Cambridge University Press, 2000, pp. 132–3. See also A. McElderry, *Shanghai Old-Style Banks (ch'ien-chuang), 1800–1935; A Traditional Institution in a Changing Society*, Ann Arbor, University of Michigan, 1976.

11 R.F. Chatham was a retired Chief Inspector of the London Clearing House. He submitted his report on the Hong Kong clearing system in March 1962. In addition to reducing the number of primary clearing banks, the changes ensured that individual cheques with a value greater than HK$10,000 would be cleared the same day as they were presented in order to speed up business activities in the colony.

12 Balance Sheet of Hong Kong Branch of Chartered Bank, Guildhall Library, MS31519/308 and MS31519/343.

13 In 1962, the Hang Seng Bank overtook the Bank of East Asia as the largest Chinese-controlled bank in Hong Kong.

14 Jao, *Banking and Currency in Hong Kong; A Study of Postwar Financial Development*, London, Macmillan, 1974, p. 194, and E. Sinn, *Growing with Hong Kong; The Bank of East Asia 1919–1994*, Hong Kong, Bank of East Asia, 1994. The Bank of Canton was the first Chinese modern bank, established in 1912 with branches in Canton and Shanghai.

15 Sinn, *Growing with Hong Kong*, p. 100.

16 Jao, *Banking and Currency*, p. 194.

17 See King, *The Hongkong Bank*, Vol. IV, Chapter 10 for details of branches.

18 For a survey of the literature and some fresh contributions from a historical perspective, see G. Jones (ed.) *Banks as Multinationals*, London, Routledge, 1990.

19 G. Jones, 'Competitive Advantages in British Multinational Banking since 1890', in G. Jones (ed.) *Banks as Multinationals*, London, Routledge, 1990, pp. 30–61, pp. 53–4.

20 Perry-Aldworth to Turner, 23 January 1959. Correspondence re: Switzerland, Chairman's Files Carton No. 4, HSBC. Turner, Chairman of the Hongkong Bank, confirmed that he shared these sentiments in his reply on 27 January 1959.

21 *Hongkong and Shanghai Banking Corporation Annual Report 1958*.

22 Perry-Aldworth (London) to M.W. Turner (HK), 6 May 1959. Chairman's Papers Carton No. 4, BBME 1959, HSBC. The historian of the Chase Bank credits Lord Cromer, Governor of the Bank of England, with discouraging Chase from acquiring the Mercantile while encouraging the Hongkong Bank to do so. J.D. Wilson, *The Chase; The Chase Manhattan Bank, N.A. 1945–85*, Boston, Harvard Business School Press, 1986, p. 100.

23 National and Overseas Grindlay was a UK bank with interests in Africa. For an account of the merger from the point of view of the BBME, see G. Jones, *Banking and Oil; The History of the British Bank of the Middle East Vol. 2*, Cambridge, Cambridge University Press, 1987, pp. 78–88.

24 See correspondence in Chairman's Papers Carton No. 4, British Bank of the Middle East 1959, HSBC.

25 In 1960 Lloyds Bank took 25 per cent of the equity of National and Grindlays and in 1968 Citibank bought a 40 per cent interest in the bank.
26 Sinn, *Growing with Hong Kong*, p. 106.
27 The Lee Wah Bank was established in 1920.
28 M. Casson, 'Evolution of Multinational Banks; A Theoretical Perspective', in G. Jones (ed.) *Banks as Multinationals*, London, Routledge, 1990, pp. 14–29, p. 20.
29 Letter from Saunders (HK) to Mealing, manager of Mercantile Bank, London, 26 July 1962. Chairman's Papers Carton No. 5, Letters between M.W. Turner and Sir Kenneth W. Mealing, HSBC.
30 For a list of the 14 banks with offices in China in September 1946, see J. Ahlers, 'Postwar Banking in Shanghai', *Pacific Affairs*, 19, 1946, pp. 384–93. Banks without branches in Hong Kong were Moscow National Bank and Banque Franco-Asiatique.
31 Balance Sheet of the Chartered Bank, Guildhall Library, MS31519.
32 In March 1962, HSBC accounted for 37 per cent of deposits, and this share was decreasing. The Hong Kong bank deposits are from Kam Hon Chu, 'Monetary and Banking System of Hong Kong', Ph.D. Thesis, University of Toronto, 1995, based on published bank balance sheets.
33 Between 1958 and 1965, the number of branches of US banks in the UK increased from 10 to 21. J. Kelly, *Bankers and Borders; The Case of American Banks in Britain*, Cambridge, Massachusetts, Ballinger Publishing, 1977, p. 23.
34 The possibility that the Chase might become embroiled in a contravention of the US Trading With The Enemy Act was the main reason for the closure of the bank in Hong Kong. During the war, the bank had undergone considerable embarrassment as a result of a case relating to the trade of one of its European customers. It was later realised that closing the Hong Kong branch had been a mistake. Wilson, *The Chase*, p. 36.
35 Sinn, *Growing with Hong Kong*, p. 90.
36 The following account draws on Shirley S. Lin, *Citicorp in China: A Colorful, Very Personal History since 1902*, New York, Citicorp/Citibank, 1990.
37 H. van B. Cleveland, Thomas F. Huertas with R. Streuber, J.L. Silverman, M. Mungibelli, M.S. Turner, C.L. Wasson, *Citibank 1812–1970*, Boston, Harvard University Press, 1985, p. 263.
38 *Far Eastern Economic Review*, 11 April 1963, p. 81.
39 Minutes of the London Consultative Committee, Hongkong Bank, 13 June 1963. Chairman's Papers Carton No. 4, HSBC. The Nationale Handelsbank sold its Tokyo and Osaka branches to the Continental Illinois National Bank and Trust Co. of Chicago the same year.
40 S.W.P. Perry-Aldworth (Senior London Manager, Hongkong Bank) to G.O.W. Stewart (Manager, Hongkong Bank, Hong Kong), 15 June 1959. Perry-Aldworth was using this as an argument that the Hongkong Bank should take over the British Bank of the Middle East in order to prevent a US bank taking control.
41 J.A.H. Saunders (Manager, Hongkong Bank, Hong Kong) to Morse (Hongkong Bank, London), 18 September 1962. Chairman's Papers Carton No. 5, Correspondence of A. Morse, HSBC.
42 Letter from Mercantile Bank Hong Kong to Mercantile Bank London, 11 February 1952. Chairman's Papers Carton No. 4, HSBC.
43 Letter from Mercantile Bank Hong Kong to Mercantile Bank London, 29 September 1952. Chairman's Papers Carton No. 4, HSBC. The Mercantile's main competition in Hong Kong came from Dutch banks engaged in trade finance in Southeast Asia. Memo by G.O.W. Stewart (Hongkong Bank, Hong Kong) to Lydall (Hongkong Bank, London), 16 January 1959, GHO 426, HSBC.
44 D. Williams, 'Hong Kong Banking', *Three Banks Review*, 59, September 1963, pp. 26–44, p. 37.
45 H.J. Tomkins, *Report on the Hong Kong Banking System and Recommendations for the Replacement of the Banking Ordinance, 1948*, Hong Kong, April 1962, p. 8.

46 J.A.H. Saunders (Manager, Hongkong Bank, Hong Kong) to Morse (Hongkong Bank, London), 24 September 1962. Chairman's Papers Carton No. 5, Correspondence of A. Morse, HSBC.

47 *Far Eastern Economic Review*, 11 April 1963, p. 81.

48 Minutes of the London Consultative Committee, Hongkong Bank, 11 February 1960, 10 March 1960, 13 October 1960. Chairman's Papers Carton No. 4, HSBC.

49 H.J. Tomkins, Confidential Supplementary Notes on draft Hong Kong Banking Ordinance, 1 April 1962, BE OV14/22.

50 Banque pour le Commerce Suisse-Israelien, Foreign Trade Bank (Israel), National Bank of Commerce of Seattle, Swiss Bank Corporation, Irving Trust Co., Marine Midland Grace Trust Co., Philippine National Bank, Royal Bank of Canada.

51 The net increase in the number of foreign companies registered in Hong Kong was 204 between 1957 and 1965. *Hong Kong Statistics, 1947–1967*, Hong Kong, Census and Statistics Department, 1969. Montes credits Hong Kong's early development as a host to MNCs for the emergence as financial centre. M.F. Montes, 'Tokyo, Hong Kong and Singapore as Competing Financial Centres', in G. de Brouwer and W. Pupphavesa (eds) *Asia Pacific Financial Deregulation*, London, Routledge, 1999, pp. 151–70, p. 152.

52 Central Bank of China, Bank of China, Bank of Communications, Farmers Bank of China, Central Trust of China, Chinese Postal Remittances and Savings Bank, Kwangtung Provincial Bank, Provincial Bank of Kwangsi, Provincial Bank of Fukien. *Far Eastern Economic Review*, 1 December 1949, pp. 702–3.

53 This was accentuated by the fact that until 1987 a railway bond issued in 1911 remained unredeemed, and prevented the bank from gaining direct admittance to the London capital market.

54 Jao, *Banking and Currency*, p. 193.

55 For an account of the development of native banks before 1939, see J.M. Chesterton and T.K. Ghose, *Merchant Banking in Hong Kong*, Hong Kong, Butterworths, 1998, pp. 19–21.

56 Letter from H.J. Tomkins to R.E. Heasman (Bank of England), 27 February 1962, BE OV14/21.

57 K.-L. Ng, 'The Native Banks; Their Structure and Interest Rates', *Far Eastern Economic Review*, 11 February 1960, pp. 307–21, p. 307.

58 *Far Eastern Economic Review*, 19 May 1948, p. 490.

59 *Far Eastern Economic Review*, 4 February 1948, p. 100.

60 Ng, 'The Native Banks'.

61 Williams, 'Hong Kong Banking', 1963, p. 28.

62 *Committee on the Working of the Monetary System, Minutes of Evidence*, London, HMSO, Q. 4637–8, p. 327. These remarks may not have referred specifically to Hong Kong. On the lack of trust between foreign and Chinese industrialists, and among Chinese of different regions, see S.-L. Wong, *Emigrant Entrepreneurs*, Hong Kong, Oxford University Press, 1988, pp. 114–7.

63 The following analysis relies on Ng Kwok-Leung, 'The Native Banks', pp. 307–21. Other native banks included in Ng's report were Dao Heng, Hang Lung, Tai Sang and Po Sang (which all reorganised into modern banks) and Wing Hang Cheong Kee Bank, Lui Hing Hop Cheung Kee Bank and Chan Man Fat Bank. The banking crisis of 1983–6 can be traced to runs on the Hang Lung Bank in 1982/3.

64 Figures for the banking system are based on 59 reporting banks at the end of 1961. Smaller banks are excluded. *Hong Kong Statistics 1947–67*.

65 'The Gold and Silver Exchange of Hongkong' by a Chinese Banker, *Far Eastern Economic Review*, 24 June 1954, p. 803.

66 For a brief survey of Hang Seng's history, see Y.P. Ngan, 'Hang Seng Bank Limited; A Brief History', in F.H.H. King (ed.) *Eastern Banking; Essays in the History of the Hongkong and Shanghai Banking Corporation*, London, Athlone Press, 1983, pp. 709–16.

67 The following account is from the Hang Seng Report of Foreign Division, April 1965, GHO322, HSBC.
68 Hang Seng was taken over by the Hongkong Bank in April 1965.
69 Report of Foreign Division, April 1965, Hang Seng 1965, GHO 322, HSBC.
70 Report of Foreign Division, April 1965, Hang Seng 1965, GHO 322, HSBC.
71 The offices of the Banca d'America e d'Italia in the following cities held Hang Seng's control documents: Agana, Amsterdam, Bangkok, Beirut, Dusseldorf, Karachi, Kobe, Kuala Lumpur, Osaka, Tokyo, Yokohama, London, Los Angeles, Manila, Naha, Paris, Singapore, New York.
72 Report of Foreign Division, April 1965, Hang Seng 1965, GHO 322, HSBC.
73 Gillian Chambers, *Hang Seng; The Evergrowing Bank*, Hong Kong, Hang Seng Bank, 1991, pp. 72–3.
74 The Hong Kong office of the Hongkong Bank's share of exports increased from 22 per cent to 26 per cent in 1958–63, and the share of imports increased from 16 per cent to 21 per cent in the same period. By 1966, the shares were 19 per cent and 14 per cent, respectively. The share of all offices of the Hongkong Bank was 5–10 per cent higher. Report on the Results of Hong Kong Office and Agencies for various years, GHO201, HSBC.
75 Report on the Results of Hong Kong Office and Agencies for 1963, GHO201, HSBC.
76 File on Tomkins Report, Chairman's Papers Carton No. 5, HSBC.
77 Y.C. Jao, 'Financing Hong Kong's Early Postwar Industrialization; The Role of the Hongkong and Shanghai Banking Corporation', in F.H.H. King (ed.) *Eastern Banking; Essays in the History of the Hongkong and Shanghai Banking Corporation*, London, Athlone Press, 1983, pp. 545–74, p. 560.
78 One account in 1959 suggested that the published figures only accounted for 40 per cent of total deposits (including inter-bank deposits). The basis for this estimate is unclear, and since many native banks did not accept considerable deposits this estimate can be discounted. T.C. Lee, 'The Economy of Hong Kong since World War II', in E.F. Szczepanik (ed.) *Symposium on Economic and Social Problems of the Far East*, Hong Kong, Hong Kong University Press, 1962, pp. 166–79.
79 V.F.S. Sit, 'Branching of the Hongkong and Shanghai Banking Corporation in Hong Kong; A Spatial Analysis', in F.H.H. King (ed.) *Eastern Banking; Essays in the History of the Hongkong and Shanghai Banking Corporation*, London, Athlone Press, 1983, pp. 629–54, p. 630. The 50 per cent estimate was also cited for the 1960s in 'Chinese Boomerang', *The Economist*, 18 November 1967, pp. 26–30. In June 1965, the Banking Commissioner stated that 'the greater part' of Hong Kong's bank deposits came from outside the colony. *South China Morning Post*, 12 June 1965. Cited in D.W. Stammer, 'Money and Finance in Hong Kong', unpublished Ph.D. Thesis, Australian National University, 1968, p. 120.
80 Tomkins, *Report on the Hong Kong Banking System*, pp. 13–4.
81 Ibid., pp. 7–9.
82 The Bank of East Asia was one of Hong Kong's most prominent banks but it had a cautious attitude to branching, opening its first branch in Mongkok in 1962 and accumulating only seven branches in total by 1968. See Sinn, *Growing with Hong Kong*, pp. 100–3 and 127–8.
83 The new licence fee of HK$1,000 for each new branch favoured the large banks over their smaller competitors.
84 Sit, 'Branching', pp. 629–54, pp. 633–4.
85 Minutes of the London Committee, Hongkong Bank, 10 December 1964. Chairman's Papers Carton No. 4, London Consultative Committee Minutes 1960–64, HSBC.
86 Sit, 'Branching', p. 645.
87 Balance Sheet of Kowloon Office, Chartered Bank, Guildhall Library, MS31519/344.
88 In the early 1970s, foreign banks bought interests in many Hong Kong banks in order to take advantage of the increasing prosperity in the colony. Thus, Mitsubishi bought part

of Liu Chong Hing Bank in 1973, and Tokai Bank bought part of the Commercial Bank of Hong Kong in 1972.

89 *Liu Chong Hing Bank Ltd 40th Anniversary*, Hong Kong, 1988.

90 Ng Kwok-Leung, 'More Banks in Hongkong', *Far Eastern Economic Review*, 12 April 1962, p. 67.

91 Minutes of the London Consultative Committee, HSBC, 13 July 1961. Chairman's Papers Carton No. 4, HSBC.

92 Letter from Tomkins (in Hong Kong) to Heasman (London), 1/3/62, BE OV14/21.

93 Liu Chong Hing Bank became an authorised exchange bank in 1967, and in October 1973 Mitsubishi Bank bought a 25 per cent interest in it. By 1987, Liu Chong Hing had assets of HK$7 billion. *Liu Chong Hing Bank Ltd 40th Anniversary*, Hong Kong, 1988.

94 Letter from Hallows to Haslam after a visit to Hong Kong, 3 June 1960, BE OV14/21.

95 Memo by Hallows of a conversation with J.A.H. Saunders, 15 June 1961, BE OV14/21.

96 For the Bank of England's role in Malaya, Ghana and Nigeria, see C.R. Schenk, 'Monetary Institutions in Newly Independent Countries: The Experience of Malaya, Ghana and Nigeria in the 1950s', *Financial History Review*, (4), 1997, pp. 181–98.

97 Memo by Hallows of a conversation with J.A.H. Saunders, 15 June 1961, BE OV14/21.

98 Letter from P.L. Hogg to Heasman, 24/8/61, BE OV14/21.

99 The bank approached the Colonial Office offering their services in September. R.I. Hallows (Bank of England) to Galsworthy (Colonial Office), 29 September 1961.

100 Cowperthwaite (HK) to Tomkins (London), 24 January 1962, BE OV14/21.

101 Memo by W.R. Allardyce, 4 April 1962, BE OV14/22.

102 Letter from Heasman to Tomkins, 6 April 1962. Tomkins was also asked to simplify the language of the draft. BE OV14/22.

103 Letter from Tomkins to Heasman, 10 April 1962, BE OV14/22.

104 The following account of the difference between the Oliphant and Tomkins drafts is from the covering memo to the draft Banking Ordinance by H.J. Tomkins for the Financial Secretary, Hong Kong, 9 March 1962, BE OV14/21, and H.J. Tomkins, Confidential Supplementary Notes on draft Hong Kong Banking Ordinance, 1 April 1962, BE OV14/22.

105 Letter from Tomkins to Heasman, 10 April 1962. The working party (Bank of East Asia, the Chartered Bank, the Bank of China, the Banque Belge pour l'Etranger, the Hang Seng Bank and the Hongkong Bank) was also discussing the reformation of the clearing house system. BE OV14/22.

106 H.J. Tomkins, Confidential Supplementary Notes on draft Hong Kong Banking Ordinance, 1 April 1962, BE OV14/22.

107 Ibid.

108 Tomkins to Cowperthwaite, 12 July 1962, BE OV14/22.

109 Williams, 'Hong Kong Banking', p. 40.

110 Sinn, *Growing with Hong Kong*, p. 124.

111 Tomkins, Confidential Supplementary Notes on draft Hong Kong Banking Ordinance, 1 April 1962, BE OV14/22.

112 Letter from Stewart (Hongkong Bank, London) to Oliphant (Hong Kong), 3 March 1964. Chairman's Papers Carton No. 4, R.G.L Oliphant's private letters file 1963–5, HSBC.

113 H.J. Tomkins, Confidential Supplementary Notes on draft Hongkong Banking Ordinance, 1 April 1962, BE OV14/22.

114 King, *HongKong Bank*, Vol. IV, p. 615. King credits the Hongkong Bank with prompting the arrival of Tomkins to draft a new banking ordinance.

115 The Chinese banks in particular objected to the restrictions on property dealing. Letter from Q.W. Lee, manager of Hang Seng Bank, to H.J. Tomkins, 18 June 1962, BE OV14/22.

116 Letter to Financial Secretary Hong Kong from Oliphant, 23 June 1962. File on Tomkins Report, Chairman's Papers Carton No. 5, HSBC. See also memo from Tomkins to Watson (Bank of England), 20 September 1962, BE OV14/22.

117 Tomkins, Confidential Supplementary Notes on draft Hong Kong Banking Ordinance, 1 April 1962, BE OV14/22.

118 Letter to Financial Secretary Hong Kong from Oliphant, 23 June 1962. File on Tomkins Report, Chairman's Papers Carton No. 5, HSBC.

119 Unsecured personal loans to directors or their families were restricted to the original 1 per cent or HK$250,000.

120 Jao, *Banking and Currency*, pp. 239–40.

121 Chairman's Statement, Hongkong and Shanghai Banking Corporation Annual Report, 1961.

122 Minutes of the London Consultative Committee of Hongkong Bank, 10 December 1964. Chairman's Papers Carton No. 4, HSBC. See also the report by S.C. Chen in the *Far Eastern Economic Review*, 30 July 1964, p. 213.

123 Oliphant to Saunders (in HK), 24 April 1964. Chairman's Files Carton No. 4, HSBC.

124 Ibid. Oliphant's frustration with the government's inaction was expressed publicly in an article for the *Far Eastern Economic Review*, 22 April 1965, in which he remarked that 'It is a pity that the Government regard with suspicion any advice given by bankers, as they thereby deny themselves the full benefit of the enormous fund of technical knowledge and experience which exists amongst the representatives of about 90 banks', p. 179.

125 Memo by M.G. Carruthers, 12 June 1965, GHO322, HSBC.

126 Ibid.

127 Q.W. Lee to M.G. Carruthers, 15 April 1965, GHO322, HSBC.

128 Jao, *Banking and Currency*, pp. 253–4.

129 Ming Tak was a sole proprietorship engaged mainly in remittances to/from the USA and later in real estate speculation. Ghose, *The Banking System of Hong Kong*, pp. 73–4.

130 Letter from Oliphant (Hong Kong) to Stewart (London), 4 February 1965. R.G.L. Oliphant's Private file, Chairman's Papers Carton No. 4, HSBC. Both the Hongkong Bank and the Bank of England urged the Government of Hong Kong to take the opportunity of the 1965 banking crisis to 'weed out some of the weaker brethren amongst the banks'. Stewart to Oliphant, 12 February 1965. R.G.L. Oliphant's Private file, Chairman's Papers Carton No. 4, HSBC.

131 Jao suggests that the announcement of support from the Hongkong Bank was misman-aged, which decreased its effect on confidence. Jao, *Banking and Currency*, p. 248. See also G. Davies, 'Hong Kong Banking after the Crisis', *The Banker*, CXV(470), April 1965, pp. 243–51, p. 246.

132 The restrictions on withdrawals were lifted in mid-February after the arrival of sterling notes to ease liquidity. Sinn, *Growing with Hong Kong*. See Jao, *Banking and Currency*, pp. 244–50 for more detail on the 1965 crisis.

133 The banking crisis of 1965 also critically weakened two other Chinese banks, the Yau Yue Commercial Bank and the Far East Bank which were also aided by the Hongkong Bank. The government asked Hongkong Bank to take over Yau Yue in August 1966. Sales of assets began in July 1967 and the bank was finally wound up in March 1969. GHO 262, HSBC. The Far East Bank was taken over by the First National City Bank in 1969. For details see Jao, *Banking and Currency*, pp. 249–50. Q.W. Lee, Chairman of Hang Seng, gives a brief account of the Hang Seng takeover in 'Banks and Bankers', in S. Blyth and I. Wotherspoon (eds) *Hong Kong Remembers*, Hong Kong, Oxford University Press, 1996, pp. 185–91.

134 Hang Seng Bank Ltd Progress Report by P.E. Hutson, Assistant Manager/Chief Accountant HSBC, 20 September 1965, GHO 322, HSBC.

135 Note by P.E. Hutson, 15 July 1965, GHO 322, HSBC.

136 *The Economist* speculated that the increase in Communist banks' deposits after the crisis was 'presumably on the theory that any bank backed by Chairman Mao would not be allowed to go under'. 'Chinese Boomerang', *The Economist*, 18 November 1967, p. 29.

137 *Far Eastern Economic Review*, 27 April 1967, pp. 187–9.
138 Y.C. Jao, 'Recent Banking Crises in Hong Kong and Taiwan; A Comparative Perspective', in M.-K. Nyaw and C.-Y. Chang (eds) *Chinese Banking in Asia's Market Economies*, Hong Kong, Chinese University of Hong Kong, 1989, pp. 15–48.
139 M.F. Montes, 'Tokyo, Hong Kong and Singapore as Competing Financial Centres', in G. de Brouwer and W. Pupphavesa (eds) *Asia Pacific Financial Deregulation*, London, Routledge, 1999, pp. 151–70, p. 160.

4 Foreign exchange markets

1 Y.C. Jao, *Hong Kong as an International Financial Centre*, Hong Kong, City University of Hong Kong, 1997, p. 38.
2 *Far Eastern Economic Review*, 3 October 1957.
3 These uses of the market were confirmed by Martin Scott's survey of the market in March 1964. Report by M.F. Culhane of a visit to Hong Kong, 2 May 1966, PRO T295/125.
4 The sterling area comprised the British Colonies and Commonwealth (except for Canada), the Persian Gulf Territories, Iraq, Jordan, Iceland, Ireland and Burma. For an analysis of the sterling area in the 1950s, see C.R. Schenk, *Britain and the Sterling Area; From Devaluation to Convertibility in the 1950s*, London, Routledge, 1994.
5 In Kuwait, a free market operated in US dollars against the rupee supplied by American oil companies' disbursements and used for unofficial imports from the dollar area.
6 Treasury Brief for UK Representatives to IMF, 29 November 1952, PRO T231/705.
7 Letter from W.A. Morris to Norman Young at Treasury, 10 November 1949, BE OV14/4.
8 *Far Eastern Economic Review*, 11 December 1946, p. 9.
9 *Far Eastern Economic Review*, 30 April 1947, p. 207.
10 Personal Report by P.L. Hogg, 11 May 1953, BE OV14/9. The gold market is considered in detail in Chapter 5.
11 A survey of the free market by Martin Scott, former Exchange Controller, in March 1964 added travellers' cheques and notes (mainly from Taiwan) and a small amount of inward investment capital as further sources of supply. Report by M.F. Culhane (BE) of a visit to Hong Kong, 2 May 1966, PRO T295/125.
12 *Far Eastern Economic Review*, 20 November 1946, p. 2. The total daily turnover was about the same value as Hong Kong–China trade per month.
13 *Far Eastern Economic Review*, 30 April 1947, pp. 203–4.
14 *Far Eastern Economic Review*, 27 May 1954, p. 676.
15 Memo by W.G. Pullen, Bank of England, 31 January 1956, BE OV65/4.
16 Letter from A.J. Bird (Hong Kong) to W.G. Pullen, 2 February 1956, BE OV65/4.
17 *Far Eastern Economic Review*, 16 October 1947, p. 5.
18 *Far Eastern Economic Review*, 16 October 1952, p. 511.
19 Fourth Meeting of Working Party on Sterling Area Free Markets, 3 May 1954, PRO T231/705. Malayan imports of dollar area goods through Hong Kong in 1952 were £7.8 million and in 1953 £8.2 million. Paper by the Bank of England, 7 May 1954, PRO T231/705.
20 Brief of UK representatives for IMF consultations, 29 November 1952, PRO T231/705.
21 Hong Kong US$ Account 1952, prepared by the Bank of England, April 1954, BE OV14/10.
22 Based on data for the unofficial gold market in the last week of each quarter reported by the *Far Eastern Economic Review*, Hong Kong. The decline in the gold trade was partly due to the opening of an official gold market in Bangkok at the end of 1952 which diverted the regional gold trade from Hong Kong, and to the fading of the regional uncertainty associated with the Korean War. See Chapter 5.

23 W.F. Beazer, *The Commercial Future of Hong Kong*, New York, Praeger, 1978, p. 139.

24 F.H.H. King, 'The Hong Kong Open Market, 1954', in F.H.H. King (ed.) *Asian Policy, History and Development; Collected Essays*, Hong Kong, University of Hong Kong, 1979, pp. 161–72, p. 166.

25 Telegram from Secretary of State for the Colonies to Grantham, 16 September 1949, BE OV14/4.

26 Ibid.

27 Telegram from Grantham to Secretary of State for the Colonies, 9 October 1949, BE OV14/4.

28 Letter by F.J. Portsmore, 31 October 1949, BE OV14/4.

29 Draft letter as sent by Chancellor of the Exchequer to Secretary of State for the Colonies, 14 January 1950, BE OV14/4.

30 See correspondence February to May 1950, PRO T236/5112.

31 E.W. Playfair (HMT) to F.C. Hawker (BE), 29 March 1954, PRO T231/705.

32 Report by P.L. Hogg of Bank of England, 10 March 1953, BE OV14/8.

33 J.G.F. Young, Colonial Regulation Section (BE), 18 March 1953, BE OV14/8.

34 'Retention of Powers to Control Security and Cheap Sterling Traffic through Free Markets', Bank of England, 18 May 1954, PRO T231/705. The Working Party on Sterling Area Free Markets nevertheless agreed to maintain DFR2A.

35 Final Report of the Working Party on Sterling Area Free Markets, 15 June 1954, BE OV14/10.

36 P.-R. Agenor, 'Parallel Currency Markets in Developing Countries: Theory, Evidence, and Policy Implications', IMF Working Paper, 90/114, 1990, p. 12.

37 Letter Kelvin Stark (Colonial Office) to J.W.S. Leonard, 29 September 1954, BE OV14/11.

38 Telegram from Sir Alexander Grantham to Secretary of State for the Colonies, 12 April 1949, P.R.O., T236/2034.

39 P.L. Hogg, 'Merchanting Facilities', 10 March 1953, BE OV14/8.

40 Ibid.

41 Beazer, *Commercial Future*, p. 72. A. Rabushka, *The Changing Face of Hong Kong*, Washington, Hoover Institution, 1973, pp. 36–7.

42 Jao, *Banking and Currency*, p. 93.

43 King, 'The Hong Kong Open Market', p. 171.

44 From October 1951, Hong Kong-owned dollar securities could be imported into the UK and sold in the London market. Before this time it was necessary to buy HK dollar securities as an intermediary step in the security switch. 'HK-Security Deals', 19 March 1952, BE OV14/8.

45 For a brief discussion of the Kuwait Gap, see S.C. Smith, *Kuwait 1950–1965; Britain, the al-Sabah, and Oil*, Oxford, Oxford University Press, 1999, pp. 75–7.

46 The figures for transactions through Kuwait in the same period were £28 million of sterling securities and £24 million in dollar securities. Working Party on Sterling Area Free Markets, Oxford, 15 June 1954, BE OV14/10.

47 Personal Report by P.L. Hogg, 11 May 1953, BE OV14/9.

48 Memorandum by P.L. Hogg, 6 February 1956, BE EC5/434.

49 For a more detailed discussion of the debate surrounding this policy, see C.R. Schenk, 'Closing the Hong Kong Gap; The Hong Kong Free Dollar Market in the 1950s', *Economic History Review*, XLVII(2), 1994, pp. 335–53.

50 *The Times*, London, 6 July 1957.

51 See correspondence in BE EC5/435. T.L. Rowan (HMT) was particularly keen to eliminate this traffic.

52 G.H. Tansley to F.W. Glaves-Smith, 27 February 1958. M. Rudd (HMT) to Tansley (BE), 25 July 1958, BE EC5/435.

53 Telegram from R. Black, Hong Kong, 12 March 1958, BE EC5/435.

54 'Hong Kong and the Kuwait Gap', 6 February 1962, PRO T295/27.

55 'The Exchange Control Gap and Security Sterling', 18 December 1963, PRO T295/27.

56 S. Goldman to Sir Denis Rickett, 19 December 1963, PRO T295/27.
57 Note from the Chancellor to the Prime Minister, 13 January 1965. The Chancellor did not want to rush new controls while sterling was weak for fear of further disrupting international confidence. PRO T295/65.
58 Brief for the Chancellor, 5 August 1965, PRO T295/65.
59 Warburg advised the Chancellor to require that all security deals through Hong Kong should be registered to stop the flow of sterling through Hong Kong. The official response to this suggestion was that since the transactions were legal, registering the deals would not curb them. Brief for the Chancellor of the Exchequer, 24 January 1966, PRO T295/123. The Kahn Enquiry on pressures on sterling during 1965/6 was another opportunity to raise the issue. Letter from I.P. Bancroft to Sir D. Rickett, 25 October 1965, PRO T295/65.
60 Minutes of Sir Dennis Rickett's Investment Group, attended by representatives of the Treasury and the Bank of England, 3 December 1965, PRO T295/123.
61 The Exchange Control Gap in the Persian Gulf and Hong Kong, January 1966, PRO T295/123.
62 At a dinner in Downing Street at the end of December 1964, Alec Cairncross (economic adviser to the government) reported that Thomas Balogh (adviser to the PM) launched into a tirade of criticism of the Hong Kong Gap. Callaghan was not convinced. A. Cairncross, *The Wilson Years; A Treasury Diary 1964–69*, Historian's Press, London, 1997, p. 27. Balogh continued to urge the Chancellor to close the gap through the next year. Balogh had been brought in by Prime Minister Wilson as special economic adviser to the Cabinet in 1964–7. Cairncross described him as 'A man of intuitive judgements that were often sound but of a violent temper and full of bile.' Ibid., p. 1.
63 'Hong Kong and the Persian Gulf', 5 April 1966, PRO T295/124.
64 A.K. Rawlinson to Radice (for the Chancellor), 12 April 1966, PRO T295/124.
65 Report on the Results of the Hong Kong Office and Agencies for June 1965, GHO 201, HSBC.
66 Report on the Results of the Hong Kong Office and Agencies for 1957, GHO 201, HSBC.
67 Report on the Results of the Hong Kong Office and Agencies for June 1958, GHO 201, HSBC.
68 'Report to the Chancellor of the Exchequer on the Currency and Exchange Position in Hong Kong' by Bank of England, 28 August 1949, BE OV14/4.
69 P.L. Hogg to Mr Connell, 1 May 1953, BE OV14/9.
70 Estimate noted in a Memo by Glover (HMT), 20 July 1967, PRO T295/201.
71 The Exchange Control Gap in the Persian Gulf and Hong Kong, January 1966, PRO T295/123.
72 Sir Maurice Parsons (BE) to Sir William Armstrong (HMT), 24 May 1966, PRO T295/125.
73 Memo by M.F. Culhane, 18 May 1966, PRO T295/125.
74 Culhane's report on his visit to Hong Kong, 2 May 1966, PRO T295/125.
75 Ibid.
76 Ibid.
77 Letter from Sir M. Parsons (BE) to Sir D. Rickett (HMT), 6 July 1966, PRO T295/125.
78 Minutes of a meeting held at HMT with the Bank of England, 16 June 1966, PRO T295/125.
79 Memo from Sir D. Rickett to A.K. Rawlinson, 9 June 1966, PRO T295/125.
80 Minute by A.K. Rawlinson, 3 August 1966, PRO T295/125.
81 A.K. Rawlinson to Goldman, 20 September 1966, PRO T295/125.
82 Memo by A.K. Rawlinson on Galsworthy's (CO) meeting with Cowperthwaite in Hong Kong, 6 September 1966. Note for the Record by A.K. Rawlinson on a meeting in London with Cowperthwaite, 19 September 1966, PRO T295/125.
83 Note for the Record by A.K. Rawlinson on a meeting in London with Cowperthwaite, 19 September 1966, PRO T295/125.

84 Note of a meeting in the Chancellor's room, 21 February 1967, PRO T295/240.

85 M.F. Culhane memo on a visit to Hong Kong in October/November 1966, 6 December 1966, PRO T295/207.

86 Memo by Glover (HMT), 20 July 1967, PRO T295/201.

5 The gold market, the stock exchange and insurance

1 Y.C. Jao, 'Hong Kong as a Regional Financial Centre: Evolution and Prospects', in C.-K. Leung *et al.* (eds) *Hong Kong: Dilemmas of Growth*, Canberra, Research School of Pacific Studies, Australia National University, 1980, p. 72.

2 Yan-Ki Ho, 'The Variability of Gold Prices in Hong Kong', in Y.-K. Ho and Cheung-Kwok Law (eds) *Hong Kong Financial Markets: Empirical Evidences*, Hong Kong, Hong Kong University Press, 1983, pp. 249–66, pp. 251–2.

3 For a fuller discussion of the Hong Kong gold market, see C.R. Schenk, 'The Hong Kong Gold Market and the Southeast Asian Gold Trade in the 1950s', *Modern Asian Studies*, 29(2), 1995, pp. 387–402. For a survey of the market's operations more recently, see R. Sitt, *The Hong Kong Gold Market*, London, Rosendale Press, 1995.

4 1.000 fine gold = 24 carat gold.

5 *Far Eastern Economic Review*, 12 February 1947, p. 87.

6 *Far Eastern Economic Review*, 30 April 1947, p. 202.

7 Ibid., p. 203.

8 Quoted in *Annual Bullion Review*, Samuel Montagu and Co., 1951, p. 4.

9 Telegram from Grantham to Secretary of State for the Colonies, 9 June 1948, PRO T236/2033.

10 Telegram from Secretary of State for the Colonies to Grantham, 6 November 1948, PRO T236/2034.

11 Telegram from Grantham to Secretary of State for the Colonies, 24 May 1949, PRO T236/2034.

12 Telegram from Grantham to Secretary of State for the Colonies, 22 April 1949, PRO T236/2034. Sterling had been under pressure for months and was eventually devalued in August 1949.

13 Letter to N.E. Young from Portsmore at Bank of England, 24 May 1949, PRO T236/2034.

14 Note of a meeting at Colonial Office, 14 September 1948, PRO T236/2034.

15 Telegram from Secretary of State for the Colonies to Grantham, 27 May 1949, PRO T236/2034.

16 Report of F.J. Portsmore's visit to Hong Kong, 27 June 1949, BE OV14/4.

17 Ibid.

18 A.R. Pratt to G.A. Haig (Ministry of Food, London), 20 May 1949, PRO T236/5111.

19 P.L. Hogg, Personal Report, 11 May 1953, BE OV14/4.

20 'Gold Refiners and Gold-smiths of Hongkong', by a Swatow Gold Dealer, 20 July 1950. *Far Eastern Economic Review*, 20 July 1950, p. 84.

21 *Far Eastern Economic Review*, 13 May 1954, p. 611. These companies still controlled the Hong Kong trade in 1968. 'Gold; A Tael of Two Cities', *The Economist*, 16 November 1968, pp. 38–40.

22 'The Gold and Silver Exchange of Hongkong', by 'a Chinese Bullion Dealer', *Far Eastern Economic Review*, 26 July 1951, pp. 123–4.

23 Personal Report by P.L. Hogg, 11 May 1953, BE OV14/9.

24 'The Gold and Silver Exchange of Hongkong', by 'a Chinese Bullion Dealer', *Far Eastern Economic Review*, 26 July 1951, pp 123–4.

25 'The Gold and Silver Exchange of Hongkong', by a Chinese Banker, *Far Eastern Economic Review*, 24 July 1954, pp. 802–3.

26 'The Gold and Silver Exchange of Hongkong', by 'a Chinese Bullion Dealer', *Far Eastern Economic Review*, 26 July 1951, pp. 123–4. One tael = 1.2033 troy ounce.

27 The dividend amounted to 8 per cent p.a. in May 1953. Personal Report by P.L. Hogg, 11 May 1953, BE OV14/9.
28 'Gold and Silver Exchange of Hongkong', by 'a Chinese Bullion Dealer', *Far Eastern Economic Review*, 26 July 1951, pp. 123–4.
29 *Far Eastern Economic Review*, 8 November 1949, p. 740.
30 The first 'bucketshop' broker in 1948 was Ming Hing. Others included Sun Kee, Yat Shing, Sang Cheong, Chun Fat, Yan Yu. *Far Eastern Economic Review*, 8 November 1949, p. 741.
31 Ibid., p. 741.
32 *Annual Bullion Review*, Samuel Montagu and Co., 1955–7.
33 The suspended banks were Fu Loon, Nam Sang, Yau Hang, Fu Kee, Man Yick, Shun Loong, Lin Cheong and Yue Tak. *Far Eastern Economic Review*, 13 May 1954, p. 611.
34 *Far Eastern Economic Review*, 20 May 1954, p. 641.
35 *Far Eastern Economic Review*, 12 October 1950, p. 449.
36 *Far Eastern Economic Review*, 20 July 1950, p. 84.
37 *Far Eastern Economic Review*, 11 January 1951, p. 58.
38 'Macao Gold Trade', *Far Eastern Economic Review*, 3 April 1952, p. 466.
39 Ibid.
40 *Far Eastern Economic Review*, 11 January 1951, p. 58.
41 'Macao Gold Trade', *Far Eastern Economic Review*, 3 April 1952, p. 466.
42 *Annual Bullion Review*, Samuel Montagu and Co., 1953, p. 5.
43 'Hong Kong: Gold', 24 December 1954, BE OV14/11.
44 Named banks in 1954 included King Fook, Chan Man Fat, Chan Man Cheung, Wing Sing Loong and Hang Seng. *Far Eastern Economic Review*, 13 May 1954, p. 611.
45 *Far Eastern Economic Review*, 13 May 1954, p. 611.
46 *Far Eastern Economic Review*, 17 June 1957, p. 769.
47 *Far Eastern Economic Review*, 20 June 1957, p. 796.
48 The revised reward to informants was only a maximum of 4 per cent of the market price of the gold throughout the 1950s.
49 *Far Eastern Economic Review*, 28 February 1952, p. 292.
50 *Annual Departmental Reports, Director of Commerce and Industry*, 1956/7, p. 30.
51 *Annual Departmental Reports, Director of Commerce and Industry*, 1957/8, Hong Kong, p. 38.
52 P.L. Hogg, Personal Report, 11 May 1953, BE OV14/9.
53 'Gold; A Tael of Two Cities', *The Economist*, 16 November 1968, pp. 38–40, p. 40.
54 *Far Eastern Economic Review*, 11 January 1951, p. 58. As noted above, the pataca was officially on a par with the HK dollar but in practice sold at a premium of 3–12 per cent in this period.
55 'Macao Gold Trade', *Far Eastern Economic Review*, 2 April 1952, p. 466.
56 T. Green, *The New World of Gold*, London, Weidenfeld and Nicolson, 1985, p. 160. This is also the view of 'Our Special Correspondent', in *The Banker*, 120, July 1970, pp. 767–70, p. 769.
57 Letter from J.M. Stevens of Bank of England to Crick at UK Treasury and Supply Delegation in Washington, 3 November 1953, BE OV14/9.
58 Ibid.
59 Hong Kong Dossier, prepared for Haslam (Bank of England), 1 October 1959, BE OV14/13.
60 *Far Eastern Economic Review*, 20 June 1957, p. 796.
61 Letter from M.W. Turner to R.E. Black, 9 March 1960. Chairman's Files Carton No. 2, Correspondence with Governor of Hong Kong, HSBC.
62 *Far Eastern Economic Review*, 17 November 1949, p. 638.
63 'A Proposed Philippine Gold Bullion Exchange', *Far Eastern Economic Review*, 11 September 1952, pp. 349–51.
64 Ibid.

65 *Far Eastern Economic Review*, 12 October 1950, p. 450.
66 'A Proposed Philippine Gold Bullion Exchange', *Far Eastern Economic Review*, 11 September 1952, pp. 349–51.
67 'Gold Trading in Thailand', *Far Eastern Economic Review*, 2 October 1952, p. 450.
68 Saigon was the second largest transhipment point for imports of gold before 1952. The Banque de l'Indochine was the main agent for importers. *Far Eastern Economic Review*, 4 September 1950, p. 255.
69 Note by A.J. Byatt, 14 October 1952, BE OV 25/11.
70 *Far Eastern Economic Review*, 6 November 1952, p. 608.
71 P.L. Hogg, 'Thailand: Gold', 24 January 1955, BE OV25/11. Phao later lost power in a coup in 1957 which placed his rival Sarit in place as Prime Minister.
72 The number of gold dealers was originally 12. *Far Eastern Economic Review*, 6 November 1952, p. 609.
73 P.L. Hogg, 'Thailand: Gold', 24 January 1955, BE OV25/11.
74 Ibid.
75 'Gold Trading in Thailand', *Far Eastern Economic Review*, 2 October 1952, p. 449.
76 *Far Eastern Economic Review*, 6 November 1952, p. 609.
77 P.L. Hogg's Personal Report on a visit to Hong Kong, 11 May 1953, BE OV14/9.
78 Ibid.
79 Ibid.
80 Ibid. This is confirmed in *Far Eastern Economic Review*, 12 October 1950, p. 450.
81 P.L. Hogg's Personal Report on a visit to Hong Kong, 11 May 1953, BE OV14/9.
82 'Where the Gold Goes', *The Economist*, 20 November 1965, pp. xix–xxiii.
83 Ibid.
84 Interview with Mr Francis R. Zimmern, member of the HKSE from its inception and Chairman 1972–7, 14 November 1996. Hong Kong Stock Market History Project, Centre for Asian Studies, University of Hong Kong.
85 The merger was performed with government encouragement. The new trading room opened on 2 January 1947 and both organisations traded there until they were merged the next month. 'Resumption of Stock Exchange Trading', *Far Eastern Economic Review*, 8 January 1947, p. 17.
86 Shanghai brokers were also attracted to the market. In February 1947, R.J.R. Elias (foreign exchange and bullion broker from Shanghai) and Aubrey Hillaly, partner of Hilally and David, Shanghai, applied for seats. *Far Eastern Economic Review*, 12 February 1947, p. 87.
87 There were reports that some brokers were charging less at the beginning of the exchange's operations. *Far Eastern Economic Review*, 12 February 1947, p. 87.
88 *Shares in Hong Kong; One Hundred Years of Stock Exchange Trading*, Hong Kong Stock Exchange, 1991, p. 51.
89 E. Sinn, *Growing with Hong Kong; The Bank of East Asia 1919–1994*, 1994, p. 93.
90 K.A. Wong, 'The Stock Market in HK; A Study of its Functions and Efficiency', Ph.D. Thesis, University of Liverpool, 1975.
91 Jao, *Banking and Currency in Hong Kong*, London, Macmillan, 1974, p. 88.
92 D.W. Stammer, 'Money and Finance in Hong Kong', unpublished Ph.D. Thesis, Australian National University, 1968, p. 193.
93 U. Tun Wai and H.H. Patrick, 'Stock and Bond Issues and Capital Markets in Less Developed Countries', *IMF Staff Papers*, 20, 1973, pp. 253–317.
94 Continuous trading was introduced in 1961. The name was changed to Stock Exchange of Malaysia in 1963 and to Stock Exchange of Malaysia and Singapore in 1965 following the vagaries of the political relationship between Malaya and Singapore.
95 P.J. Drake, 'The New-Issue Boom in Malaya and Singapore 1961–64', *Economic Development and Cultural Change*, 18(8), October 1969, pp. 75–91.
96 Report of the Industrial Bank Committee, 1960, p. 5.
97 Wong, The Stock Market in HK, pp. 89–90.
98 'Unit Trusts for Hong Kong?', *Far Eastern Economic Review*, 11 February 1960, pp. 329–31.

99 Interview with Francis R. Zimmern, member of the HKSE from its inception and Chairman 1972–7, 14 November 1996. Hong Kong Stock Market History Project, Centre for Asian Studies, Hong Kong University.

100 *Shares in Hong Kong*, Hong Kong Stock Exchange, pp. 55–6.

101 The 'Sticking List' which set the negotiable amount of shares for each listing was published in the *Far Eastern Economic Review*, 16 April 1947, p. 189.

102 'Stock Market Report', *Hong Kong Exporter*, 1962, pp. 89–93. Zimmern claimed that this policy by the Hongkong Bank of keeping its unit share price low was a disincentive for overseas investors who preferred high value, low volatility shares. Interview with Francis R. Zimmern, member of the HKSE from its inception and Chairman 1972–7, 14 November 1996. Hong Kong Stock Market History Project, Centre for Asian Studies, Hong Kong University.

103 Minutes of the London Consultative Committee, Hongkong Bank, 8 September 1960. Chairman's Papers Carton No. 4, HSBC.

104 Minutes of the London Consultative Committee, Hongkong Bank, 8 June 1961. Chairman's Papers Carton No. 4, HSBC.

105 'Stock Market Report', *Hong Kong Exporter*, 1956–7, pp. 229–33.

106 This pushed up the value of dock and wharf listings.

107 'Stock Market Report', *Hong Kong Exporter*, 1962, pp. 89–93.

108 D. Wolfstone, 'Eighty-two Banks and Over a Hundred Branches', *Far Eastern Economic Review*, 11 February 1960, p. 303.

109 Wong, The Stock Market in HK, pp. 83–4.

110 *Shares in Hong Kong*, Hong Kong Stock Exchange, pp. 57–8.

111 *Nigel Ruscoe's Hong Kong Register*, 1962, p. 338, 1963, p. 210.

112 R.G.L. Oliphant (HK) to G.P. Stubbs (Singapore), 5 November 1962. Chairman's Papers Carton No. 4, Correspondence with Singapore, HSBC.

113 *Hongkong and Shanghai Banking Corporation Annual Report, 1961*. The bank that needed rescuing was the Liu Chong Hing Bank, which is discussed below.

114 *Nigel Ruscoe's Annual Hong Kong Register*, 1963, p. 207.

115 For a list of the companies, see *Far Eastern Economic Review*, 3 January 1963, p. 43.

116 Interview with Francis R. Zimmern, member of the HKSE from its inception and Chairman 1972–7, 14 November 1996. Hong Kong Stock Market History Project, Centre for Asian Studies, Hong Kong University.

117 See, for example, *Nigel Ruscoe's Hong Kong Register*, and *Hong Kong Exporter*, Stock Market Reports.

118 *Hongkong and Shanghai Banking Corporation Annual Report, 1960*.

119 *Hongkong and Shanghai Banking Corporation Annual Report, 1959*.

120 *Far Eastern Economic Review*, 18 December 1946.

121 The companies were the Loan and Investment Co. Ltd, International Investment Corporation, Allied Investors Corporation, Victoria International Investment Co. Ltd, and Hong Kong and Far Eastern Investment. The latter was managed by the investment department of Jardine Matheson. *Far Eastern Economic Review*, 11 June 1964, pp. 556–7.

122 The Hong Kong directors were A.K.W. Eu, Managing Director of Pearl Investment Managers, Ltd, and G.K. Taylor, partner of Taylor International Co. *Far Eastern Economic Review*, 11 June 1964, pp. 556–7.

123 D. Williams, 'Foreign Currency Issues on European Security Markets', *IMF Staff Papers*, 14, 1967, pp. 43–77.

124 *Far Eastern Economic Review*, 20 October 1966, p. 137.

125 Williams, 'Foreign Currency Issues', p. 63.

126 In 1938, there were 124 foreign insurance offices in Shanghai (of which 60 per cent were British) and a further 20 Chinese companies. C. Trebilcock, *Phoenix Assurance and the Development of British Insurance, Vol. 2*, Cambridge, Cambridge University Press, 1998, p. 780.

127 *Far Eastern Economic Review*, 30 October 1946, p. 8. The companies were American International Underwriters, International Assurance, and Pagoda Insurance.
128 *Hong Kong Hong List, 1947*, Hong Kong, Hong Kong Trade and Industry Publishing Co.
129 The firms were Alliance, Atlas, Guardian, Lombard, Employers' Liability Assurance Companies and Queensland, Bankers and Traders, Triton, Economic, and Merchants' Marine Insurance Companies. *Far Eastern Economic Review*, 22 March 1951. Dominion Insurance was a subsidiary of Wheelock Marden and Co.
130 P.H.M. Jones, 'Rapid Expansion in Hong Kong', *Far Eastern Economic Review*, 19 May 1960, p. 981.
131 The *Hong Kong Directory* of 1964 listed the local offices of 105 general insurers (excluding companies represented by agents), 11 life insurance companies and 34 accountants.
132 P.H.M. Jones, 'Rapid Expansion in Hong Kong', *Far Eastern Economic Review*, 19 May 1960, p. 981.
133 From Company Reports in the *Far Eastern Economic Review*.
134 Jones, 'Rapid Expansion in Hong Kong', p. 981.
135 Hong Kong Company Meetings, *Far Eastern Economic Review*, 5 July 1956, p. 23.
136 The following account is from the *Far Eastern Economic Review*, 11 June 1964, p. 559.
137 *Far Eastern Economic Review*, 19 May 1960, p. 983.
138 Jao, *Banking and Currency*, p. 99.

6 Hong Kong as an international financial centre

1 For a selection of research on IFCs, see R. Roberts (ed.) *International Financial Centres*, Vols 1–4, Edward Elgar, 1994. For the classic account of the historical development of IFCs, see C.P. Kindleberger, *The Formation of Financial Centers; A Study in Comparative Economic History*, Princeton, NJ, International Finance Section, Princeton University, Cheltenham, 1974.
2 G. Dufey and I.H. Giddy, *The International Money Market*, Englewood Cliffs, NJ, Prentice-Hall, 1978, p. 43. See also R.C. Bryant, *International Financial Intermediation*, Washington, Brookings Institution, 1987, and M.F. Montes, 'Tokyo, Hong Kong and Singapore as Competing Financial Centres', in G. de Brouwer and W. Pupphavesa (eds) *Asia Pacific Financial Deregulation*, London, Routledge, 1999, pp. 151–70.
3 R. Michie, *The City of London*, London, Macmillan, 1992, pp. 30–1.
4 Ibid., Table 4, p. 26 and pp. 30–8.
5 D.R. Meyer, *Hong Kong as a Global Metropolis*, Cambridge, Cambridge University Press, 2000, p. 199.
6 G. Dufey and I.H. Giddy, *The International Money Market*, pp. 37–8, 51.
7 H.C. Reed, *The Pre-Eminence of International Financial Centres*, New York, Praeger, 1981.
8 Jones, for example, describes the Hongkong Bank as 'British-managed'. G. Jones, 'International Financial Centres in Asia, the Middle East and Australia; A Historical Perspective', in Y. Cassis (ed.) *Finance and Financiers in European History, 1880–1960*, Cambridge, Cambridge University Press, 1992, pp. 405–28, p. 417.
9 On the location of Head Office and relation with London in the post-war period, see F.H.H. King, *The Hongkong Bank in the Period of Development and Nationalism 1941–84; From Regional Bank to Multinational Group. Vol. IV of The History of the Hongkong and Shanghai Banking Corporation*, Cambridge, Cambridge University Press, 1991, pp. 247–50.
10 For an account of this expansion into London, see J. Kelly, *Bankers and Borders; The Case of American Banks in Britain*, Cambridge, Massachusetts, Ballinger, 1977.
11 *Hong Kong Government Gazette*, Supplement No. 4.
12 The IMF figures exaggerate the decline in assets in 1964 compared with Hong Kong's official statistics, both because of a slightly higher point for 1963 (US$0.37 billion vs US$0.36 billion) and a somewhat lower figure for 1964 (the Hong Kong statistics state the 1964 level as US$0.34 billion compared to the IMF estimate of US$0.31).

13 H.G. Johnson, 'Panama as a Regional Financial Center; A Preliminary Analysis of Development Contribution', *Economic Development and Cultural Change*, 24(2), January 1976, pp. 261–86.

14 Y.C. Jao, *Hong Kong as an International Financial Centre; Evolution, Prospects and Policies*, Hong Kong, City University of Hong Kong, 1997, pp. 24–5. See also Jao, 'The Financial Structure', in D.G. Lethbridge (ed.) *The Business Environment in Hong Kong*, Hong Kong, Hong Kong University Press, 1980, pp. 159–99. Also, 'Hong Kong as a Regional Financial Centre; Evolution and Prospects', in C.-K. Leung *et al.* (eds) *Hong Kong: Dilemmas of Growth*, Canberra, Research School of Pacific Studies, Australian National University, 1980, pp. 161–94.

15 Jao, 'Hong Kong as a Regional Financial Centre', p. 163. The analysis in Jao, *Banking and Currency in Hong Kong; A Study of Postwar Financial Development*, London, Macmilan, 1974, includes material from the 1950s but is primarily focused on the late 1960s and early 1970s.

16 G. Jones, 'International Financial Centres', pp. 405–28.

17 Ibid., p. 408.

18 Ibid., p. 409.

19 Chartered Bank Balance Sheets, Guildhall Library, MS31519.

20 G. Jones, *Banking and Oil; The History of the British Bank of the Middle East, Vol. 2*, Cambridge, Cambridge University Press, 1987, pp. 190–1.

21 J.-P. Abraham, N. Bervaes, A. Guinotte and Y. Lacroix, *The Competitiveness of European International Financial Centres*, Bangor, Institute of European Finance, 1993, p. 43. Jao also highlights these features, Jao, *Hong Kong as an International Financial Centre*, pp. 3–8. See also his entry on Hong Kong in The Banker Research Unit (ed.) *Banking Structures and Sources of Finance in the Far East*, 3rd edition, London, Financial Times Publishing, 1980, pp. 180–219. In this earlier piece, he put more emphasis on freedom from exchange control, low tax rates and liberal government policy. The same attributes are identified with entrepot financial centres by Dufey and Giddy, *The International Money Market*, pp. 45–7.

22 Tokyo was a notable exception to political instability in the region, but its banking system was tightly regulated.

23 J.J. Cowperthwaite (Financial Secretary) apparently refused to join the Hong Kong Club because it did not admit Asians. Personal Report, J. Tomkins, 9 May 1962, BE OV14/22.

24 C.-Y. Chang, 'Localization and Chinese Banking in Southeast Asia', in M.-K. Nyaw and C.-Y. Chang (eds) *Chinese Banking in Asia's Market Economies*, Hong Kong, Chinese University of Hong Kong, 1989.

25 See, for example, D. Williams, 'Commercial Banking in the Far East', *The Banker*, CXIII, June 1963, pp. 418–30. For the Hongkong Bank's experience, Correspondence with Singapore 1962–6, Chairman's Papers Carton No. 4, HSBC.

26 For an account of the debate surrounding the establishment of a central bank in Malaya, see C.R. Schenk, 'The Origins of a Central Bank in Malaya and the Transition to Independence, 1954–59', *Journal of Imperial and Commonwealth History*, 21(2), 1993, pp. 409–31. On its early operations, see C.R. Schenk, 'Monetary Institutions in Newly Independent Countries: The Experience of Malaya, Ghana and Nigeria in the 1950s', *Financial History Review*, 4(4), 1997, pp. 181–98.

27 R. Amatayakul and S.A. Pandit, 'Financial Institutions in Thailand', *IMF Staff Papers*, VIII(4), 1961, pp. 464–89.

28 For a survey of the restrictions on ethnic Chinese economic activities in Indonesia, Malaysia, the Philippines and Thailand, see Y.L. Wu and C.H. Wu, *Economic Development in Southeast Asia; The Chinese Dimension*, Stanford, Hoover Institution Press, 1980, pp. 173–9.

29 Interview with J.J. Cowperthwaite in *The Banker*, 120, July 1970, pp. 734–45, p. 743.

30 T.K. Ghose, *The Banking System of Hong Kong*, Singapore, Butterworths, 1987, pp. 80–1. J.M. Chesterton and T.K. Ghose, *Merchant Banking in Hong Kong*, Singapore, Butterworths, 1998, pp 22–4. As well as the external regulation of the moratorium on

licences, the internal self-regulation of the Exchange Banks' interest rate agreement was an important contributor to the rise of new forms of non-bank institutions.

31 Personal Report by H.J. Tomkins, 9 May 1962, BE OV14/22. The United Commercial Bank was registered in India.

32 The Hong Kong government issued a 3.5 per cent loan in 1940 to raise HK$1 million. This was followed in 1948 by a 3.5 per cent loan for HK$46 million.

33 The financial year 1961/2 finished with a surplus of HK$76 million.

34 Tomkins (HK) letter to R. Haslam (Bank of England), 17 February 1962, BE OV14/21.

35 Minute by Tomkins, 28 June 1962, BE OV14/22.

36 The lottery was expected to raise HK$2 million. *HSBC Annual Report 1961*.

37 S.W.K. Chiu, K.C. Ho and T.-L. Lui, *City-States in the Global Economy; Industrial Restructuring in Hong Kong and Singapore*, Boulder, Westview Press, 1997, p. 21.

38 The Bank of Indonesia opened in 1955 but was closed in 1963 due to the 'confrontation'.

39 The Singapore banks in Hong Kong by 1965 were OCBC, Overseas Union Bank, Four Seas Communications Bank (named Sze Hai Tong Bank until 1964), and Chung Khiaw Bank.

40 Williams, 'Commercial Banking in the Far East', p. 420. The Chartered Bank had the most aggressive branching policy with 15 offices in Singapore by 1963. This was resented by the Singapore Inspector of Banks, the Hongkong Bank, and by the Overseas Chinese Banking Corporation. R.G. Oliphant (HK) to G.P. Stubbs (Singapore), 28 August 1963, and Stubbs' reply 3 September 1963. Correspondence with Singapore 1962–6, Chairman's Papers Carton No. 4, HSBC.

41 D. Williams, 'Money Markets of Southeast Asia', *The Banker*, VXIII(449), July 1963, pp. 484–91, p. 489.

42 S.Y. Lee, 'The Development of Commercial Banking in Singapore and the States of Malaya', *Malayan Economic Review*, XI(1), April 1946, pp. 85–100, p. 93.

43 S.W.K. Chiu, K.C. Ho and T.-L. Lui, *City-States in the Global Economy; Industrial Restructuring in Hong Kong and Singapore*, Boulder, Westview Press, 1997, p. 35.

44 Ibid.

45 Volume of traffic is Telex/Telegrams sent and received. *UN Statistical Yearbook for Asia and the Far East*, 1970.

46 Report by P.J. Keogh on his visit to Australia and the Far East, November 1948–February 1949, BE OV66/1.

47 Letter from Emmanuel (Colonial Office) to Simons (Treasury) 23 January 1956, BE OV65/4.

48 Bank of England explanation 25 January 1956, given to the Finance Committee of the Malayan Constitutional Conference on 26 January 1956, BE OV65/4.

49 Note for G.M. Watson, 30 January 1956, BE OV65/4.

50 Letter from Colonel H.S. Lee to Morford, Chief General Manager of Chartered Bank, 27 January 1956, BE OV65/4. Lee was appointed the first Minister of Finance for the Federation of Malaya after the constitutional conference. The explanation for his query is in Memo by Fisher of a meeting with Morford, 6 February 1956, BE OV65/4.

51 Memorandum for Fisher's meeting with Morford, 4 February 1956, BE OV65/4.

52 Memorandum for Fisher's meeting with Morford, 4 February 1956, BE OV65/4.

53 See, for example, correspondence between the Central Bank and Singapore, 24–26 April 1956. The head of the Overseas Chinese Bank believed rumours about the new central bank was an important factor in Chinese flight capital. BE OV65/10.

54 Quoted in Lee Kuan-yew, *The Singapore Story*, New York, Prentice-Hall, 1998, pp. 296–7.

55 This view was expressed by representatives of the Mercantile Bank, Citibank, Hongkong Bank and Chartered Bank. See briefs in February 1956, BE OV65/10. The Chartered Bank blamed the Hongkong Bank for the delay in implementing a clearing system. A clearing system was not established in Singapore until 1964.

56 In Singapore, Watson met with representatives of the European Chamber of Commerce, Straits Trading Company, and rubber brokers Holiday, Cutler and Bath in February 1956. Their views are recorded in BE OV65/10.

57 Report of a meeting with Holiday, Cutler and Bath Co., 23 February 1956, BE OV65/10.
58 Minutes of a meeting in the Financial Secretary of Singapore with representatives of Hongkong Bank, Chartered Bank and the Singapore, Singapore Chinese, and Indian Chambers of Commerce, 15 and 23 August 1957, BE OV65/10.
59 See correspondence in Chairman's Papers Carton No. 4, Correspondence with Singapore 1962–6, HSBC. The Hong Kong manager believed that Stubbs was unduly pessimistic and cautious, and he was subsequently recalled to Hong Kong. The Mercantile Bank in Malaya and Singapore made consistent losses from 1962 to 1967, due to devaluation of the rupee and high administration costs. Mercantile Bank Ltd Preliminary Survey Report May/June 1967, HSBC.
60 When Singapore joined Malaysia in 1963, Indonesia imposed a trade embargo on the basis that Singapore was aligning itself with British neo-colonialism.
61 The classic early examples are R.W. Goldsmith, *Financial Structure and Development*, New Haven, Yale University Press, 1969, R.I. McKinnon, *Money and Capital in Economic Development*, Washington, Brookings Institute, 1973, and E.S. Shaw, *Financial Deepening in Economic Development*, Oxford, Oxford University Press, 1973. For more recent surveys of the literature, see J. de Gregorio and P.E. Guidotti, 'Financial Development and Economic Growth', *World Development*, 23(3), 1995, pp. 433–48, and R. Levine, 'Financial Development and Economic Growth; Views and Agenda', *Journal of Economic Literature*, 35, 1997, pp. 668–726.
62 D.H. Brooks and S.-N. Oh, 'Asia's Financial Crisis; Is Financial Liberalisation the Villain?', in D.H. Brooks and M. Queisser (eds) *Financial Liberalisation in Asia; Analysis and Prospects*, Paris, OECD/Asian Development Bank, 1999, pp. 85–100. B. Bosworth, 'The East Asian Financial Crisis; What Happened and What We Can Learn From It', *Brookings Review*, Summer 1998, pp. 6–9.
63 A. Tsui, 'Lessons from Hong Kong's Experience of the Crisis', in D.H. Brooks and M. Queisser (eds) *Financial Liberalisation in Asia; Analysis and Prospects*, Paris, OECD/Asian Development Bank, 1999, pp. 43–7.
64 C. Tuan and L.F.Y. Ng, 'Regionalization of the Financial Market and the Manufacturing Evolution in Hong Kong; Contributions and Significance', *Journal of Asian Economics*, 9(1), 1998, pp. 119–37.
65 Jao, *Hong Kong as an International Financial Centre*, pp. 77–8.
66 Reed, *The Preeminence of International Financial Centres*, pp. 77–8.
67 Tuan and Ng, 'Regionalization of the Financial Market and the Manufacturing Evolution in Hong Kong', p. 133.
68 X. Gorostiaga, *The Role of the International Financial Centres in Underdeveloped Countries*, Beckenham, Kent, Croom Helm, 1984.
69 E. Szczepanik, *The Economic Growth of Hong Kong*, Oxford, Oxford University Press, 1958, p. 142.
70 Y.L. Wu and C.H. Wu, *Economic Development in Southeast Asia; The Chinese Dimension*, Stanford, Hoover Institution Press, 1980, p. 95.
71 Ibid., p. 96.
72 Ibid.
73 Y.C. Jao, 'Financing Hong Kong's Early Postwar Industrialisation; The Role of the Hongkong and Shanghai Banking Corporation', in F.H.H. King (ed.) *Eastern Banking; Essays in the History of the Hongkong and Shanghai Banking Corporation*, London, Athlone Press, 1983, pp. 545–74, p. 552.
74 V.F.S. Sit, 'Dynamism in Small Industries – The Case of Hong Kong', *Asian Survey*, 22(4), April 1982, pp. 399–409, p. 404. For the original survey, see V.F. Sit, S.-L. Wong and T.-S. Kiang, *Small Scale Industry in a Laissez-Faire Economy; A Hong Kong Case Study*, Hong Kong, University of Hong Kong Press, 1980. The importance of subcontracting for trading companies in the early stages of industrialisation is also cited in K.-M. Lee, 'Flexible Manufacturing in a Colonial Economy', in T.-K. Ngo (ed.) *Hong Kong's History; State and Society Under Colonial Rule*, London, Routledge, 1999, pp. 162–79, pp. 172–3.

75 D.R. Meyer, *Hong Kong as a Global Metropolis*, Cambridge, Cambridge University Press, 2000, p. 150.
76 A.H. Choi, 'State-Business Relations and Industrial Restructuring', in T.-K. Ngo (ed.) *Hong Kong's History; State and Society Under Colonial Rule*, London, Routledge, 1999, pp. 141–61. Ngo agrees that banks were interested in financing industrial exports but not industrial production. T.-W. Ngo, 'The East Asian Anomaly Revisited; The Politics of Laissez-Faire in Hong Kong 1945–85', Ph.D. Thesis, London, School of Oriental and African Studies, August 1996, p. 104.
77 A.H. Choi, 'State-Business Relations and Industrial Restructuring', p. 155. The phrase 'lap-dog' is from a contemporary article in the *Far Eastern Economic Review*. On the relationship between Shanghai and Cantonese industrialists, see S.-L. Wong, *Emigrant Entrepreneurs*, Hong Kong, Oxford University Press, 1988.
78 Choi assumes that the decision was bound to be negative because no industrialists were represented on the committee. There is no empirical support for Choi's contention that an industrial bank was rejected because it would compete with existing commercial banks. Choi, 'State-Business Relations and Industrial Restructuring', p. 151.
79 *Report of the Industrial Bank Committee*, 1960, p. 15.
80 The Chinese Manufacturers' Association had offered assistance to firms seeking finance from banks and had been inundated with requests, but was unable to supply the Committee with the details of these applicants. *Report of the Industrial Bank Committee*, 1960, pp. 14–5.
81 Letter of 4 June 1959, from the Director of Commerce and Industry, *Report of the Industrial Bank Committee*, 1960, Appendix pp. 10–1.
82 Ibid.
83 Letter of 22 September 1959, from the Hong Kong General Chamber of Commerce, *Report of the Industrial Bank Committee*, 1960, Appendix pp. 5–9. The Federation of Hong Kong Industries Working Party agreed with the views of the Chamber of Commerce.
84 Economist Intelligence Unit, *Industry in Hong Kong*, 1962, p. 15.
85 This argument is partly circular since an inability to attract large-scale finance may have necessitated small units of production.
86 V.F.-S. Sit and S.-L. Wong, *Small and Medium Industries in an Export-Oriented Economy; The Case of Hong Kong*, Hong Kong, Centre of Asian Studies, 1989, pp. 147–9. Those who raised capital from a variety of sources depended primarily on their own savings.
87 Sit, Wong and Kiang, *Small Scale Industry in a Laissez-Faire Economy*, p. 214.
88 Cited in Tuan and Ng, 'Regionalization of the Financial Market and the Manufacturing Evolution in Hong Kong', p. 126.
89 The Macmillan Gap was identified in the UK in 1931 to describe the failure of British banks to lend to small and new businesses. Economist Intelligence Unit, *Industry in Hong Kong*, 1962, p. 20.
90 M. Collins, *Banks and Industrial Finance in Britain 1800–1939*, Cambridge, Cambridge University Press, 1995. S. Pollard, *Britain's Prime and Britain's Decline; The British Economy 1870–1914*, London, Edward Arnold, 1989.
91 Sit, Wong and Kiang, *Small Scale Industry in a Laissez-Faire Economy*, pp. 231–4.
92 Letter of 27 July 1959, from the Chinese Manufacturers' Association to the Industrial Bank Committee, *Report of the Industrial Bank Committee*, 1960, Appendix p. 4.
93 Hang Seng 1965, GHO 322, HSBC.
94 Note by P.E. Hutson, 15 July 1965. Emphasis in the original. Hang Seng 1965, GHO 322, HSBC.
95 Hang Seng Bank Ltd Progress Report by Hutson, 20 September 1965. Hang Seng 1965, GHO 322, HSBC.
96 Wong, *Emigrant Entrepreneurs*, pp. 117–9.
97 Minutes of the London Consultative Committee, 10 December 1964. W.T. Wilkinson, the industrial consultant, for example, visited Birmingham in March 1964 to drum up

such business. Memo by Birmingham Chamber of Commerce, 9 March 1964, R.G.L. Oliphant private file 1963–5, Chairman's Papers Carton No. 4, HSBC.

98 The term 'Compradore' was officially dropped by the bank in 1960. See C.T. Smith, 'Compradores of the Hongkong Bank', in F.H.H. King (ed.) *Eastern Banking; Essays in the History of the Hongkong and Shanghai Banking Corporation*, London Athlone Press, 1983, pp. 93–111.

99 For an account of the activities of the IDB, see Jao, 'Financing Hong Kong's Early Postwar Industrialisation', pp. 554–7.

100 Chartered Bank Balance Sheet, Guildhall Library, MS31519/344.

101 Chartered Bank Balance Sheet, Guildhall Library, MS31519/343 and MS31519/344.

102 Chinese in this context means Hong Kong Chinese as opposed to European, Australian or Indian.

103 Letter from J.H. Saunders to Sir K.W. Mealing (Mercantile Bank in London), 12 May 1965, Letters between Turner and Sir Kenneth W. Mealing (Mercantile), Chairman's Papers Carton No. 5, HSBC.

104 Jao, 'Financing Hong Kong's Early Postwar Industrialisation', pp. 545–74.

105 An analysis of King's sample of joint board memberships shows an increase in the links between the directors of the Hongkong Bank and the insurance industry (rising from four links in 1950 to 11 by 1960). The large representation on the boards of utilities (seven by 1960) was reflected in the Hongkong Bank's domination of lending to this sector. F.H.H. King, *The Hongkong Bank in the Period of Development and Nationalism 1941–84; From Regional Bank to Multinational Group. Vol. IV of The History of the Hongkong and Shanghai Banking Corporation*, 1991, pp. 253–4.

106 E. Sinn, *Growing with Hong Kong; The Bank of East Asia 1919–1994*, 1994, pp. 91–2.

107 *Report of the Industrial Bank Committee*, 1960, p. 9. The survey included 62 out of 83 licensed banks 'including all banks of importance'.

108 Balance Sheets of the Hong Kong Office of Chartered Bank, Guildhall Library, MS31519. Jao states that similar data are not available in the archives of the Hongkong Bank before 1966. Jao, 'Financing Hong Kong's Early Postwar Industrialisation'.

109 Chairman's Files Carton No. 5, Tomkins Report, HSBC. By 1969, the Hongkong Bank's share had fallen to 26.5 per cent. Jao, 'Financing Hong Kong's Early Postwar Industrialisation', pp. 545–74, p. 560.

110 Jao, 'Financing Hong Kong's Early Postwar Industrialisation', p. 561.

111 Sinn, *Growing with Hong Kong*, p. 135.

112 K.-L. Ng, 'The Native Banks; Their Structure and Interest Rates', *Far Eastern Economic Review*, 11 February 1960, pp. 316–7.

113 See, for example, S.W.K. Chiu, K.C. Ho and T.-L. Lui, *City-States in the Global Economy; Industrial Restructuring in Hong Kong and Singapore*, Boulder Westview Press, 1997, p. 133–4.

114 Jao, *Banking and Currency*, p. 274.

115 From the Hong Kong Annual Report 1987/88, cited in Sit and Wong, *Small and Medium Industries in an Export-Oriented Economy*, p. 43.

116 D.W. Stammer, 'Financial Development and Economic Growth in Underdeveloped Countries; Comment', *Economic Development and Cultural Change*, 20(2), January 1972, pp. 318–25.

117 The 'demand-leading' and 'supply-leading' framework was developed by H. Patrick, 'Financial Development and Economic Growth in Developing Countries', *Economic Development and Cultural Change*, XIV(2), January 1966, pp. 174–89.

7 Epilogue and summary

1 Results of Hong Kong Office and Agencies for December 1967, HSBC GHO201.

2 Report by N.H.T. Bennett (Hong Kong), 26 May 1967. Chairman's Papers Carton No. 4, HSBC.

3 See correspondence in PRO T295/240.
4 The stock market crashed again in 1987, prompting more thorough regulatory reforms.
5 T.K. Ghose, *The Banking System of Hong Kong*, Butterworths, Singapore, 1987, p. 84.
6 For a comparison of Hong Kong and Singapore in the 1990s, see F. Wu, 'Hong Kong and Singapore; A Tale of Two Asian Business Hubs', *Journal of Asian Business*, 13(2), 1997, pp. 1–17, M.F. Montes, 'Tokyo, Hong Kong and Singapore As Competing Financial Centres', in G. de Brouwer and W. Pupphavesa (eds) *Asia Pacific Financial Deregulation*, London, Routledge, 1999, pp. 151–70, and K.-J. Ngiam, 'Singapore as a Financial Center; New Developments, Challenges and Prospects', in T. Ito and A.O. Kreuger (eds) *Financial Deregulation and Integration in East Asia*, Chicago, University of Chicago Press, 1996, pp. 359–85.
7 Interview with J.J. Cowperthwaite in *The Banker*, 120, July 1970, pp. 734–45, p. 739.
8 Interview with J.J. Cowperthwaite in *The Banker*, 120, July 1970, pp. 734–45, p. 744.
9 S.Y. Lee, 'The Asian Dollar Market, Asian Bond Market, and the Hongkong Bank Group', in F.H.H. King (ed.) *Eastern Banking*, London, Athlone Press, 1983, pp. 575–90, pp. 577–8. The same observation is made in S.-Y. Lee, 'Developing Asian Financial Centres', in A.H.H. Tan and B. Kapur, (eds) *Pacific Growth and Financial Interdependence*, Sydney, Allen and Unwin, 1986, pp. 205–36, p. 216. For a comparison of Hong Kong and Singapore in the early 1970s, see Y.C. Jao, *Banking and Currency in Hong Kong; A Study of Postwar Financial Development*, Macmillan, 1974, Chapter 5.
10 Cain and Hopkins use Sir Charles Addis, London manager of the Hongkong Bank at the turn of the century, as an example of a gentleman imperialist capitalist. P.J. Cain and A.G. Hopkins, *British Imperialism; Crisis and Deconstruction 1914–1990*, London, Longman, 1993, pp. 241–2.
11 A.H. Choi, 'State Business Relations and Industrial Restructuring', in T.-W. Ngo (ed.) *Hong Kong's History; State and Society Under Colonial Rule*, London, Routledge, 1999, pp. 141–61.
12 Given the nature of Hong Kong's manufacturing, many firms were both importers and producers.

Bibliography

Archival sources

Bank of England – London
UK Treasury – Public Records Office, Kew, London
UK Foreign Office – Public Records Office, Kew, London
UK Colonial Office – Public Records Office, Kew, London
Hongkong and Shanghai Banking Group – London
Chartered Bank of India, Australia and China – Guildhall Library, London
US Joint Chiefs of Staff
US State Department, Office of International Research, China Files

Periodicals

The Economist
Far Eastern Economic Review
Hong Kong Directory
Hong Kong Exporter
Hong Kong Hong List, 1947
Hong Kong Legislative Council
Hong Kong Stock Exchange, *Handbook of Stocks and Shares of the Principal Public Companies of Hong Kong*
Hong Kong Textile Annual
Nigel Ruscoe's Annual Hong Kong Register
Samuel Montagu and Co. Ltd, *Annual Bullion Review*

Government publications

Board of Trade, *Report of the United Kingdom Trade Mission to China, October to December 1946*, London, HMSO, 1948.
Chinese People's Association for Foreign Cultural Relations, *Kuang-chou*, Canton, Kuang-chou Literary Press, 1959. US Government translation published by Joint Publication Research Service.
Colonial Office, *Hong Kong Annual Report*.
Committee on the Working of the Monetary System; Minutes of Evidence, London, HMSO, 1960.
Hong Kong Census and Statistics Department, *Estimates of Gross Domestic Product 1961–1994*, Hong Kong, 1995.

Hong Kong Census and Statistics Department, *Hong Kong Statistics, 1947–1967*, Hong Kong, 1969.

Hong Kong Department of Commerce and Industry, *Annual Report of the Director.*

Hong Kong Department of Supplies, Trade and Industry, *Annual Report.*

Hong Kong Government Gazette.

International Monetary Fund, *International Financial Statistics.*

Report on the National Income Survey of Hong Kong, 1969.

Tomkins, H.J., *Report on the Hong Kong Banking System and Recommendations for the Replacement of the Banking Ordinance, 1948*, Hong Kong, April 1962.

UN Statistical Yearbook for Asia and the Far East, 1970.

Books and articles

Abraham, J.-P., N. Bervaes, A. Guinotte and Y. Lacroix, *The Competitiveness of European International Financial Centres*, Bangor, Institute of European Finance, 1993.

Agenor, P.-R., 'Parallel Currency Markets in Developing Countries: Theory, Evidence, and Policy Implications', IMF Working Paper, 90/114, 1990.

Ahlers, J., 'Postwar Banking in Shanghai', *Pacific Affairs*, 19, 1946, pp. 384–93.

Amatayakul, R. and S.A. Pandit, 'Financial Institutions in Thailand', *IMF Staff Papers*, VIII(4), 1961, pp. 464–89.

Beazer, W.F., *The Commercial Future of Hong Kong*, New York, Praeger, 1978.

Bergere, M.-C., ' "The Other China"; Shanghai from 1919 to 1949', in C. Howe (ed.) *Shanghai: Revolution and Development in an Asian Metropolis*, Cambridge, Cambridge University Press, 1981, pp. 26–30.

Boardman, R., *Britain and the People's Republic of China 1949–72*, London, Macmillan, 1976.

Bosworth, B., 'The East Asian Financial Crisis; What Happened and What We Can Learn from It', *Brookings Review*, Summer 1998, pp. 6–9.

Brooks, D.H. and S.-N. Oh, 'Asia's Financial Crisis; Is Financial Liberalisation the Villain?', in D.H. Brooks and M. Queisser (eds) *Financial Liberalisation in Asia; Analysis and Prospects*, Paris, OECD/Asian Development Bank, 1999, pp. 85–100.

Bryant, R.C., *International Financial Intermediation*, Washington, Brookings Institution, 1987.

Buckley, R., *Hong Kong; The Road to 1997*, Cambridge, Cambridge University Press, 1997.

Cain, P.J. and A.G. Hopkins, *British Imperialism; Crisis and Deconstruction 1914–1990*, London, Longman, 1993.

Cairncross, A., *The Wilson Years; A Treasury Diary 1964–69*, London, Historian's Press, 1997.

Casson, M., 'Evolution of Multinational Banks; A Theoretical Perspective', in G. Jones (ed.) *Banks as Multinationals*, London, Routledge, 1990.

Chambers, G., *Hang Seng; The Evergrowing Bank*, Hong Kong, Hang Seng Bank, 1991.

Chang, C.-Y., 'Localization and Chinese Banking in Southeast Asia', in M.-K. Nyaw and C.-Y. Chang (eds) *Chinese Banking in Asia's Market Economies*, Hong Kong, Chinese University of Hong Kong, 1989.

Chang, K.N., *The Inflationary Spiral: The Experience in China, 1939–50*, Cambridge, Massachusetts, Technology Press of Massachusetts Institute of Technology, 1958.

Chau, L.C., 'Estimates of Hong Kong's Gross Domestic Product 1959–69', *Hong Kong Economic Papers*, 7, September 1972, pp. 11–33.

Chau, L.C., *Hong Kong; A Unique Case of Development*, Washington, World Bank, 1993.

Chen, A.H.Y., 'The Legal System', in J.Y.S. Cheng (ed.) *Hong Kong in Transition*, Hong Kong, Oxford University Press, 1986, pp. 88–119.

Chen, E.K.Y., 'The Economic Setting', in D. Lethbridge (ed.) *The Business Environment in Hong Kong*, Oxford, Oxford University Press, Hong Kong, 1980.

Chen, E.K.Y., 'Foreign Trade and Economic Growth in Hong Kong; Experience and Prospects', in C. Bradford and W. Branson (eds) *Trade and Structural Change in Pacific Asia*, Chicago, University of Chicago Press, 1987, pp. 333–78.

Chesterton, J.M. and T.K. Ghose, *Merchant Banking in Hong Kong*, Singapore, Butterworths, 1998.

Chiu, S.W.K., K.C. Ho and T.-L. Lui, *City-States in the Global Economy; Industrial Restructuring in Hong Kong and Singapore*, New York, Westview, 1997.

Choi, A.H., 'State-Business Relations and Industrial Restructuring', in T.-W. Ngo (ed.) *Hong Kong's History; State and Society Under Colonial Rule*, London, Routledge, 1999, pp. 141–61.

Chou, K.R., *The Hong Kong Economy; A Miracle of Growth*, Hong Kong, Academic Publications, 1966.

Chung, S.P.-Y., *Business Groups in Hong Kong and Political Change in South China, 1900–25*, London, Macmillan, 1998.

Clayton, D., *Imperialism Revisited; Political and Economic Relations Between Britain and China, 1950–54*, London, Macmillan, 1997.

Cleveland, H. van B. and T.F. Huertas with R. Streuber, J.L. Silverman, M. Mungibelli, M.S. Turner, C.L. Wasson, *Citibank 1812–1970*, Boston, Harvard University Press, 1985.

Collins, M., *Banks and Industrial Finance in Britain 1800–1939*, Cambridge, Cambridge University Press, 1995.

Davies, G., 'Hong Kong Banking After the Crisis', *The Banker*, CXV, no. 470, April 1965, pp. 243–51.

Drake, P.J., 'The New-Issue Boom in Malaya and Singapore 1961–64', *Economic Development and Cultural Change*, 18(8), October 1969, pp. 75–91.

Dufey, G. and I.H. Giddy, *The International Money Market*, New Jersey, Prentice-Hall, 1978.

Dwyer, D.J. (ed.) *Asian Urbanization; A Hong Kong Casebook*, Hong Kong, Hong Kong University Press, 1971.

Economist Intelligence Unit, *Industry in Hong Kong*, Hong Kong, 1962.

Enright, M., E.E. Scott and D. Dodwell, *The Hong Kong Advantage*, Oxford, Oxford University Press, 1997.

Ghose, T.K., *The Banking System of Hong Kong*, Singapore, Butterworths, 1987.

Goldsmith, R.W., *Financial Structure and Development*, New Haven, Yale University Press, 1969.

Gorostiaga, X., *The Role of the International Financial Centres in Underdeveloped Countries*, Beckenham, Kent, Croom Helm, 1984.

Green, T., *The New World of Gold*, London, Weidenfeld and Nicolson, 1985.

de Gregorio, J. and P.E. Guidotti, 'Financial Development and Economic Growth', *World Development*, 23(3), 1995, pp. 433–48.

Haggard, S., *Pathways from the Periphery; The Politics of Growth in the Newly Industrializing Countries*, New York, Cornell University Press, 1990.

Ho, Yan-Ki, 'The Variability of Gold Prices in Hong Kong', in Y.-K. Ho and Cheung-Kwok Law (eds) *Hong Kong Financial Markets: Empirical Evidences*, Hong Kong, Hong Kong University Press, 1983, pp. 249–66.

Ho, Y.P., *Trade, Industrial Restructuring and Development in Hong Kong*, London, Macmillan, 1992.

Hong Kong Cotton Spinners Association, *Twenty Five Years of the Hong Kong Cotton Spinning Industry*, Hong Kong, 1973.

Hong Kong Stock Exchange, *Shares in Hong Kong; One Hundred Years of Stock Exchange Trading*, Hong Kong, Hong Kong Stock Exchange, 1991.

Hooper, B., *China Stands Up; Ending the Western Presence 1948–50*, London, Allen and Unwin, 1986.

Hsiao, Liang-lin, *China's Foreign Trade Statistics 1864–1949*, Boston, Harvard University Press, 1974.

Huggins, T. and C. Greene, 'The Economic Contribution of the Financial Sector in the Bahamas; A Ten Year Overview 1977–1987', *Central Bank of the Bahamas Quarterly Review*, 15(2), June 1988, pp. 31–40.

Hui, G.W.L., 'Ranking Hong Kong as an International Financial Centre', *Hong Kong Economic Papers*, 22, 1992, pp. 35–51.

Islam, I. and A. Chowdhury, *Asia-Pacific Economies; A Survey*, Routledge, 1997.

Jao, Y.C., *Banking and Currency in Hong Kong; A Study of Postwar Financial Development*, London, Macmillan, 1974.

Jao, Y.C., 'The Financial Structure', in D.G. Lethbridge (ed.) *The Business Environment in Hong Kong*, Hong Kong, Hong Kong University Press, 1980, pp. 159–99.

Jao, Y.C., 'Hong Kong', in The Banker Research Unit (ed.) *Banking Structures and Sources of Finance in the Far East*, 3rd edition, London, Financial Times Publishing, 1980, pp. 180–219.

Jao, Y.C., 'Hong Kong as a Regional Financial Centre; Evolution and Prospects', in C.-K. Leung *et al.* (eds) *Hong Kong; Dilemmas of Growth*, Canberra, Australian National University, 1980, pp. 67–73.

Jao, Y.C., 'Financing Hong Kong's Early Postwar Industrialisation; The Role of the Hongkong and Shanghai Banking Corporation', in F.H.H. King (ed.) *Eastern Banking; Essays in the History of the Hongkong and Shanghai Banking Corporation*, London, Athlone Press, 1983, pp. 545–74.

Jao, Y.C., 'Hong Kong's Role in Financing China's Modernization', in A.J. Youngson (ed.) *China and Hong Kong; The Economic Nexus*, Hong Kong, Oxford University Press, 1983, pp. 12–76.

Jao, Y.C., 'Recent Banking Crises in Hong Kong and Taiwan; A Comparative Perspective', in M.-K. Nyaw and C.-Y. Chang (eds) *Chinese Banking in Asia's Market Economies*, Hong Kong, Chinese University of Hong Kong, 1989, pp. 15–48.

Jao, Y.C., *Hong Kong as an International Financial Centre; Evolution, Prospects and Policies*, Hong Kong, City University of Hong Kong, 1997.

Johnson, H.G., 'Panama as a Regional Financial Center', *Economic Development and Cultural Change*, January 1976.

Jones, G., *Banking and Oil. The History of the British Bank of the Middle East, Vol. 2*, Cambridge, Cambridge University Press, 1987.

Jones, G. (ed.) *Banks as Multinationals*, London, Routledge, 1990.

Jones, G., 'Competitive Advantages in British Multinational Banking since 1890', in G. Jones (ed.) *Banks as Multinationals*, London, Routledge, 1990, pp. 30–61.

Jones, G., 'International Financial Centres in Asia, the Middle East and Australia; A Historical Perspective', in Y. Cassis (ed.) *Finance and Financiers in European History, 1880–1960*, Cambridge, Cambridge University Press, 1992, pp. 405–28.

Jones, P.H.M., 'Rapid Expansion in Hong Kong', *Far Eastern Economic Review*, 19 May 1960, p. 981.

Kam Hon Chu, 'Monetary and Banking System of Hong Kong', Ph.D. Thesis, university of Toronto, 1995.

Kelly, J., *Bankers and Borders; The Case of American Banks in Britain*, Cambridge, Massachusetts, Ballinger, 1977.

Kindleberger, C.P., *The Formation of Financial Centers; A Study in Comparative Economic History*, Princeton Studies in International Finance, 36, Princeton University, 1974.

King, F.H.H., *The Monetary System of Hong Kong*, Hong Kong, Oxford University Press, 1953.

King, F.H.H., 'The Hong Kong Open Market, 1954', in F.H.H. King (ed.) *Asian Policy, History and Development; Collected Essays*, Hong Kong, University of Hong Kong, 1979, pp. 161–72, p. 166.

King, F.H.H., *The Hongkong Bank in the Period of Development and Nationalism, 1941–1984; From Regional Bank to Multinational Group*, Vol. IV of the History of the Hongkong and Shanghai Banking Corporation, Cambridge, Cambridge University Press, 1991.

Lee, K.-M., 'Flexible Manufacturing in a Colonial Economy', in T.-K. Ngo (ed.) *Hong Kong's History; State and Society Under Colonial Rule*, London, Routledge, 1999, pp. 162–79.

Lee, K.-Y., *The Singapore Story*, New York, Prentice-Hall, 1998.

Lee, Q.W., 'Banks and Bankers', in S. Blyth and I. Wotherspoon (eds) *Hong Kong Remembers*, Hong Kong, Oxford University Press, 1996, pp. 185–91.

Lee, S.Y., 'The Asian Dollar Market, Asian Bond Market, and the Hongkong Bank Group', in F.H.H. King (ed.) *Eastern Banking*, 1983, pp. 575–600.

Lee, S.-Y., 'Developing Asian Financial Centres', in A.H.H. Tan and B. Kapur (eds) *Pacific Growth and Financial Interdependence*, Sydney, Allen and Unwin, 1986, pp. 205–36.

Lee, S.Y., 'The Development of Commercial Banking in Singapore and the States of Malaya', *Malayan Economic Review*, XI(1), April 1946, pp. 85–100.

Lee, T.C., 'The Economy of Hong Kong Since World War II', in E.F. Szczepanik (ed.) *Symposium on Economic and Social Problems of the Far East*, Hong Kong, Hong Kong University Press, 1962, pp. 166–79.

Levine, R., 'Financial Development and Economic Growth; Views and Agenda', *Journal of Economic Literature*, 35, 1997, pp. 668–726.

Li, C.-H., *Economic Development of Communist China; An Appraisal of the First Five Years of Industrialisation*, Berkley, University of California Press, 1959.

Lin, S.S., *Citicorp in China: A Colorful, Very Personal History Since 1902*, New York, Citicorp/Citibank, 1990.

Ling, T. and H. Lei, *The Circulation of Money in the People's Republic of China*, translated by Joint Publications Research Service, 1959.

Liu Chong Hing Bank Ltd 40th Anniversary, Hong Kong, 1988.

Louis, Wm. R., 'Hong Kong; The Critical Phase, 1945–49', *American Historical Review*, 102(4), October 1997, pp. 1052–84.

Mah, F.-H., *The Foreign Trade of Mainland China*, Edinburgh, University of Edinburgh Press, 1972.

McCarthy, I., 'Offshore Banking Centers; Benefits and Costs', *Finance and Development*, 16(4), December 1979, pp. 45–58.

McElderry, A., *Shanghai Old-Style Banks (ch'ien-chuang), 1800–1935; A Traditional Institution in a Changing Society*, Ann Arbor, University of Michigan, 1976.

McKinnon, R.I., *Money and Capital in Economic Development*, Washington, Brookings Institute, 1973.

Meyer, D.R., *Hong Kong as a Global Metropolis*, Cambridge, Cambridge University Press, 2000.

Michie, R. *The City of London*, London, Macmillan, 1992.

Montes, M.F., 'Tokyo, Hong Kong and Singapore as Competing Financial Centres', in G. de Brouwer and W. Pupphavesa (eds) *Asia Pacific Financial Deregulation*, London, Routledge, 1999, pp. 151–70.

Ng, K.-L., 'The Native Banks; Their Structure and Interest Rates', *Far Eastern Economic Review*, 11 February 1960, pp. 307–21.

Ng, K.-L., 'More Banks in Hongkong', *Far Eastern Economic Review*, 12 April 1962, p. 67.

Ngan, Y.P., 'Hang Seng Bank Limited; A Brief History', in F.H.H. King (ed.) *Eastern Banking; Essays in the History of the Hongkong and Shanghai Banking Corporation*, London, Athlone Press, 1983, pp. 709–16.

Ngiam, K.-J., 'Singapore as a Financial Center; New Developments, Challenges and Prospects', in T. Ito and A.O. Kreuger (eds) *Financial Deregulation and Integration in East Asia*, Chicago, University of Chicago Press, 1996, pp. 359–85.

Ngo, T.-W., 'The East Asian Anomaly Revisited; The Politics of Laissez-Faire in Hong Kong 1945–85', Ph.D. Thesis, London, School of Oriental and African Studies, August 1996.

Ngo, T.-W., 'Industrial History and the Artifice of Laissez-Faire Colonialism', in T.-W. Ngo (ed.) *Hong Kong's History; State and Society under Colonial Rule*, London, Routledge, 1999, pp. 119–40.

Owen, N.C., 'Economic Policy in Hong Kong', in K. Hopkins (ed.) *Hong Kong The Industrial Colony: A Political, Social and Economic Survey*, Hong Kong, Oxford University Press, 1971, pp. 141–206.

Patrick H.H., 'Financial Development and Economic Growth in Developing Countries', *Economic Development and Cultural Change*, XIV(2), January 1966, pp. 174–89.

Patrikeeff, F., *Mouldering Pearl; Hong Kong at the Crossroads*, London, Coronet Books, 1989.

Patten, C., *East and West; China, Power and the Future of Asia*, New York, Times Books, 1998.

Pollard, S., *Britain's Prime and Britain's Decline; The British Economy 1870–1914*, London, Edward Arnold, 1989.

Rabushka, A., *The Changing Face of Hong Kong*, Washington, Hoover Institution, 1973.

Rabushka, A., *Hong Kong; A Study in Economic Freedom*, Chicago, University of Chicago Press, 1979.

Reed, H.C., *The Pre-eminence of International Financial Centres*, New York, Praeger, 1981.

Riedel, J., *The Industrialization of Hong Kong*, Tubingen, J.C.B. Mohr, 1974.

Roberts, R., *International Financial Centres, Vols 1–4*, Hants, Edward Elgar, 1994.

Schenk, C.R., 'The Origins of a Central Bank in Malaya and the Transition to Independence, 1954–59', *Journal of Imperial and Commonwealth History*, 21(2), 1993, pp. 409–31.

Schenk, C.R., *Britain and the Sterling Area; From Devaluation to Convertibility in the 1950s*, London, Routledge, 1994.

Schenk, C.R., 'Closing the Hong Kong Gap; The Hong Kong Free Dollar Market in the 1950s', *Economic History Review*, XLVII(2), 1994, 335–53.

Schenk, C.R., 'Monetary Institutions in Newly Independent Countries: The Experience of Malaya, Ghana and Nigeria in the 1950s', *Financial History Review*, (4), 1997, pp. 181–98.

Schenk, C.R., 'Commercial Rivalry between Shanghai and Hong Kong during the Collapse of the Nationalist Regime in China, 1945–1949', *International History Review*, XX(1), March 1998, pp. 68–88.

Schenk, C.R., 'Le passe d'Une Region; Les relations monetaires entre Hong Kong et la Chine dans les annees quarante', *Economie Internationale*, 78(2), 1999, pp. 155–78.

Schenk, C.R., 'Another Asian Financial Crisis: Monetary Links between Hong Kong and China 1945–50', *Modern Asian Studies*, 34(3), 2000, pp. 739–64.

Shai, A., *The Fate of British and French Firms in China 1949–54; Imperialism Imprisoned*, London, Macmillan, 1997.

Shao, W., *China, Britain and Businessmen; Political and Commercial Relations, 1949–57*, London, Macmillan, 1991.

Shaw, E.S., *Financial Deepening in Economic Development*, Oxford, Oxford University Press, 1973.

Sit, V.F.S., 'Dynamism in Small Industries – The Case of Hong Kong', *Asian Survey*, 22(4), April 1982, pp. 399–409.

Sit, V.F.S., 'Branching of the Hongkong and Shanghai Banking Corporation in Hong Kong; A Spatial Analysis', in F.H.H. King (ed.) *Eastern Banking; Essays in the History of the Hongkong and Shanghai Banking Corporation*, London, Athlone Press, 1983, pp. 629–54.

Sit, V.F.S., S.-L. Wong and T.-S. Kiang, *Small Scale Industry in a Laissez-Faire Economy; A Hong Kong Case Study*, Hong Kong, University of Hong Kong Press, 1980.

Sit, V.F.-S. and S.-L. Wong, *Small and Medium Industries in an Export-Oriented Economy; The Case of Hong Kong*, Hong Kong, Centre of Asian Studies, 1989, pp. 147–49.

Sitt, R., *The Hong Kong Gold Market*, London, Rosendale Press, 1995.

Smith, C.T., 'Compradores of the Hongkong Bank', in F.H.H. King (ed.) *Eastern Banking; Essays in the History of the Hongkong and Shanghai Banking Corporation*, London, Athlone Press, 1983, pp. 93–111.

Smith, H., *John Stuart Mill's Other Island; A Study of the Economic Development of Hong Kong*, London, Institute of Economic Affairs, 1966.

Smith, S.C., *Kuwait 1950–1965; Britain, the al-Sabah, and Oil*, Oxford University Press, Oxford, 1999.

Stammer, D.W., 'Money and Finance in Hong Kong', unpublished Ph.D. Thesis, Australian National University, 1968.

Stammer, D.W., 'Financial Development and Economic Growth in Underdeveloped Countries; Comment', *Economic Development and Cultural Change*, 20(2), January 1972, pp. 318–25.

Sung, Y.W., 'Fiscal and Economic Policies in Hong Kong', in J.Y.S. Cheng (ed.) *Hong Kong in Transition*, Oxford, Oxford University Press, 1986, pp. 120–41.

Szczepanik, E., *The Economic Growth of Hong Kong*, Oxford, Oxford University Press, 1958.

Szczepanik, E., 'The Embargo Effect on China's Trade with Hong Kong', *Contemporary China*, II, 1956–7, pp. 85–93.

Trebilcock, C., *Phoenix Assurance and the Development of British Insurance, Vol. 2*, Cambridge, Cambridge University Press, 1998.

Tsang, S.Y.-S., *Democracy Shelved; Great Britain, China, and Attempts at Constitutional Reform in Hong Kong, 1945–1952*, Oxford University Press, Oxford, 1988.

Tsang, S., *Hong Kong; An Appointment With China*, London, I.B. Taurus, 1997.

Tsui, A., 'Lessons from Hong Kong's Experience of the Crisis', in D.H. Brooks and M. Queisser (eds) *Financial Liberalisation in Asia; Analysis and Prospects*, Paris, OECD/Asian Development Bank, 1999.

Tuan, C. and L.F.Y. Ng, 'Regionalization of the Financial Market and the Manufacturing Evolution in Hong Kong; Contributions and Significance', *Journal of Asian Economics*, 9(1), 1988, pp. 119–37.

Wai, U. Tun and H.H. Patrick, 'Stock and Bond Issues and Capital Markets in Less Developed Countries', *IMF Staff Papers*, 20, 1973, pp. 253–317.

Welsh, F., *A History of Hong Kong*, London, Harper Collins, 1997.

Williams, D., 'Commercial Banking in the Far East', *The Banker*, CXIII, June 1963, pp. 418–30.

Williams, D., 'Money Markets of Southeast Asia', *The Banker*, VXIII(449), July, 1963, pp. 484–91.

Williams, D., 'Hong Kong Banking', *Three Banks Review*, 59, September 1963, pp. 26–44.

Williams, D., 'Foreign Currency Issues on European Security Markets', *IMF Staff Papers*, 14, 1967, pp. 43–77.

Wilson, J.D., *The Chase; The Chase Manhattan Bank, N.A. 1945–85*, Boston, Harvard Business School Press, 1986.

Wolfstone, D., 'Eighty-Two Banks and Over a Hundred Branches', *Far Eastern Economic Review*, 11 February 1960, pp. 297–305.

Wong, K.A., 'The Stock Market in HK; A Study of Its Functions and Efficiency', unpublished Ph.D. Thesis, University of Liverpool, 1975.

Wong, S.-L., *Emigrant Entrepreneurs; Shanghai Industrialists in Hong Kong*, Hong Kong, Oxford University Press, 1988.

Wu, F., 'Hong Kong and Singapore; A Tale of Two Asian Business Hubs', *Journal of Asian Business*, 13(2), 1997, pp. 1–17Y.

Wu, L. and C.H. Wu, *Economic Development in Southeast Asia; The Chinese Dimension*, Stanford, Hoover Institution Press, 1980.

Yu, T.F.-L., *Entrepreneurship and Economic Development in Hong Kong*, London, Routledge, 1997.

Index